A CHARTWELL-BRATT STUDENT TEXT

Databases and Database Systems

Concepts and Issues: 2nd Edition

Elizabeth Oxborrow

Computing Laboratory,
University of Kent at Canterbury

Chartwell-Bratt   Studentlitteratur

British Library Cataloguing in Publication Data
Oxborrow, E. A. (Elizabeth A)
    Databases and database systems: concepts and issues. - (A
    Chartwell-Bratt student text)
    1. Databases
    I. Title
    005.74

ISBN 0-86238-237-8

All rights reserved. No part of this publication may be reproduced or transmitted in any form or by any means, electronic or mechanical, including photocopying, recording, or any information storage and retrieval system, without permission in writing from the publisher.

© Elizabeth Oxborrow and Chartwell-Bratt Ltd, 1989

Chartwell-Bratt (Publishing and Training) Ltd
ISBN 0-86238-237-8

Printed in Sweden,
Studentlitteratur, Lund
ISBN 91-44-25372-9

3 4 5 6 7 8 9 10 | 1993 92

Contents

Preface

Acknowledgements

1	**Database Systems: Concepts and Architecture**	1
1.1	Introduction	1
1.2	The Emergence of Database Technology	2
1.3	The Traditional file Approach versus the Database Approach	4
1.4	Traditional File Problems and Database Solutions	6
1.5	The Different Views of the Database	9
1.6	Architecture of a Typical Database System	11
1.7	Summary	13

2	**Data Modelling: The Conceptual Model**	15
2.1	Introduction	15
2.2	Data Modelling and Database Development	16
2.3	The Purpose of Data Modelling	20
2.4	The Components of Data Modelling	22
2.5	Data Model Diagrams and the Top-Down Data Modelling Methodology	27
2.6	The Normalisation Methodology for Data Modelling	37
2.7	Further Semantic Aspects of Conceptual Models	48
2.8	Summary	56

3	**Database Design: Mapping from the Conceptual Model to the Database Schema**	57
3.1	Introduction	57
3.2	The Relational Model	59
3.3	The Network Model	68
3.4	The Hierarchical Model	77
3.5	The Binary Relationship Model	81
3.6	The Conceptual Model Revisited	90
3.7	Views and the External Schema	93
3.8	Summary	97

4	**Database Query and Manipulation Languages**	98
4.1	Introduction	98
4.2	The Nature of Queries	101
4.3	Natural Language Interfaces	104
4.4	Graphics-orientated Interfaces	109
4.5	Formal Query Languages	115
4.6	High-level Procedural Languages	125
4.7	Database Manipulation Languages	131
4.8	Views and the External Schema Revisited	139
4.9	Summary	140
5	**Database Management Systems: Facilities and Implementation Aspects**	142
5.1	Introduction	142
5.2	Database Management Systems	143
5.3	Database Organisation and Storage	148
5.4	Query Processing	163
5.5	Database Protection: Reliability, Security and Integrity	179
5.6	Summary	188
6	**Distributed Database Systems**	189
6.1	Introduction	189
6.2	Major Issues in Distributed Database Systems (DDBSs)	190
6.3	Centralised Database versus Distributed Database	191
6.4	Communications Network Architecture for DDBSs	194
6.5	DDBS Software Architecture	196
6.6	Data Distribution	207
6.7	Data Models, Languages and Protocols in a DDBS	210
6.8	Coordination and Control: The DDBS Nucleus	215
6.9	Summary	225
7	**New Directions**	227
7.1	Introduction	227
7.2	From Databases to Knowledge Bases	228
7.3	Advanced User Interfaces	232
7.4	Database Machines	236
7.5	The Intelligent Knowledge Based System of the Future	239

7.6	Conclusion	241
	Index	**242**
	Reference	**247**
	Appendix A: Object-Oriented Database Systems	**255**
A.1	Introduction	255
A.2	Object-Oriented Concepts	258
A.3	The Future for Object-Oriented Database Systems	270

Preface

This book is designed to give broad coverage to a wide range of topics in the database field. The main objective is to provide a basic awareness of concepts and issues relating to databases and database management systems, in order that readers may understand the nature and purpose of databases, and ways in which database systems may be implemented and used efficiently, both now and in the future. The book introduces all the major database topics, comparing different approaches, and highlighting similarities and differences.

In order to provide this broad coverage, it is not possible to discuss every aspect in full detail, but examples are provided to illustrate the basic concepts, approaches, and techniques. References to specialist texts and papers are provided where relevant for those who wish to develop their knowledge or expertise in specific topics beyond the scope of this book.

The book is suitable not only for students who are taking a first course on databases, but also for those taking a more advanced or specialist course, such as one on database design or on distributed database systems. It should also be of use to database researchers in providing background information for their research and an initial source of references.

The material in this book is organised around topics; the topics included are: data modelling, database design, database query and manipulation languages, database management system implementation aspects, distributed database systems, and new directions in database technology. Many academic institutions adopt such a topic-oriented approach to teaching the subject, and hence this book should provide a useful text for these database courses. The book is not based on specific systems, as it is recognised that educational institutions will have access to different database systems, so detailed aspects of specific systems are not covered. Examples are, of course, provided from some systems for illustrative and comparative purposes. This approach thus leaves course lecturers free to design their own case study material to complement the book, based on the database systems to which they and their students have access.

A brief outline of the book is given below.

The first chapter is introductory in nature, providing a background for the detailed discussions of the various aspects of databases and database management systems (DBMSs) in the rest of the book.

The next two chapters are related, and are concerned with conceptual data modelling and database design respectively. In Chapter 2, a generalised conceptual data model is developed, first using a top-down approach and then using the normalisation approach; semantic aspects of conceptual models are also discussed in detail. In Chapter 3, the conceptual model is mapped into the data models of the different DBMS approaches — relational, network, hierarchical, and binary relationship.

Chapter 4 discusses the different types of language which may be used to access the data in databases, including natural language, graphics-oriented languages, formal query languages, procedural query languages (e.g. relational algebra), and database manipulation languages.

Chapters 5 and 6 are, to a certain extent, related. Chapter 5 first looks at the general facilities provided by current DBMSs and briefly introduces some actual systems to illustrate the different approaches. It then covers various implementation aspects, including database organisation and storage, query processing, and database protection (including concurrency control). Chapter 6 discusses various aspects relating to distributed database systems (DDBSs). The main concepts and issues are first introduced, and the query processing and concurrency control techniques which were introduced in Chapter 5 are extended for use in a DDBS environment.

Chapter 7 looks at new directions in database technology, including the move towards intelligent knowledge based systems, advanced user interfaces, and database machines.

A library system is used as a basis for all the main examples in the book, in order to provide continuity and a basis for the comparison of different approaches.

In conclusion, the main features of this book which distinguish it from most of the other database texts are:

. the material in the book is organised around database topics, rather than systems

. it provides broad coverage of the database field, including:
- a complete chapter on data modelling and database semantics, as well as a chapter on database design
- substantial material on the binary relationship approach, and the use of Prolog in a database environment, in addition to coverage of the traditional approaches — relational, network, and hierarchical
- implementation aspects such as organisation and storage of data, query processing, and concurrency control
- a complete chapter on distributed database systems

. it provides substantial references to specialist papers and books relating to particular topics and subtopics

E.A. Oxborrow
18.2.86

Preface to the Second Edition

A number of significant developments have been taking place in the field of database technology since the first publication of this book in 1986. The additional material in this second edition is designed to provide an indication of the nature of these developments, and to provide an introduction to one of the most important — the object-oriented approach to data management. This new material is provided in Appendix A.

The introductory section of the Appendix explains why there has been recent interest in new approaches to data management, and mentions three specific approaches: logic-based, enhanced relational, and object-oriented. Object-oriented concepts are then covered in detail in the second section. The discussion is supported by examples which are mainly based on the library example of the main text. Where appropriate, comparisons are made with traditional database systems (relational, network, hierarchical) to highlight both the limitations of these approaches to data management and the flexibility of the object-oriented approach. The final section summarises the possibilities offered by the object-oriented approach and the current problems. A number of supporting references are provided at the end.

E.A. Oxborrow
September 1989

Acknowledgements

I am indebted to a number of people for their advice and assistance regarding the production of this book. Firstly, many thanks to Peter Gray from Aberdeen University, Chris Keen from the University of Tasmania, and Richard Cooper from the University of Canterbury, New Zealand, for their very helpful comments and suggestions for improvements.

Next, I wish to thank Pam Blackman for assistance with some of the diagrams, and Janet Bayfield for assistance with some of the typing. I am also grateful to Jim Higham, Trevor Potts, and other computer operations staff, who helped to get the Canon laserprinter in working order when it had its periodic 'hiccups'!

Thanks must also go to the VAX 11/780 known as 'eagle' at the University of Kent, to the text processor 'troff', and to the troff preprocessor 'pic' (responsible for a few hours of frustration while I learnt how to produce diagrams!), and last, but definitely not least, the Canon laserprinter.

Finally, I must not forget John, who not only provided some valuable assistance, but also provided some much-needed moral support.

E.A. Oxborrow
18.2.86

Appendix Acknowledgements

I would like to thank Roy Thearle for some useful discussions on terminology which have helped to clarify the issues involved and highlight the inconsistencies. Thanks also should go to Janet Bayfield who did some of the typing, including drawing most of the diagrams using 'pic'.

E.A. Oxborrow
September 1989

Dedication

To Bruin and Chi-Chi

CHAPTER ONE

Database Systems: Concepts and Architecture

1.1 Introduction

This book discusses various aspects of databases and database systems. It aims to provide an introduction to the major concepts and issues in the field of databases, and a comparison of different approaches, highlighting the similarities and differences. It provides broad coverage of a wide range of different concepts, approaches and facilities, rather than detailed coverage of only the main approaches to database systems. Hence it does not describe in detail any specific database systems, but introduces examples from a number of them in order to illustrate certain features. Readers who are particularly interested in a specific topic will find a number of references to specialist papers on the subject.

In this first chapter, an overview of the subject of databases and database systems provides a background for the detailed discussion of the various topics in the rest of the book.

Chapter 2 first briefly discusses the processes involved in the construction of a database, including data investigation, data modelling, database design, implementation (i.e. setting up the database), and database monitoring and tuning. A detailed discussion of the data modelling process then follows. The objective of this process is to develop a conceptual model of that part of the real world which is of interest. Some basic data modelling concepts are introduced, and a top-down approach to data modelling is described by means of an example. An alternative approach, normalisation, is then described and compared with the top-down approach. Finally, further semantic aspects of data models are discussed.

Chapter 3 discusses the database design stage, which involves mapping the conceptual model (the real world oriented view of the database) into a model supported by a specific database system. Database systems may support different underlying data models; the four main ones are relational, network, hierarchical, and binary relationship, and each of these are discussed. Database systems are generally relatively weak in their support for real world semantics, and this aspect is discussed at the end of this chapter.

Chapter 4 considers the different types and levels of language used for accessing databases, from natural language, through graphics-oriented languages, formal query languages and procedural query languages, to the relatively low level database manipulation languages for application programming. The chapter commences with an introduction to the nature of queries, and to predicate and relational calculus. The different languages which are then discussed are related to the concepts introduced at the beginning of the chapter, and examples are used to compare and contrast the languages.

Chapter 5 takes a look at the facilities provided by database systems, in addition to those discussed in the book already, and considers some implementation aspects, including database organisation, query processing, and database protection techniques.

Chapter 6 considers the important issues in the field of distributed database systems. Interest has been increasing in this rapidly developing field, due to the now widespread availability of wide area and local area communications networks.

The final chapter looks at new directions in databases. The vast increase in the number of casual non-specialist users due to the widespread availability of inexpensive micros over the past few years is providing the impetus for research into more user-friendly interfaces. Much research is also currently being undertaken into ways of putting more semantic information into databases and more intelligence into systems designed to manage such databases. This final chapter considers the current developments in both of these areas, together with database hardware developments aimed at improving the performance of DBMSs.

1.2 The Emergence of Database Technology

Database technology emerged in the late 1960's as a result of a combination of circumstances. Firstly, as computer users in organisations became more aware of the potentials of computers, there was a growing demand for more information to be provided by the computer — not only information relating to the day-to-day running of the organisation, but also information for planning and control purposes. This demand coincided with advances in computer technology which, amongst other things, made disc-based computer systems economically feasible and gave rise to a move away from magnetic tape to disc as the main file medium. It also coincided with increasing expertise in the computer data processing area rendering it possible to design and implement more complex software.

It was soon recognised however that more advanced data processing techniques would be required if all information requirements were to be satisfied. While file-based systems are adequate for providing information relating to the routine day-to-day activities of an organisation, they prove to be deficient when it comes to providing other types of information. High-level planning and control information relates to the whole organisation and it is therefore necessary to consider the totality of an organisation's data as a single unit, not as a set of independent units stored in separate files. Effort was put into considering how this could be done, and from this effort emerged the idea of collecting together relevant data belonging to an organisation into a large conceptual file, maintained by special-purpose systems software. The 'large conceptual file' was termed a *database* and the 'special-purpose systems software' was termed a *database management system* (or DBMS for short). Thus, a database can be considered to be an organised collection of related sets of data, managed in such a way as to enable the user or application program to view the complete collection, or a logical subset of the collection, as a single unit. Also, a database management system can be defined as a system which facilitates shared access to data in a database, and which maintains the reliability, security and integrity of the database by controlling access to it and supervising updates. These definitions are summarised in Table 1.1.

Database (DB)	Organised collection of related sets of data. Complete collection or any logical subset may be viewed as a single unit.
Database management system (DBMS)	Facilitates shared access to data in a database. Maintains reliability, security and integrity of data.

Table 1.1 Definitions

1.3 The Traditional File Approach versus the Database Approach

Figures 1.1 and 1.2 highlight the differences between file-based applications and database applications by means of an example. Consider a very simplified library system, consisting of three applications: one for book loans, one for book reservations, and one to recall overdue loans. In the traditional file approach (Figure 1.1), the reservation program uses data from a reservation file, a loan file and a book file; the loan program uses the loan file, the book file, and a person file (containing information about borrowers); and the overdue loans program uses the loan and person files.

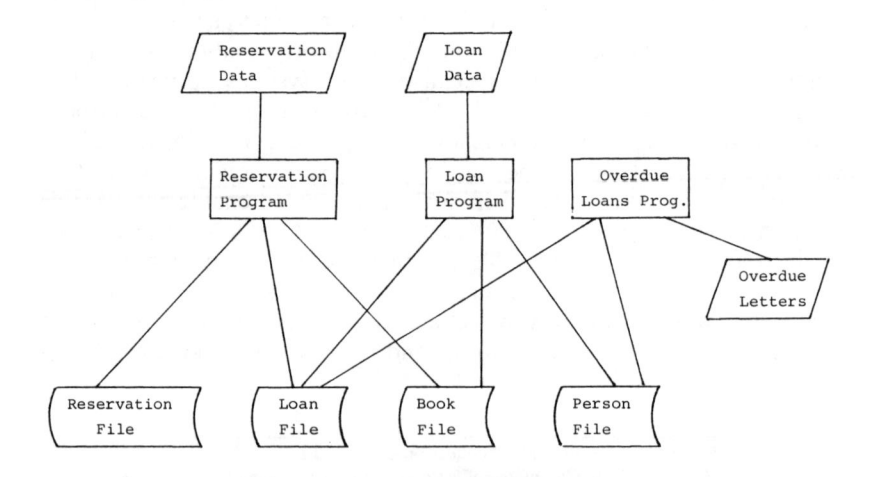

Figure 1.1 Traditional File Approach — Simplified Library Example

As can be seen, some files are shared by different programs, and each program uses a number of apparently independent files. However, the files are not really independent; they are in fact related. For example, the loan file will contain information about the person who has borrowed a book, and about the actual book which has been borrowed. In the traditional file approach it is the application program which has to relate data between files as relevant and when necessary. A number of problems arise from this, which will be discussed later in this chapter.

In the database approach (Figure 1.2), all the data is conceptually stored in a single database.

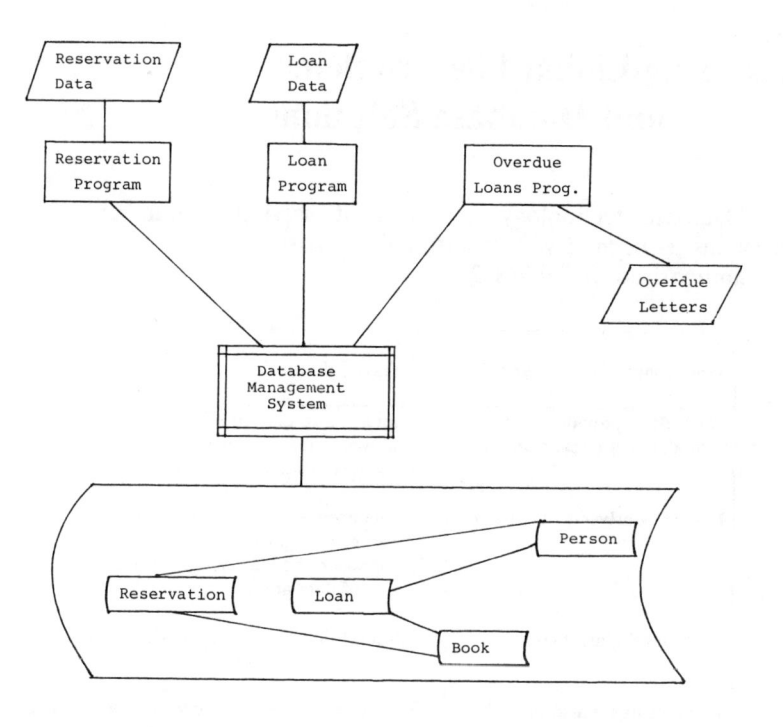

Figure 1.2 Database Approach — Simplified Library Example

The database will probably be physically stored in a set of files, but users and applications do not need to know anything about the physical storage. Relationships between sets of data are represented in the database (illustrated by lines in the diagram). Stored with the actual data will be a description of the database — like a complex directory — enabling the database management system to retrieve information from the database and to store new data in the appropriate place in the database, establishing relationships with other data if relevant. The applications do not directly access the database; instead they pass requests to the database system to retrieve or store data.

In summary, the traditional file approach may be seen as a program-oriented approach, while the database approach is essentially data-oriented. This difference has resulted in a change in emphasis at the systems analysis and design stages of information systems development; much more importance is now attached to data modelling and database design than was the case previously.

1.4 Traditional File Problems and Database Solutions

Database technology is aimed at solving a number of specific problems associated with traditional file-based systems. These problems are summarised in Table 1.2.

Traditional File Problems	Database Solutions
Difficult to provide adequate model of the real world.	Comprehensive data structuring facilities enable real world objects and relationships to be represented in the data model.
Low responsiveness to change	Data independence facilities enable the effect of changes to be minimised. Data is separated from programs and multiple views of data are permitted.
High development costs	High-level database manipulation languages make it easier to build applications.
Difficult to get answers to ad-hoc queries	Simple query languages are generally available. Query facilities are made possible by the existence of a single database and an interface to it (the DBMS).
Low data reliability, security and integrity due to the decentralised data and hence decentralised control.	Centralised control of reliability, security and integrity by the DBMS. Integrity protection includes concurrency control permitting shared access.

Table 1.2 Database Solutions to Traditional File Problems

Modelling the real world

The first problem concerns the *modelling of real world information*. The collection of data stored in files or databases is intended to represent real world facts and to record real world events. If such stored data is to be capable of providing high level information, the data must be structured in such as way as to reflect real world structure. For example, the separate functions and departments in an organisation are interdependent — they are related to each other in various ways. Such relationships should be reflected in the data structure which underlies the organisation's data. This data structure is commonly referred to as the *data model*. In the traditional file approach, represented in Figure 1.1, the files appear to be unrelated — the collection of data has no structure. The required structure has to be built in to any application program which uses the data. The database approach provides comprehensive data structuring facilities aimed at enabling data models to be constructed which reflect the interrelationships in the organisation. Facilities are provided for representing not only entities and attributes (cf. records and data items in traditional files) but also the relationships amongst them.

Responding to change

The second problem is that of low *responsiveness to change*. An organisation is continually subject to change — it exists in a dynamic environment. In a file-based system modifying programs to allow for such changes is not usually a trivial task. A change made to the structure of a file often produces side-effects in many programs which means that they have to be modified. One of the important database concepts is that of *data independence*; that is, the separation of structural information about the data from the programs which manipulate and use the data, and the provision for multiple views of the data. A well-designed and structured data model is important for data independence in eliminating dependencies which might otherwise produce undesirable side-effects when the database is updated. Also, it is important from the data independence viewpoint that different users should be permitted to have their own *view* of the data so that if they are not interested in part of the database that part need not be included in their view. This feature is also important for controlling access to parts of the database. With multiple views and separation of data structure from programs, structural changes may be made to parts of the database without affecting most of the users' views of the data and their programs.

Application systems development

A third problem is that of high *development costs*. Standard data processing languages such as Cobol, Fortran, and RPG2, although high-level in relation to machine language, are low-level in relation to data processing operations. Hence program development is complex, time-consuming and costly. Much higher level data manipulation languages are provided by DBMSs making it easier to develop application programs. Many DBMSs are 'hosted' by a standard compiler such as Cobol, Fortran or Pascal; in this case the host language is used for straightforward manipulation of individual data items once they have been retrieved from the database, while the database manipulation language is used to store data in, modify data in, and retrieve data from the database. Database manipulation language statements are embedded within the host language program either as standard host language function calls, or alternatively in some other format in which case a preprocessor will be used to convert these statements to standard function calls to appropriate DBMS routines.

Query facilities

A fourth problem is that of getting answers to *ad hoc questions* such as: What quantity of this particular item do we currently have in stock? In a file-based system in order to answer a question involving data from a number of separate files it is necessary to write a program to access each of the files and find and retrieve the relevant data in the files. When data is stored in a database and managed by DBMS software, it is possible to provide easier access to data in the database and hence it is also possible to provide query facilities. Such facilities enable users to get information from the database without needing to write an application program.

Database protection and data sharing

The final problem considered here relates to *database protection* — with shared data it is particularly important to maintain high data reliability, security, and integrity. *Reliability* relates to the protection of the data against unexpected loss, damage or destruction; the objective is to ensure that the database is always available when it is required, or at least quickly recovered in the event of unexpected damage of some sort. *Security* concerns the prevention of unauthorised access to data, while *integrity* relates to the maintenance of high-quality, consistent, and up-to-date data. In a file-based system data is stored in a number of files and many different programs may have direct access to these files. The data is decentralised and so is control of the data, giving rise to low data reliability, integrity and security.

Most DBMSs provide facilities for centralised control of these aspects. Backup copies and transaction logs are maintained for recovery purposes in the event of any failure, however small or large. Privacy locks are attached to objects in the database, and the issue of keys and passwords is controlled, to maintain the security of the database. The most important integrity protection facility is concurrency control; this enables users to access and update the database at the same time without the updates interfering with each other. This database protection is managed by the DBMS, usually under the direction of a Database Administrator — an individual responsible for the overall control of the database and DBMS.

Disadvantages of the database approach

Despite all these desirable characteristics of the database approach there are, of course, disadvantages.

Complexity: inevitably, the DBMS is a complex piece of software and requires database experts both to look after it and also to design and develop the database and applications.

Cost: comprehensive DBMSs are expensive to purchase and give rise to additional overheads when in operation — overheads in terms of processing time and storage space.

Inefficiencies in processing: unexpected database usage patterns or changes in usage may give rise to inefficiencies in processing data requests; it is essential to monitor the use of the database to detect such inefficiencies and if necessary restructure the database.

Rigidity: most current DBMSs were designed to manage a particular type of data: fixed format records; until recently, other types of data, such as text and graphics, have had to be excluded from databases and even now the ability to include them is rare and limited.

In addition to the above disadvantages, the creation of a single database containing all the organisation's data is not always feasible. Some large organisations are too complex to be modelled in a single database and multiple databases have to be accepted.

The overall picture

As far as databases are concerned, the overall picture can probably be summarised as follows: much expertise gained in the past (but not without mistakes!), some substantial benefits gained in the present, and great potential for the future when new developments in the database field and other related fields become widely available.

1.5 The Different Views of the Database

In the previous section it was mentioned that one of the aspects of data independence in database systems is the provision for multiple views of the data. Different views of the database may exist at the user level, with different users and applications viewing, and hence having access to, different subsets of the complete database. The user views, however, are not the only views which may exist; they are at the top level and other views of the database also exist at lower levels.

Figure 1.3 illustrates the now well-established ANSI/SPARC three-level data model architecture (Yormark 1977, Jardine 1977). The most important level is the middle level in which the logical view of the complete database is modelled. This view may be referred to as the *conceptual model*. Data modelling at this level will be discussed in detail in the next chapter.

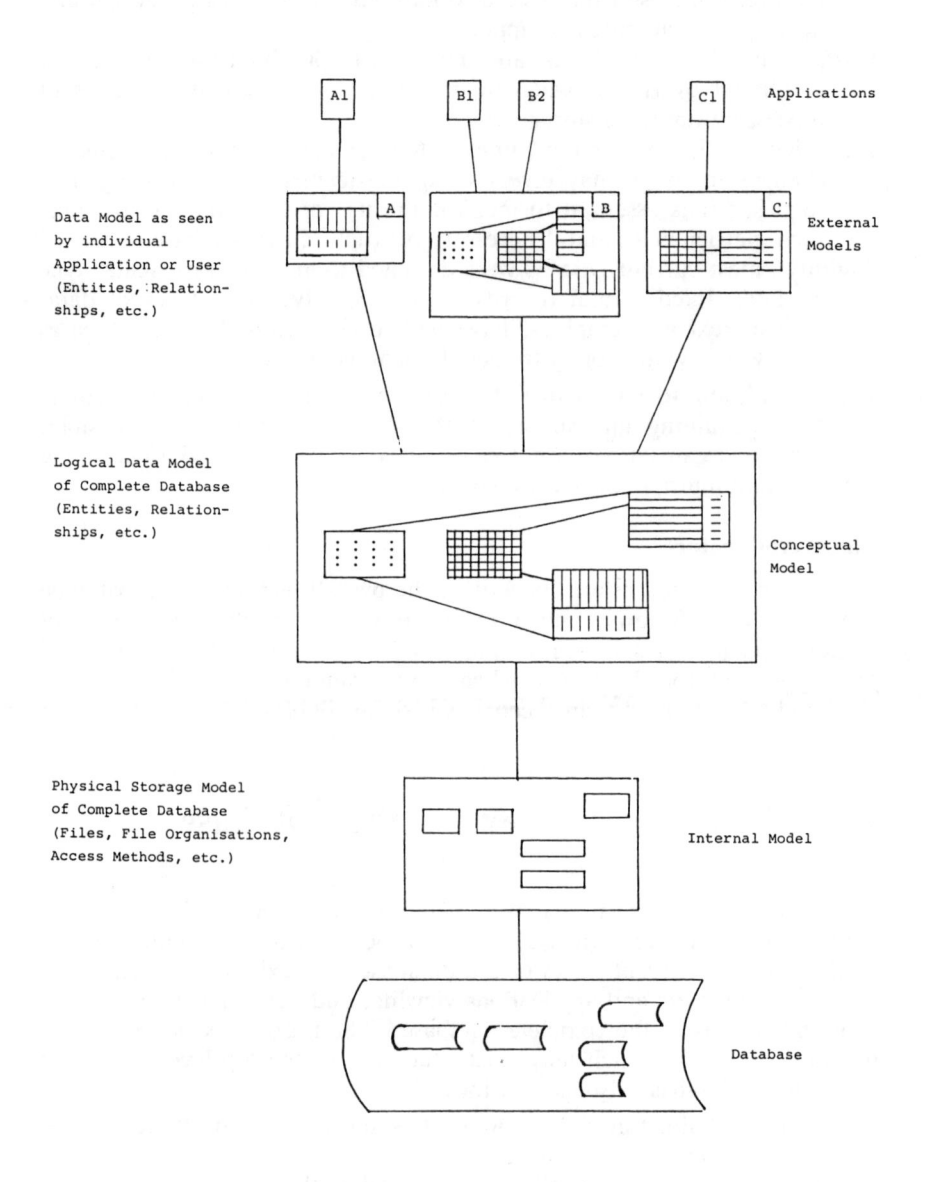

Figure 1.3 Different Levels of Data Model

At the top level we have the user views or *external models* already mentioned above. These represent subsets of the conceptual model. For a better understanding of the relationship between the external and conceptual models it will be useful to fit an example to the diagram in Figure 1.3. Consider external model A; it might represent only the book data from the library database referred to earlier in this chapter, and application A1 might be a catalogue enquiry program. External model B might represent all the reservation and loan data, together with a subset of the person data (excluding persons' addresses, for example, and other data not relevant to the B applications) and a subset of the book data (excluding books confined to the library which cannot be lent out). Applications B1 and B2 could be the loans and reservations applications, sharing the same external model. Finally, external model C might represent the loan and person data only, with application C1 being the program for the recall of overdue loans. Note that relevant relationships amongst the sets of data are represented in the external models as well as in the conceptual model.

At the bottom level we have the physical storage view of the database — the *internal model*. Such physical storage aspects as filenames, file organisations, access methods, etc. will be represented at this level; it could also therefore be referred to as the 'file level'. This is a similar level to that used by standard programming languages such as Cobol and Fortran; file-based application programs written in such languages would interface with files at a level such as this.

It should be noted that there is not necessarily a one-to-one correspondence between files and conceptual sets of data. For example, the conceptual book data may physically be split into two files: one for books which can be lent out and one for confined books. The internal model, then, reflects the data as actually stored in database files.

1.6 Architecture of a Typical Database System

The way in which the different data models fit into the overall architecture of a typical database system will now be considered. Figure 1.4 illustrates the interaction between the DBMS, the users or applications, the data models and the database. In place of the data models shown in Figure 1.3 we have the corresponding schema. The term *schema* is used to indicate the description of a data model. The language used for this data model description will depend on the actual DBMS used. Mapping from a data model to a DBMS-specific schema will be discussed in a later chapter.

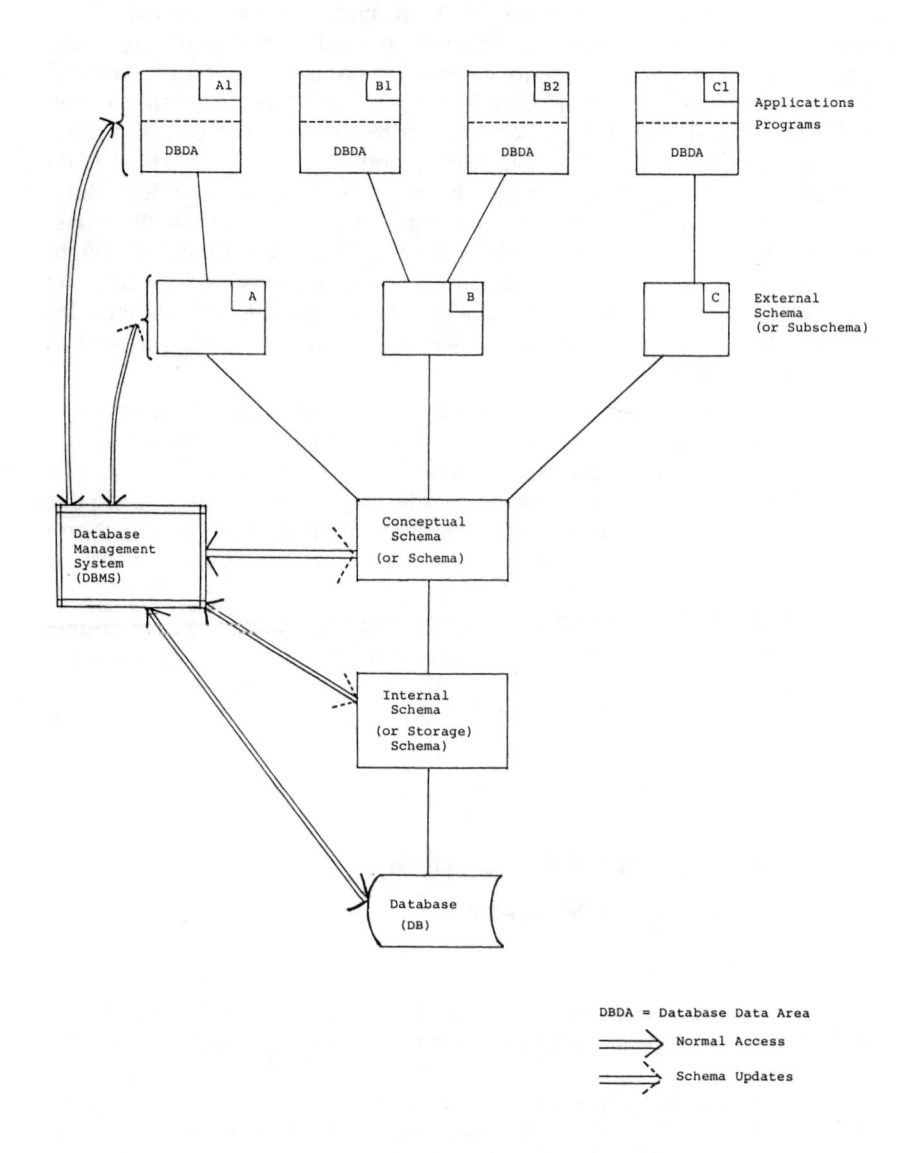

Figure 1.4 Architecture of a Typical Database System

The applications are shown to include a Database Data Area (sometimes referred to as the User Working Area). In a typical system, a special area such as this will be used for the communication of data between the DBMS and the applications. It may be compared to the File Section in a Cobol program, or the Common data area in a Fortran program. It is an area where an application can place data such as records for storage in the database, or key values for retrieval of data by means of a key or keys, and it is also an area where the DBMS can place data which has been retrieved from the database for the application.

It can be seen from the diagram that the applications communicate with the DBMS and reference the *external schema* only. The DBMS performs the mapping from items in the external schema to the associated items in the *conceptual schema*, and thence references the *internal schema* for information about the physical storage of the items referred to. The DBMS also accesses the database itself to store/retrieve data, and communicates the results of the database access to the applications. The DBMS is in control.

Figure 1.4 highlights this very important feature of a database environment: the centralised control of database access by the DBMS. It was mentioned earlier that centralised control is important for the protection of the data against such events as unexpected loss of or damage to the database, the prevention of unauthorised access, and the maintenance of consistent and up-to-date data.

1.7 Summary

In this chapter the reasons why database technology emerged in the late 1960's as an important field of research and development were first considered. Users' demand for more information coincided both with advances in computer technology, especially in relation to disc files, and also with increased expertise in the software engineering area. Traditional file-based systems were found to be inadequate to satisfy users' needs and the concept of an integrated database managed by special-purpose software, the DBMS, emerged.

Database technology addressed itself to some specific problems associated with traditional files: inadequate data modelling capabilities, low responsiveness to change, high development costs, difficulty of answering ad hoc queries, and low degree of data reliability, security and integrity. Certain standard facilities are available in nearly all DBMSs to provide solutions to these problems; these are: comprehensive data structuring facilities, data independence (that is, the separation of data structure from programs, and multiple views of data), high-level database manipulation languages and query languages, and centralised database protection.

A typical database environment consists not only of the DBMS and the database, but also the different views of the data — the user views (referred to as the external models and described by the external schema), the overall logical view of the database (referred to as the conceptual model and described by the conceptual schema), and the physical storage view of the database (the internal model described by the internal schema). DBMSs may provide self-contained database manipulation and programming languages, but are often hosted by a standard compiler (such as Cobol), in which case each application typically consists of database manipulation language (DML) statements relating to access to the database, embedded in host language statements. DBMSs also provide end-user query languages, some of which are very powerful and are in reality more than just query languages; such languages can substantially reduce the need for application programming.

During the remaining chapters, all the special database facilities will be covered. Concepts and terms introduced in this chapter will be discussed in more detail. In the next chapter various aspects of data modelling will be discussed.

CHAPTER TWO

Data Modelling: The Conceptual Model

2.1 Introduction

The main topic of this chapter is data modelling — the process of structuring real world facts into real world concepts. Data modelling is one of the tasks involved in building a database. It is a very important task since it has an impact not only on the effectiveness of the resulting database in supporting existing requirements, but also on the extent to which it can support future changes without necessitating major restructuring.

Data modelling will first be put into its proper context by briefly considering all the tasks involved in building a database. The purpose of data modelling will then be discussed in detail. Data models are made up from different components and these will be described. The result of the data modelling task is the production of data structure diagrams representing the data model. A specific diagrammatic notation will be introduced and used to illustrate how real world facts can be modelled. An example will then be used to illustrate two data modelling methodologies — the top-down methodology and the normalisation methodology. The example will be based on the library system introduced in Chapter 1. Finally, further semantic aspects of conceptual models will be discussed.

2.2 Data Modelling and Database Development

Data modelling is just one process, but a very important one, amongst a number of processes involved in database development. Before discussing data modelling in detail, however, database development will be viewed as a whole in order to place data modelling in its proper context.

Database development involves the construction of an actual database and it can be viewed as a number of processes. In this book five processes will be identified: *data investigation, data modelling, database design, database implementation*, and *database monitoring and tuning*. The term *data analysis* is sometimes used to describe part of the database development process, but this term has been avoided here as it is not always used consistently. In some cases it is used to embrace the data investigation process only, while in other cases it is used to embrace both data investigation and data modelling.

Database development usually takes place in conjunction with information systems development, in particular the investigation, analysis/modelling, and design stages. Traditional systems development methodologies were almost entirely function or process oriented (reflecting the program orientation of the traditional file approach). More recent methodologies are much more data oriented and combine data and functional analysis, though some still put more emphasis on the latter. Systems development methodologies will not be discussed here, but readers interested in this area will find descriptions of a number of important methodologies in Olle (1982, 1983), and feature analyses of some of them in Maddison (1983) and Fitzgerald (1985). Amongst the methodologies which emphasise data analysis are: DDSS (and a variant: D2S2) which uses an entity-relationship data model with notation similar to the notation introduced later in this chapter, LBMS-SDM which also uses an entity-relationship model, ACM/PCM which is based on the Semantic Hierarchy Model of Smith & Smith (Smith 1977), and Niam which is based on a binary relationship data model. Descriptions of Niam, D2S2 and ACM/PCM may be found in Olle (1982).

In any particular database development exercise, the five processes will not necessarily be carried out in strict sequence. It is quite likely that an iterative process will be necessary. For example, if, during data modelling, some information appears to be missing or ambiguous, it may be necessary to carry out some further data investigation and then recommence the modelling process. As a further example, the process of database monitoring may highlight inefficiencies or inadequacies, and suggest that some design alterations would be desirable; further database development may then be commenced from the database design stage or even the data investigation stage.

Each of these processes will now be considered in a little more detail. Table 2.1 summarises the tasks involved and the end-result of each process.

Process	Tasks involved	End-result
Data Investigation	Identification of nature and use of data	Skeleton Data Dictionary
Data Modelling	Shaping real world facts into real world concepts	Generalised Conceptual Model
Database Design	Mapping conceptual model into DBMS-specific data model	DBMS-Specific Conceptual Schema & External Schema
Database Implementation	Structuring the actual data in the physical database	Internal Schema & Database
Database Monitoring & Tuning	Monitoring database usage and restructuring the database if necessary	Optimised Database

Table 2.1   Database Development

Data investigation

Data investigation is a fact finding process. It involves the identification of the nature and use of data in an organisation. Information to be collected would include details of the objects in the system, constraints on the objects, the relationships between them, their physical characteristics, etc. Facts may be divided into 3 main categories: basic facts, constraints (including domain, integrity, and representation constraints), and rules (including inference and derivation rules, and other types of rule which will be considered at a later stage). In the library example, the following facts would be amongst those which are relevant:

. basic facts:
  . a book has a title, author, publisher, and year of publication; it also has a classmark (e.g. QA76) associated with it;
  . a book is allocated a unique International Standard Book No. (ISBN) when it is first published;

- when a copy of a book is purchased it is allocated a unique number (sometimes referred to as an accesssion number);
- each loan status has a loan period and maximum number of books on loan associated with it;
- constraints:
  - the ISBN is a 13-character item with formats which include: n-nnn-nnnnn-x or n-nnnnn-nnn-x, where n is a decimal digit and x is a decimal digit or the character 'x';
  - loan status values may be undergraduate, postgraduate, staff and visitor only;
  - a copy of a book must not exist without a catalogue entry
  - the loan period for a book depends on the status of the individual borrowing it;
- rules:
  - if date due back of loan is less than current date then loan is overdue.

The facts indicated above would be some of those which are relevant to the library example, but there would be many others which would be identified during the data investigation stage. In addition, this stage would provide functional information about the use of the data, i.e. the processing which is to be carried out on it. The main use of the functional information is in the design and development of the application systems which will use the database. As far as database development is concerned, though, the functional information is important for determining what data is required for particular user and application views, and will be used at the database design stage when the external models are derived. This information is also used at the conceptual modelling stage, for ensuring that all relevant data objects and relationships are included in the model and for providing the basis for determining relevant derivation rules.

All the facts gathered at the data investigation stage represent 'data about data' and are often referred to as *metadata*; they provide important semantic and other information about the data which is to be held in the database. The metadata will be used not only during the data modelling and database design stages as indicated above, but also during database implementation and it will provide much useful information for application system development. The metadata will not be complete at the end of this process; further information will be added during other processes, either as a result of clarification or refinement of facts, or as a result of decisions made on design and implementation aspects.

The subject of metadata is an important one and many DBMSs now provide automated and integrated data dictionary facilities. Data dictionary systems provide for the storage and retrieval of certain types of metadata; they of course vary in comprehensiveness and sophistication. A controversial issue is whether metadata should be considered as separate from, or as part of, the database itself. It is beyond the scope of this book to discuss this issue in detail. Suffice it to say that it is important that the facts collected at the data investigation stage and expanded/refined during later stages should be organised and stored in such a way as to provide for easy reference by database designers and administrators, application system developers, and also end-users. The end result of this organisation and storage of the metadata will be referred to as the *data dictionary*; it will not be of concern here whether the data dictionary is manual, partially automated, or fully integrated. The subject of metadata and data dictionaries will be considered again in the last chapter.

Data modelling

Data modelling involves shaping the facts collected during the data investigation process into data model concepts, deriving a conceptual model as a result. The basic facts, plus some of the constraints and rules, are of primary importance for this process, but functional information is also of interest, as indicated earlier. However, as Shave indicates: "The functional viewpoint is inevitably more application dependent .... and should therefore play a secondary role in the construction of a conceptual model." (Shave 1981). The conceptual model is required to support not only present applications and requirements, but also unknown future ones and its design should not be constrained by specific applications. It must be a global model reflecting the company-wide view of the data, rather than reflecting a collection of local departmental views, some of which may conflict. It should also reflect, to a certain extent, future company plans as well as present activities, to avoid the need for database restructuring as far as possible. The model derived will be a generalised model, independent of any specific DBMS. This process will be considered in detail later in this chapter.

Database design

Different database management systems will have their own specific constructs, rules and limitations which apply to the data model. The process of *database design* is that of mapping the generalised data model into the DBMS-specific data model. At this stage, the conceptual schema (or schema) will be derived; this is the description of the database written in the data description language provided by the DBMS. In addition, some (or all) of the external schema (or subschema) may be derived; these are the descriptions of the individual user and application views.

Database implementation

At the *database implementation* stage the internal or storage schema will be created, by reference to the DBMS data model and other information obtained during the data investigation stage. Decisions will be made regarding the physical database characteristics; for example, file sizes, file organisations, access methods, and any other physical aspects which are not fixed by the DBMS. The actual database will also be initially created.

Database monitoring and tuning

Finally, when the database is in operation, its usage should be monitored to detect any inefficiencies, errors or omissions. Inefficiencies may arise due to unexpected changes in usage patterns, or due to inadequate investigation into usage patterns in the early stages of database development. It may be necessary, therefore, to *restructure* the database, but such restructuring should be transparent to the users and should not affect the existing applications which use the database. This is the essence of the *database monitoring and tuning* process and is an important result of the database concept of *data independence* which was mentioned in Chapter 1. It is possible though that the monitoring process may highlight certain errors and omissions which may give rise to some redevelopment. Further database development will also need to be undertaken if changes take place either in the company or outside it which affect the structure of the data. Database development is therefore likely to be an on-going process.

2.3 The Purpose of Data Modelling

Returning now to consider data modelling in more detail, the purpose of data modelling is to transform aspects of the real world into a formal data model — the *conceptual model*. If the information requirements of an organisation are to be satisfied it is essential that the formal data model, which will form the basis of the database, adequately reflects reality.

What is this reality which we are trying to model? Reality is effectively boundless; hence in Figure 2.1 reality is shown with no horizon. But only perceived reality can, of course, be modelled and perceived reality is bounded. However, we all have our own, necessarily incomplete, views of reality. It is perceived differently by different individuals, and from different viewpoints. For example, the reality of a particular university is unique, but each individual's perception of that reality is different. Those who work or study in the university view it quite differently from those who do not. Even those people whose positions in the university are very similar have their own very different perceptions of it. These differences are partly due to inherent differences in individuals. Some of us are more generally aware than others; but,

REALITY

(no horizon)

PERCEIVED

REALITY

Limited views of reality   'Best' limited view

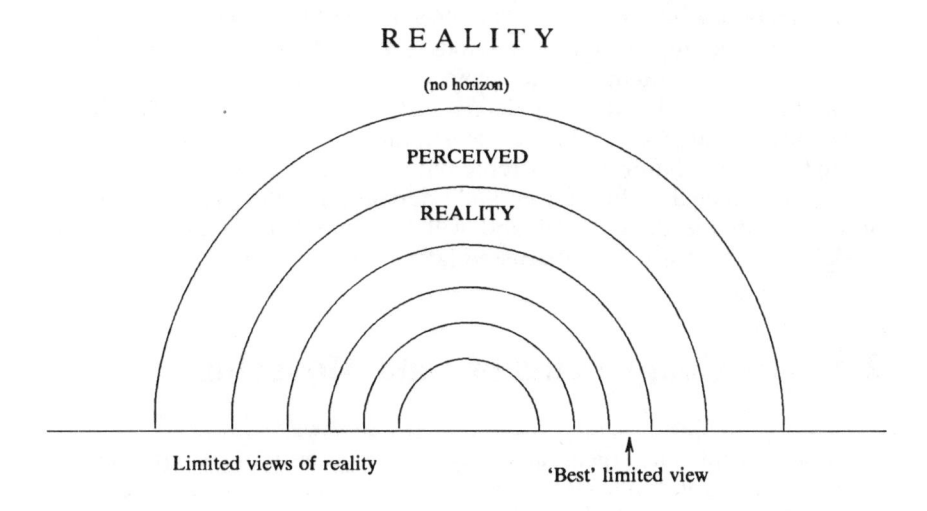

Figure 2.1   Data Modelling Horizons

more importantly, we all have different backgrounds and experiences.

Despite individual differences in perceived reality, the conceptual model which is derived from perceived reality must attempt to embrace all the views of those who wish to use the database, but inevitably some compromises have to be made. The conceptual model must be as comprehensive as possible, and hence the data modeller must ensure that his view of reality is sufficiently broad to meet this objective. It is the data investigation process (briefly discussed earlier) which is, of course, the means by which the data modeller obtains the information for this task.

After data investigation, then, the data modeller's view will be broad and complex, and although this may represent the best model as far as reflecting reality is concerned, it may not be the best model from the information system viewpoint. The data modeller will abstract from reality, reducing his complex view to some simpler and more limited view (as illustrated in Figure 2.1), which will form the basis of the formal conceptual model. From the conceptual model, and using other information obtained previously, the different user views (the *external models*) and the storage structure (the *internal model*) can be derived, but this is done in separate processes, as mentioned earlier.

The main purpose of the data modelling stage is to provide an overall and user-oriented view of the database. For this purpose the use of a diagrammatic notation is an important aid to communication between all those involved with the database including database specialists and end-users. Many different notations exist which support various different data modelling methodologies. The objective will be to represent as much of the semantic information as possible in the data model diagram, while at the same time attempting to avoid cluttering it up so much that the visual impact of the data model is lost. All the basic facts will be represented and some of the constraints. Certain constraints (for example, those relating to data representation) are not the concern of the conceptual model. Inference and derivation rules add a further dimension to the data model and will be omitted from the basic data model diagram, but will be discussed later in the chapter.

2.4 The Components of Data Modelling

Real world facts generally describe relationships or associations between real world objects — people, cars, books, courses, etc. The *relationship* (or *association*) is a very important data modelling component, and will be considered first; this will be followed by a discussion of two other important components: the *entity* and *attribute*. Finally, two subsidiary components associated with entities and attributes will be discussed: the *domain* and the *identifier*.

2.4.1 Relationships

There are a number of different notations currently in use for representing the relationships between modelled objects. For instance, all of the examples in Figure 2.2 below represent a simple one-to-many relationship between object A and object B.

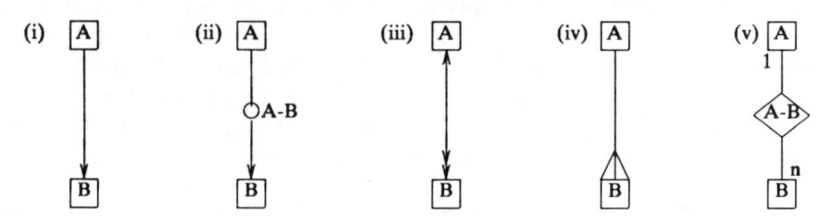

Figure 2.2 Different One-to-many Relationship Notations

Some notations (such as (i) and (ii)) are somewhat restrictive, partly for historical reasons. Notation (ii) was designed by Charles Bachman for the diagrammatic representation of Codasyl database descriptions, and hence carries similar restrictions to those of Codasyl data models which will be discussed in the next chapter. Other notations (such as (iii), (iv) and (v)) are capable of supporting different types of relationship, not just the simple one-to-many relationship. Notation (iii) is described in detail by Robinson (1981); notation (iv) was first proposed by Baker and has subsequently been taken up and developed by others including CACI and Rock-Evans (1981); notation (v) was designed by Chen (1976) and has gained in popularity over the years (Chen 1980).

Simple notations such as (i) and (ii) were those used in the early days of databases when the representation of one-to-many relationships was considered to be of prime importance. But it was soon recognised that the real world has more to it than just one-to-many relationships between objects. The need to bridge the gap between the real world view and the restricted view represented by the data model led to research into database design methodology and notation, and techniques such as those described in Robinson (1981), Rock-Evans (1981), Chen (1976), are now available which enable data structure diagrams to be drawn which contain a vast amount of real world information. In this chapter a hybrid notation based on (iii) and (v) will be used; this will be discussed in more detail later. The basic notation for relationships is given in Figure 2.3 together with some examples.

The *type* of a relationship consists of two main characteristics: the *degree* of the relationship and its *existence*. To determine the type, the possible situations which might exist at any point in time need to be considered. In the first example in Figure 2.3, there is a one-to-one mandatory relationship between book and title, and the relationship itself has been called 'is-named' in the 'book —> title' direction and 'is-name-of' in the 'title —> book' direction. The fact being modelled is that a book is named by a title, and more specifically a book must always have just one title and a title belongs to one book only, assuming unique titles. (Note: in general it cannot be assumed that titles are unique; this assumption is made here for illustrative purposes but will be dropped later.) In the second example, there is a one-to-many optional relationship between a trade-union and employee, reflecting the fact that a trade-union may have many employees as members (though it need not in fact have any), while an employee may be a member of a trade-union but need not be. This relationship only applies, of course, to trade-unions which are not 'closed-shops'; the third example models the closed-shop situation with a one-to-many mandatory relationship between trade-union and employee. Already the power of the notation in enabling us to represent real world information can be seen. The next two examples show contingent relationships; these are relationships in which there is an optional relationship in one direction and a mandatory relationship in the other direction, giving a contingent relationship

a) Notation

Degree of relationship
(represented by arrowheads)

```
————————  undefined
<————————>  one-to-one
<————————>>  one-to-many
<<————————>>  many-to-many
```

Existence of relationship
(represented by lines
  between arrowheads)

```
————————  mandatory
- - - - - - - -  optional
————  - - - -  contingent
```

b) Examples

(i) Book
  ↑ is-named
  |
  ↓ is-name-of
  Title

(ii) Trade-Union
  ↑ has-member
  ¦
  ↓ is-member-of
  Employee

(iii) Closed-shop Trade-Union
  ↑ has-member
  |
  ↓ is-member-of
  Employee

(iv) Person
  ↑ owns
  ¦
  ↓ is-owned-by
  Car

(v) Student
  ↑ registered-for
  ¦
  ↓ has-registration
  Degree

(vi) Degree
  ↑ contains
  |
  ↓ contained-in
  Lecture-Course

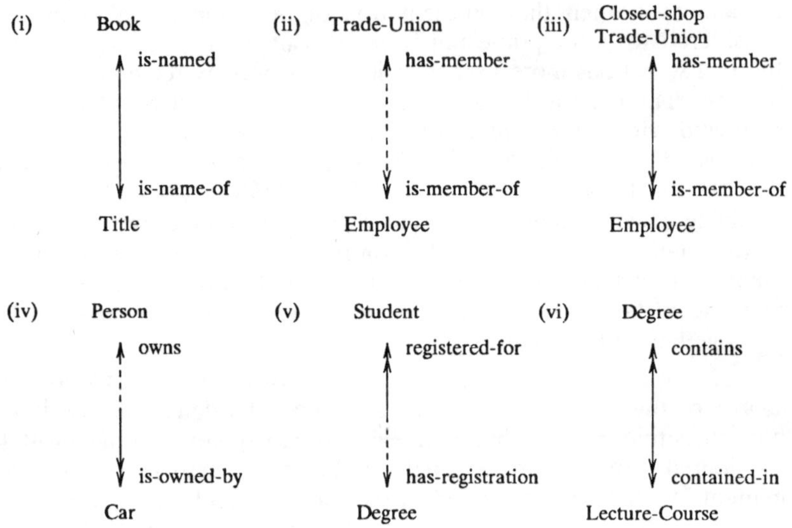

Figure 2.3 Relationships — Notation and Examples

overall. In (iv) a person may or may not own one or more cars, but a car must always have just one owner, hence the relationship is optional in the person —> car direction, mandatory in the car —> person direction, and contingent overall. In (v) a student must always be registered for just one degree, but a particular degree may or may not have students registered for it. The final example shows a many-to-many mandatory relationship. A degree must always contain lecture courses, and a lecture course must always be associated with at least one degree and may be associated with many degrees.

Finally, the undefined relationship type (a line with no arrowheads, illustrated in Figure 2.3 a) Notation) is worth mentioning. It may be found to be useful in the early stages of building a data model for enabling a rough initial version to be drawn, which shows objects in the model with an indication of the relationships but no details; it may also be used when the type of a particular relationship has not been fully determined.

2.4.2 Entities and Attributes

The next two data modelling components to be considered are: the *entity* and the *attribute*. When discussing relationships in the previous section no mention was made of the types of objects which were being related to each other. This was because the notation for relationships may be considered to be independent of the types of the related objects. But many DBMSs do require one to distinguish between objects which are entities and those which are attributes in the context of the database application area being modelled. Hence the significance of this section. It should, however, be stressed that, whereas objects may exist completely independently in a database, relationships cannot exist on their own; they are dependent on the existence of at least one object in the database.

An entity may be defined as a person or thing which exists in the real world and which possesses characteristics in which we are interested. An attribute may be defined as a quality, feature or characteristic of an entity. The distinction between an entity and an attribute is often obvious. For example, a book, person, or aircraft would normally be identified as entities; on the other hand, a title, name, or aircraft type might be identified as respective attributes of each of those entities. However, the distinction sometimes depends on context. Consider the case of the object: colour. To a car salesman, colour may simply be an attribute of a car, while to a paint manufacturer, colour is an entity in its own right which possesses characteristics such as chemical composition. As another example, to a travel agent dealing with holiday flats a television may be an attribute of the flats, while to a TV manufacturer a television is an entity possessing characteristics such as cathode ray tube type, screen size, etc.

Many DBMSs are record-oriented systems and force one to distinguish between entities and attributes. In such systems, records are the physical means of representing entities and their associated attributes. Systems based on binary relationships (such as logic, fact-based, and functional systems) are not record-oriented; instead, entities and attributes are represented as atomic objects and are associated with each other by means of binary relationships or functions. Such systems will be considered in the next chapter, together with different types of record-oriented system. Due to the current importance of the entity concept in existing DBMSs, the conceptual modelling approach to be adopted in this chapter will be based on entities, attributes and relationships, but it will be seen in the next chapter that this approach is easily mapped into a binary relationship model as well as entity-based models.

2.4.3 Domains and Identifiers

Each entity and attribute is a member of a set of objects of a particular type; that is, each one belongs to a particular class or *domain*. At any one time the actual entities or attribute values represented in a database are most likely only to be a subset of all possible objects of that type. Consider the case of books. In a library database the set of books represented in the database will only be a subset of the set of all published books; and if the publisher is included as an attribute of each book, the set of publishers represented may also be a subset of the set of all publishers.

Names given to attributes are often the same as the names of the underlying domains. However, this is not always the case. Members of a particular domain may play different *roles* in different contexts, and in this case it is useful to name the attributes according to the roles they play. Suppose, for example, that colour is identified as a domain in a car retailers database. It may be required to associate three colour attributes with the car entity: the exterior colour, the interior colour, and the upholstery colour. These are three attributes drawn from the same domain, but playing different roles in relation to the entity with which they are associated.

An important feature of an entity is its *identifier*. It is essential to be able to uniquely identify particular entity occurrences. For example, if we consider 'people', we humans are able to uniquely identify others by their appearance (facial appearance, height, build, etc.), except of course for identical twins. It is, of course, important to be able to do so. However, until it is feasible to store image data in conventional databases, we need some other means of identifying individuals. Furthermore, visual appearance is inappropriate in the case of inanimate objects such as books.

A solution is to select one or more attributes of an entity to act as the identifier of that entity. In some situations, a single attribute may provide a unique identifier, in others it may be necessary to combine two or more attributes to form the unique identifier. For example, the name of a person is very unlikely to be unique except in the most limited of environments, and even then uniqueness could not be guaranteed. Similarly, we cannot guarantee that the title of a book is unique; only by specifying the author as well can we be sure to be able to identify a particular book, and even then there may be a problem with many different editions of the same book.

An alternative to a multi-attribute identifier is the use of a unique coding scheme. In some cases such a coding scheme may already be available. An example is the International Standard Book Number (ISBN); this is a 10-character code which is assigned to each published book and which uniquely identifies a particular book by a particular author published by a particular publisher in a particular year. An advantage of using a code as an identifier is its conciseness as compared to more natural means of identification such as names and titles. It may be necessary to invent a coding scheme if no suitable one exists, but coding schemes are quite commonly used in existing manual or file-based systems. Codes used purely for identifying entities are sometimes referred to as *surrogates*. There is some controversy as to whether user-controlled attributes in a conceptual model should be used by the system as permanent surrogates (system identifiers) (Codd 1979, Kent 1979), but since no distinction is made in many systems between user-defined identifiers and system identifiers this will not be discussed further here. Since unique identification is important in later stages of the database development process, use will be made of surrogates where relevant.

2.5 Data Model Diagrams and the Top-down Data Modelling Methodology

Data model diagrams are built up from the components discussed in the previous section. Before a data model diagram can be drawn, however, the entities, attributes and relationships in the system to be modelled must be identified. Many different methodologies have been proposed for this purpose but only two will be considered in this book: the top-down approach and the more formal relation normalisation approach. The former is discussed in this section and the latter in the next.

The term *entity set* will be used to refer to a class of entities of the same type. The term *relationship set* will be used to refer to a class of relationships between entities, which have attributes dependent on the relationship and not just on the separate entities (Vetter 1981, Chen 1976). Relationship sets have some similar characteristics to entity sets and do commonly relate to actual real world objects. Some methodologies use the same diagrammatic notation for these two types of set and refer to them both as entity sets (Robinson 1981, and others), but different diagrammatic notation will be used in this book in order to be able to distinguish between them when relevant.

The basic notation to be used in this section will consist of the notation for relationships given in Figure 2.3 and the notation for objects which is given below. Names of entity and relationship sets will be shown in uppercase, names of attributes will be in lowercase with an initial uppercase letter, and names of relationships will be in lowercase. Extensions to support additional semantics are discussed later in the chapter.

```
┌──────────┐      ╱╲                    ╱─────────────╲
│ ENTITY   │    ╱ RELATIONSHIP ╲       (  Attribute Set )
│   SET    │    ╲     SET      ╱        ╲─────────────╱
└──────────┘      ╲╱
```

Figure 2.4   Diagrammatic Notation for Objects

The top-down approach involves initially identifying the main entity sets in the system and determining the relationships between them. The process of determining the relationships may lead to further refinement of the entities and relationships already identified, or to the identification of new entities and relationships. This process results in an entity-relationship diagram being built. The attributes associated with the entities can then be considered and an entity-attribute diagram built. These two diagrams — the entity-relationship and the entity-attribute diagrams — represent our data model, and can be combined into one composite diagram.

In more detail, the steps involved in the top-down methodology are as follows:

Step 1: Identify entity sets and the relationships between them.
Start with major entities, then gradually build up the model by introducing other entities until a basic entity-relationship model has been developed.

Step 2: Identify attributes associated with the entity sets and develop an entity-attribute model.

Step 3: Determine whether any attributes are associated with relationships identified in step 1. If so, create relationship sets from these relationships and hence produce a refined version of the entity-relationship and entity-attribute models.

Step 4: Select identifiers for each entity set.

Step 5: Determine the domains from which each attribute is drawn.

Step 6: Combine the entity-relationship and entity-attribute diagram into one data model diagram.

The top-down approach will be illustrated by means of an example, which will be based on the library system introduced in Chapter 1.†

Step 1: Identify entity sets and relationships

Step 1 involves identifying the major entities and the relationships between them. Two types of entity can immediately be identified in a library system: book and person (borrower), and the basic relationship between them is the loan relationship. The first version of the data model is based on the following observations:

a book can only be lent to one person at a time;

a person may borrow more than one book at a time; and

at any point in time, it is not necessary for all books to be out on loan, nor is it necessary for all persons to have a book on loan.

The model may be depicted diagrammatically as follows:

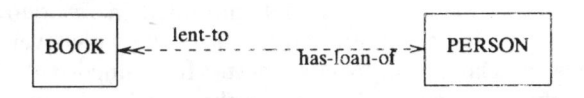

```
┌──────┐    lent-to      ┌────────┐
│ BOOK │◄─ ─ ─ ─ ─ ─ ─ ─ │ PERSON │
│      │    has-loan-of ►│        │
└──────┘                 └────────┘
```

Figure 2.5 The Loan Relationship

Note that the relationship between book and person has been named in both directions. This enables the nature of the relationship to be 'read' directly from the diagram; for example, from the above diagram it can be seen that:

optionally, a book is lent to a person,

and also optionally, a person has the loan of many books.

It is obviously useful to name the relationships in both directions, but when the data model is large and complex the data model diagram can become rather cluttered and the impact of a diagrammatic representation can be lost as a result. Some older data modelling methodologies do not name relationships at all, but it is now generally recognised that naming is essential, not only to distinguish between multiple relationships between two entities, but also to provide more useful information in the model (cf. Nijssen's Niam notation, which names relationships in both directions (Verheijen 1982)). In this chapter relationships will be named in both directions when the examples are simple, but with more complex examples relationships will be named in one direction only.

If more aspects of the library system are considered it will be realised that people may reserve books when they are out on loan to others, so

---

† The author acknowledges the similarity between the library example in this book and one in Howe (1983), chs. 14 & 15; the similarity is a pure coincidence as the author has been using this for some years.

there are actually two relationships between book and person: loan and reservation.

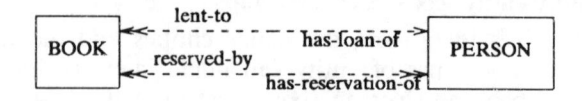

Figure 2.6 The Loan and Reservation Relationships

Note that the reservation relationship is many-to-many since a book may be reserved by many people at a time.

Now, if the library system being modelled is a university library, it is likely that multiple copies of some books will be available. Whereas a loan will relate to a physical book, a reservation will relate to a particular title and author — the reserver is not interested in reserving a specific copy of a book; he is only interested in borrowing whichever copy of the book becomes available for loan soonest. It is important therefore to distinguish between a physical book on the one hand, and a catalogue entry relating to that book and all other copies of it on the other hand. The next refinement, then, incorporates the result of this analysis.

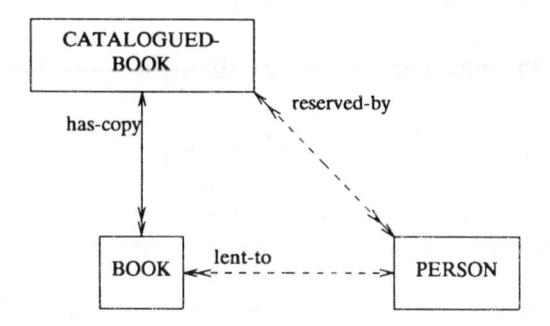

Figure 2.7 Refined Loan and Reservation Relationships

The relationship between catalogued book and book is mandatory since it is assumed that a catalogue entry for a book is only made in the library database if at least one copy of the book exists in the library, and also a book cannot exist in our database without a catalogue entry for it.

From the facts listed in section 2.2 a further entity can be identified: loan status. It will be remembered from the discussion of entities and attributes in section 2.4 that the distinction between what is an entity and what is an attribute is not always obvious. Whereas it may at first sight appear that loan status should be an attribute rather than an entity, from the facts it can be seen that loan status possesses characteristics which are of interest (for example, loan period and maximum number of books on loan). Hence loan status in this library context needs to be represented as an entity, and since borrowers will be assigned a particular status, this entity will be related to the person entity.

At the end of step 1 the entity-relationship model is as indicated in Figure 2.8.

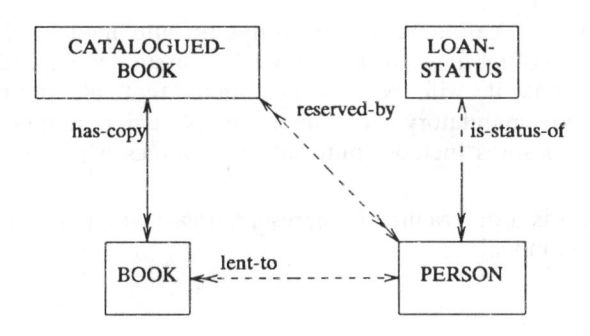

Figure 2.8 The Entity-Relationship Model at the end of Step 1

The contingent relationship between person and loan status assumes that a loan status can exist without there being any borrowers in the database with that status at a particular point in time.

Step 2: Identify attributes

Step 2 in the top-down approach to data modelling involves identifying attributes associated with the entities. It is, of course, only necessary to consider attributes relevant to the application. For example, in the library system, a book's title and author are of interest but not its size; if, however, a book mail order system were being modelled, size would be relevant since it would determine what sort of packaging was required. The identification of attributes will enable an entity-attribute diagram to be built. The facts listed in section 2.2 help to determine an initial list of attributes for the four entities in Figure 2.8 as follows:

CATALOGUED-BOOK: Author, Title, Publisher, Year, Classmark, Isbn

BOOK: Book#, Shelf

Note: each book is assumed to be allocated a unique number when purchased.

PERSON: Name, Address

LOAN-STATUS: Status, Loan-period, Max-num-books

From this list we can develop an entity-attribute model. The entity-attribute relationships need to be analysed in a similar manner to entity relationships but it will be assumed here that all entity-attribute relationships are mandatory. The implications of non-mandatory entity-attribute relationships include 'null' attribute values which are discussed in section 2.7.

Figure 2.9 is a diagrammatic representation of the first version of the entity-attribute model.

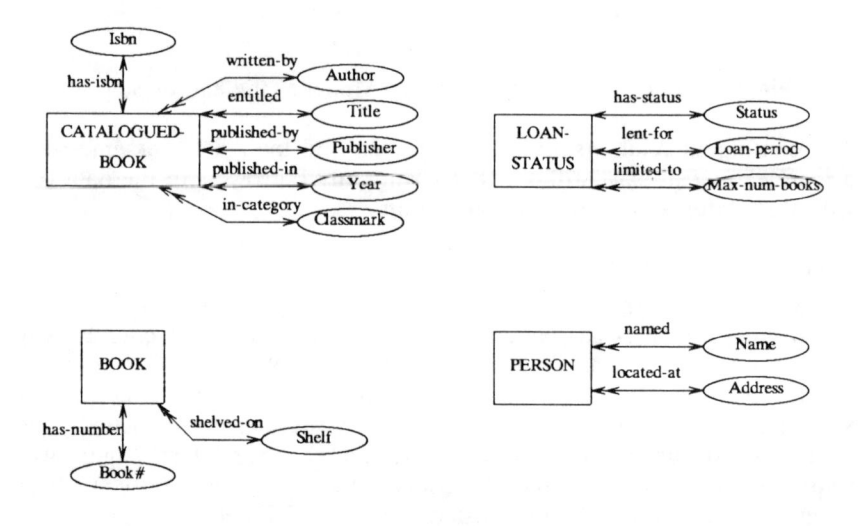

Figure 2.9 The Entity-Attribute Model (first version)

The entity-attribute relationships have been named in one direction only in this diagram, i.e. the entity to attribute direction. Note that all of the relationships are either one-to-one or many-to-one in the entity-to-attribute direction. It is assumed here that only one author is recorded for each book in the catalogue. It is left as an exercise for the reader, after he has read this chapter and the next, to work through a revised library database example in which books may have multiple authors recorded in the catalogue.

Step 3: Identify relationship sets

Step 3 concerns the entity relationships identified in step 1. We are interested in those relationships which logically have attributes associated with them. As far as the loan and reservation relationships are concerned, the loan of a book to a specific person will have a date due back associated with it, while a reservation of a book by a person will have a date of reservation associated with it in order that reservations may be dealt with on a 'first come, first served' basis. Thus loans and reservations should be considered as relationship sets. In a manual library system they would in fact be objects in their own right; there would actually exist physical objects such as loan and reservation slips on which would be recorded the loan of a book to, or reservation of a book by, a person. Some would argue that loan and reservation slips are truly entities, but although they are real world objects they represent two different relationships between two entities. It is often useful to distinguish between objects which are basic entities and objects derived from relationships, so the distinction is maintained by referring to the former as entity sets and the latter as relationship sets.

The entity-relationship model is thus further refined as illustrated in Figure 2.10.

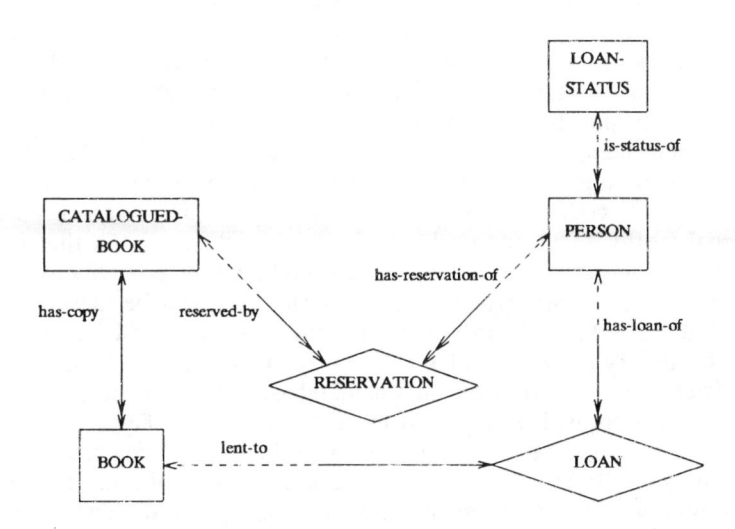

Figure 2.10 The Entity-Relationship Diagram for the Library Example

Note that the existence characteristics of the new relationships involving loan and reservation are contingent, and not optional as in the previous version. This is due to the fact that a reservation or a loan must always be associated with a book (physical or catalogue entry) and a person, but it is not necessary for a book or person to have a loan or reservation associated with it. Note also that the degree of the relationship between book and loan is one-to-one, and that the original many-to-many reservation relationship has become two one-to-many relationships.

The entity-attribute list must also be revised to include attributes associated with the relationship sets: loan and reservation, as follows:

    LOAN: Date-due-back
    RESERVATION: Date-reserved

Step 4: Select identifiers

In the next two steps of the top-down approach identifiers are selected for each entity set and the underlying domains of the attributes are identified. Firstly, how can each of the entities be uniquely identified? An attribute which has a one-to-one relationship with an entity can be used as a unique identifier. If more than one unique attribute exists for a particular entity then the most 'natural' or the most concise one should be selected. It can be seen from the entity-attribute diagram in Figure 2.9 that the Isbn can be used to identify catalogued book, the book number to identify book, and the status to identify loan status. When the person entity is considered however, the name may not be unique, so cannot be used on its own. Either it can be combined with the address, or alternatively a coding scheme can be devised for identification purposes. As mentioned earlier, the advantage of the latter is its conciseness; the disadvantage is the fact that it is less 'natural' than using a name and address to identify a person. However as indicated in section 2.4.3, coding schemes for identifying entities commonly exist in the real world. The approach which will be taken here is that in cases where unique attributes or appropriate coding schemes already exist in our sphere of interest (for example, Isbn), these will be made use of as entity identifiers, while in other cases the symbol # will be used on its own to signify a 'ghost' identifier — a currently non-existent unique identifier. At a later stage in the database development process these ghost identifiers will be replaced by real identifiers. The real identifiers will either be specially devised coding schemes (surrogates) or multi-attribute identifiers; the choice between these two alternatives depends on a number of factors which are not conceptual design aspects and therefore the choice is not made at this stage.

Step 5: Determine domains

Before drawing the complete data model diagram the domains underlying the attributes should be determined. Most of the attributes in the library model come from independent domains. For example, Isbn will come from the domain of all ISBNs, a person's address from the domain of addresses, loan-period from a domain representing numbers of weeks, and the title of a book from a title domain. Such attribute-domain associations can be represented as illustrated below (with domains in uppercase italics):

    Isbn ∈ *ISBN*
    Address ∈ *ADDRESS*
    Loan-period ∈ *NUM-OF-WEEKS*
    Title ∈ *TITLE*

However, some different attributes do share the same domain. For example, assuming that Author will be represented as a single name only, then Author and Name (of person) will both come from the same domain of person names. Also Date-reserved and Date-due-back will come from the domain of dates.

There may be some constraints on the values in a domain. For example, the *STATUS* domain may be limited to the values: staff, undergraduate, postgraduate, or visitor. There may also be additional constraints on the values of specific attributes. Any additional information concerning domains and constraints which is obtained at this stage will be added to the data dictionary.

It is now possible to draw a complete entity-attribute diagram, but this task is left to the reader. The diagram for Catalogued Book is shown in Figure 2.11 as a guide.

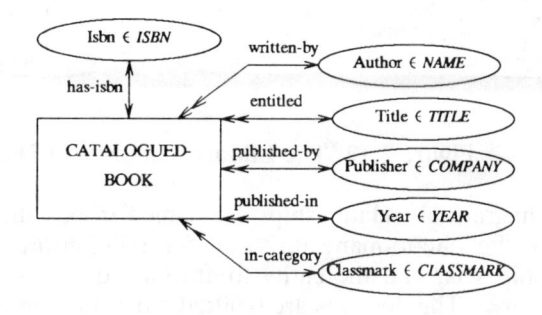

Figure 2.11 Catalogued Book Entity-Attribute Diagram

Step 6: Construct the complete conceptual model

To complete this section on data model diagrams, the two types of diagram which have just been derived — entity-relationship and entity-attribute — are combined into one data model diagram in Figure 2.12.

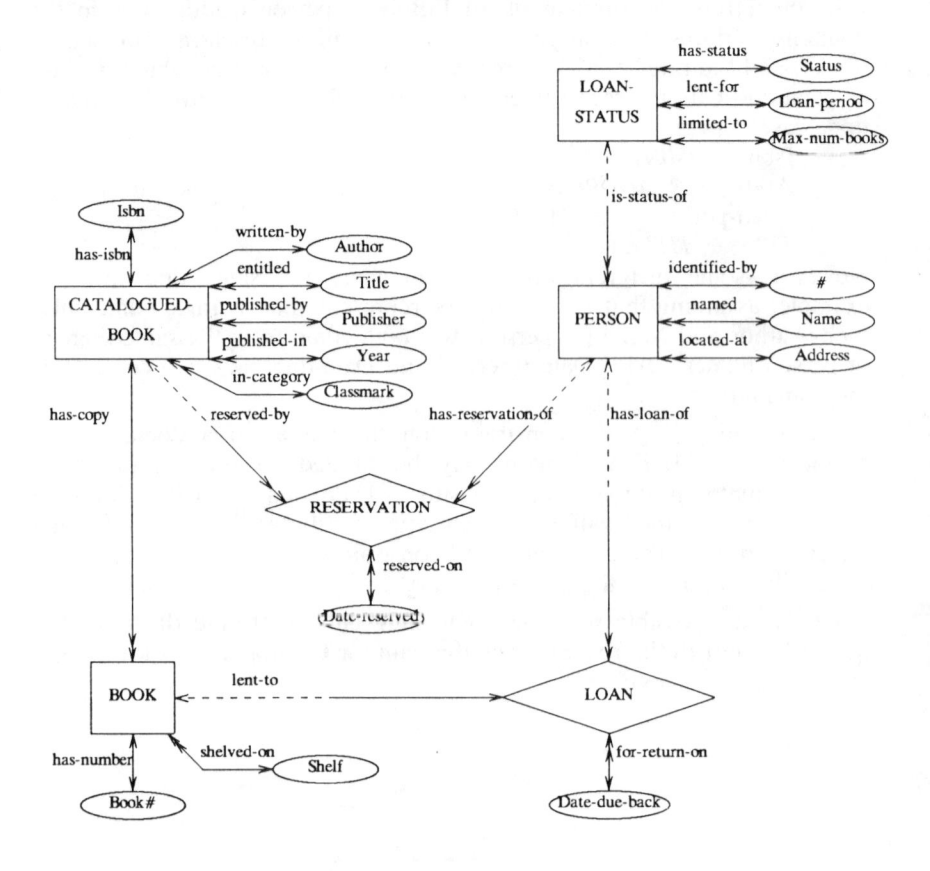

Figure 2.12 The Library Data Model Diagram

In this diagram all relationships are named in one direction only; this is generally the one-to-many direction for relationships between entity or relationship sets, and the entity to attribute direction for entity-attribute relationships. The domains are omitted from this composite diagram.

Although the composite diagram is complex, it identifies in one diagram the important features of the conceptual model which represents a particular view of the real world, and it is semantically quite rich. From such a diagram, DBMS-specific data models can be derived (as will be seen in the next chapter), including binary relationship models, even though such models do not distinguish between entities and attributes. It should be noted, however, that in the case of large and complex databases it will not always be feasible to produce a composite diagram. In this case one can either omit this last data modelling step, or alternatively divide the data model into sections and link the sections together as appropriate.

There is one final point to mention before concluding this section, and that is the concept of an *access path* or *navigational route*. In the entity-relationship diagram, the arrows indicating the relationships provide an access path or navigational route from one entity or relationship set to another. For example, although book and person are not directly linked, a book can be accessed from a person (assuming that person has a book on loan) by following the path from person to loan and then from loan to book. Access paths are important in relation to retrieval of data from the database, and this will be considered in more detail in a later chapter.

2.6 The Normalisation Methodology for Data Modelling

2.6.1 An Introduction to Normalisation

The data modelling approach used in the previous section was a top-down approach. An alternative which has been widely used in the past is the *normalisation* methodology, which can be considered as a bottom-up approach. It was originally devised as a database design tool for relational databases but has been found to be a useful tool for conceptual modelling for other types of database. As it has been used successfully for conceptual modelling and is an accepted technique, it is discussed in this chapter. Relational databases are discussed in detail in the next chapter.

There are various normal forms. The first three are the most well known: First (1NF), Second (2NF), and Third (3NF), and these were first introduced by Codd (1972a), but higher normal forms such as Boyce-Codd (BCNF) which is an extension of 3NF, Fourth (4NF) and Fifth (5NF) also exist.

What are the advantages of the normalisation methodology? Firstly, it is a formal technique, with each stage of the normalisation process eliminating a particular type of undesirable dependency. Secondly, it highlights constraints and dependencies in the data, and hence it is an aid to a better understanding of the nature of the data. Thirdly, 3NF and higher normal forms produce well-designed databases which provide a high degree of data independence. This section will concentrate on the first three normal forms since relations in 3NF are satisfactory for many applications. Some undesirable dependencies may still exist in 3NF however, in particular in the case of large and complex databases, and it is these which can benefit from the greater degree of data independence of the higher normal forms, rendering them less likely to be affected by changes in the real world environment underlying the database. A full discussion of the five normal forms may be found in Date (1981), Kent (1983).

For the purpose of discussing the normalisation methodology, it is not necessary to introduce the full relational terminology (this will be done in the next chapter). A *relation* will be simply defined here as a named object together with its associated attributes, and the *primary key* of the relation will be defined as one or more attributes of the relation which enable record occurrences in the relation to be uniquely identified. Normal form definitions will first be introduced, with simple examples as illustrations, and then the library example will be used to illustrate the complete normalisation methodology.

An unnormalised relation

A relation is said to be *unnormalised* if it has repeated values for particular attributes within a single record, while a *normalised* relation contains records with atomic (single) values only. A normalised relation may be thought of as a 'flat file'. An example of the description of an unnormalised relation is as follows:

DEPARTMENT (Dept# , Dept-name,
 repeated group for employee { Employee#, Name, Address,
 Project, Deadline })

which represents a relation containing details of departments (number and name), the employees working in each department (number, name, and address), and the project assigned to each employee together with the project's deadline. The Dept# (department number) attribute has been underlined as it is the primary key of the relation (i.e. each record occurrence in the relation can be uniquely identified by means of Dept#). This relation is unnormalised since for each department it contains repeated information relating to employees within the department.

From unnormalised form to first normal form

A *first normal form* (1NF) relation is one which satisfies the normalised relation condition, but may not necessarily satisfy the conditions for higher normal forms. To convert an unnormalised relation to 1NF, the repeated groups must be removed. If there is a single repeated group only, or the repeated groups are all nested, this can be done simply by basing the relation on the lowest level of repeated group, while if there is more than one independent repeated group the relation must be split so that the repeated groups each form a separate relation. The Department relation above has a single repeated group, so it can be converted to 1NF simply by basing the relation on employee instead of department, as follows:

EMPLOYEE (Dept# , Dept-name, Employee# ,
Name, Address, Project, Deadline)

Employee# is assumed to be unique only within a department, and therefore must be combined with Dept# to form the primary key.

From first to second normal form

A *second normal form* (2NF) relation is in 1NF but also has an additional property — it satisfies the *full functional dependency* rule which states that all non-key attributes must be fully functionally dependent on the primary key. Functional dependency is concerned with the determinancy of attribute values. If a relation has a single-attribute primary key then it must be in 2NF. However, if it has a multi-attribute primary key it is only in 2NF if the complete key is essential for determining all the non-key attributes. If it is possible for a non-key attribute to be determined by a subset of the attributes which form the primary key, it is not in 2NF. Considering the Employee relation introduced above, although it is in 1NF it is not in 2NF. Whereas the Employee# and Dept# are needed to determine a particular employee's name, address, project and deadline, only the Dept# is needed to determine the department name. The following two relations can be formed from the original Employee relation, and are both in 2NF.

EMPLOYEE (Dept# , Employee# , Name, Address,
Project, Deadline)
DEPARTMENT (Dept# , Dept-name)

From second to third normal form

A *third normal form* (3NF) relation is in 2NF but also has an additional property — it satisfies the *non-transitive dependency* rule which states that every non-key attribute must be non-transitively dependent on the primary key, i.e. non-key attributes must be mutually independent. If two non-key attributes in a relation are directly related to each other, the relation is not in 3NF. The new 2NF Employee relation is not in 3NF as there are two mutually dependent attributes in the relation: Project and Deadline. The Deadline attribute is associated with a particular project, and hence it is dependent on project and said to be transitively dependent on Dept#, Employee# (the Employee primary key) via Project; if an employee is assigned a different project, his project deadline will change according to the deadline for the new project. The following two relations can be formed from the previous Employee relation, and are both in 3NF.

EMPLOYEE (<u>Dept#</u> , <u>Employee#</u> , Name, Address, Project)
PROJECT (<u>Project</u> , Deadline)

In the process of splitting the previous relation in two, the Project attribute remains in Employee as well as being the primary key attribute of its own relation. If the Project attribute were not retained within the Employee relation the association between an employee and the project assigned to him would be lost. The Project attribute in the Employee relation is referred to as a *foreign key*. A foreign key is the primary key of some other relation (the Project relation in this example).

In general it is the case that in splitting a relation in two, the primary key attribute of one of the new relations must be retained in the other, in order to maintain the relevant association (relationship) and avoid losing information in the normalisation process. Note that this happened automatically in the conversion of the Employee relation from 1NF to 2NF since both Dept# and Employee# were necessary to uniquely identify an employee. If Employee# had been unique within the database as a whole, Dept# (the primary key of Department) would have been retained in the new Employee relation as a foreign key to maintain the association between an employee and his department, but it would not have formed part of the primary key of Employee.

At some stage in the normalisation process it is important to identify the domains underlying the attributes. Ideally this should be done at the initial (unnormalised) stage, and the attribute-domain associations should be maintained throughout the normalisation process. In this way, when relations are split during normalisation, attributes which exist in more than one relation in order to maintain relevant associations (relationships) may be renamed if required without losing sight of the associations, since these will be reflected in the common underlying domains of the attribute. Domains have not been introduced in the simple examples in this section since the primary objective is to illustrate the normalisation process.

The 3NF objective is to arrive at a set of relations such that the attributes of the relations are atomic, and all non-key attributes are fully functionally dependent on the primary key and mutually independent. The last two relations above — Employee and Project — together with the Department relation are all in 3NF and reflect the same real world information as the original unnormalised Department relation. The 3NF data model of the Department database is thus:

DEPARTMENT (Dept# , Dept-name)
EMPLOYEE (Dept# , Employee# , Name, Address, Project)
PROJECT (Project , Deadline)

Primary, candidate, and alternate keys

Before briefly mentioning the higher normal forms two terms will be defined: *candidate key* and *alternate key*. A candidate key is such that it could be chosen as the primary key of a relation. An attribute or set of attributes is referred to as a candidate key if it can uniquely identify records in a relation and, in the case of a set of attributes, no subset of that set is itself a candidate key. There may be more than one candidate key for a relation and if so, one is chosen to be the primary key, the remaining candidate key(s) being referred to as alternate keys. Consider the Employee relation. Employee# plus Dept# is one candidate key and the combination of Name and Address forms another candidate key. Employee# plus Dept# is chosen as the primary key and hence Name and Address form an alternate key. In the normal form definitions, a non-key attribute is one that is neither part of the primary key nor part of any alternate key.

Higher normal forms

As mentioned earlier full discussions of all the normal forms may be found elsewhere, but BCNF, 4NF and 5NF will be mentioned briefly. BCNF is a stronger form of 3NF and concerns attributes which are determinants, i.e. which are capable of determining other attributes in a relation. The BCNF rule states that all determinants in a relation must be candidate keys. In the 2NF Employee relation above, Name and Address together are a determinant of Project and Deadline but they also form a candidate key. However Project is a determinant of Deadline but it is not a candidate key; hence, in addition to not being in 3NF the relation is also not in BCNF as might be expected. The 3NF relations derived above are also in BCNF. The 4NF and 5NF rules are concerned with dependencies within a multi-attribute key itself. For such dependencies to exist the key must consist of at least three attributes. None of the above 3NF relations have more than two attributes in the key and hence they must be in 4NF and in 5NF.

Normal form transformations and relational algebra

The transformation of relations from one normal form to another may more formally be expressed in terms of relational algebra operations. This will be mentioned again after relational algebra has been introduced in Chapter 4.

2.6.2 Normalisation and the Library Example

The normalisation process will now be applied to the library example. It will be remembered that data modelling takes place after the data investigation stage has been carried out. Sufficient information should have been obtained from the data investigation stage to enable a relation to be created which contains attributes representing all the real world objects of interest; this is referred to as a *universal relation*, and is the first version of the data model relating to the database application area. It may not always be easy or possible to start with a single relation, in particular if the database application area is complex and a large number of attributes are involved, but it should be possible to define the initial data model by means of a very small number of relations.

Below is a universal relation representing the library database.

BOOK-DATA (<u>Isbn</u> , Author, Title, Publisher,
                Year, Classmark,
    repeated group for loans { Book#, Shelf, Name, Address,
        Status, Loan-period, Max-num-books, Date-due-back }
    repeated group for reservations { Name, Address,
        Status, Loan-period, Max-num-books, Date-reserved })

The relation has been named Book-Data and is based on a library catalogue, with one record per catalogue entry, identified by the Isbn, containing details relating to the catalogued book, copies held and lent out, and reservations. At this stage, status information is considered to be part of the recorded personal information; it is needed for reservations as well as loans since in general reservations will at some time become loans and this information is then important. It should be noted that it is not the only universal relation which could be created in this case; it is also possible to create a universal relation based on the physical books, rather than the catalogue entries. It is left to the reader to try out the normalisation methodology using this alternative universal relation, after he has worked through this section.

The Book-Data relation shows that for each Isbn there will be repeated information relating to specific copies and associated loans, and also repeated information relating to persons who have reserved the book. Note that when a copy of a book exists which is not currently on loan, the Book# and Shelf information will exist but there will be null values in the remaining loan attributes. Since non-atomic, repeated attributes exist the relation is unnormalised.

To convert the unnormalised relation to 1NF, the repeated groups must be removed. If there is a single repeated group only, or the repeated groups are all nested, this can be done simply by basing the relation on the lowest level of repeated group, as mentioned earlier, but in this case there are two independent repeated groups. The universal relation is therefore split into three in this case. One relation contains only the catalogue information, the second contains the physical book and loan information together with a copy of the Isbn to maintain the association with the catalogue information, and the third contains the reservation information again with a copy of the Isbn. The 1NF relations thus derived are as follows:

CATALOGUED-BOOK (<u>Isbn</u> , Author, Title,
        Publisher, Year, Classmark)
BOOK-LOAN-DATA (<u>Book#</u> , Isbn, Shelf, Name, Address,
        Status, Loan-period, Max-num-books, Date-due-back)
BOOK-RESERVED-DATA (<u>Isbn</u> , <u>Name</u> , <u>Address</u> ,
        Status, Loan-period, Max-num-books, Date-reserved)

Note that since the number assigned to the book is unique (as indicated in section 2.2), it can be used as the primary key for the Book-Loan-Data relation. However, the Book-Reserved-Data relation contains the information about reservations of catalogued books by persons, and since a specific book may be reserved by more than one person and a specific person may reserve more than one book, neither Isbn on its own, nor the name and address of a person on their own can uniquely identify a particular reservation; hence the primary key of this relation must be formed by the combination of Isbn, Name and Address attributes.

The above relations are in 1NF but they may not be in 2NF. It was stated earlier that if a relation has a single-attribute primary key it must be in 2NF. Hence Catalogued-Book and Book-Loan-Data are already in 2NF, but Book-Reserved-Data may not be. To find out if it is, each non-key attribute must be considered in turn to see if it can be determined by a subset of the primary key. If all attributes in the relation require the whole key to determine them, then it is in 2NF, otherwise it must be split into a set of relations, each of which satisfy the 2NF rule. Date-reserved depends on both the book reserved and the person reserving it and hence the complete primary key is required to determine it. But clearly the status information relates purely to the individual reserving the book, and hence Isbn is not needed for its determination, only the person's Name and Address are required. Thus Book-Reserved-Data is not in 2NF.

To convert Book-Reserved-Data to 2NF it is split into two relations, one with the original composite primary key together with Date-reserved which depends on it, and the other with Name and Address as the primary key together with the status information which depends on that key. The following are the resulting 2NF relations:

RESERVATION (Isbn , Name , Address , Date-reserved)
PERSON-DATA (Name , Address , Status,
   Loan-period, Max-num-books)

These, together with Catalogued-Book and Book-Loan-Data, are the four relations forming the 2NF version of the library data model.

To determine whether the 2NF relations are also in 3NF, the non-key attributes must be considered to assess whether they are mutually independent or not. If all non-key attributes in a relation are mutually independent (i.e. no transitive dependencies exist), the relation is in 3NF; if not, the relation must again be split so that the related attributes form a separate relation. In Book-Loan-Data, the status information is related to the Name and Address (which identifies the person borrowing the book); the status attributes are only dependent on the primary key Book# via Name and Address. Thus, Book-Loan-Data in not in 3NF. When this relation is split, it is found that a relation already exists containing the Name, Address and status information — Person-Data. It will sometimes happen, in particular with a large data model, that in the process of decomposing relations into higher normal forms, duplicate (or nearly equivalent) relations will be created; duplicates may be removed and nearly equivalent relations may be combined if they have the same primary key. Splitting Book-Loan-Data will therefore result in just one new relation in this case:

BOOK-LOAN (Book# , Isbn, Shelf,
   Name, Address, Date-due-back)

Further analysis of the other 2NF relations shows that Person-Data is not in 3NF. Loan-period and Max-num-books are dependent on the primary key (Name and Address) only via Status; hence Status, Loan-period and Max-num-books are not mutually independent. This relation, then, must also be split so that the status information is in a relation of its own. The resulting two relations are:

PERSON (Name , Address , Status)
LOAN-STATUS (Status , Loan-period, Max-num-books)

These two relations, together with Book-Loan above and the other two relations: Catalogued-Book and Reservation, are the five relations forming the 3NF version of the library data model. It is worth pointing out that the resulting 3NF relations are also in 5NF. The complete set of relations is shown in Figure 2.13.

It should be noted that the normalisation approach requires all relations to be uniquely identified by a primary key. In some cases, multi-attribute identifiers will be formed, as in the case of Name and Address in the library example. It is left to the data modeller to decide whether to introduce coding schemes to replace multi-attribute identifiers, but as mentioned in the previous section this decision is based on factors which are not conceptual design aspects so is not considered here.

CATALOGUED-BOOK (<u>Isbn</u> , Author, Title,
    Publisher, Year, Classmark)
RESERVATION (<u>Isbn</u> , <u>Name</u> , <u>Address</u> , Date-reserved)
BOOK-LOAN (<u>Book#</u> , Isbn, Shelf,
    Name, Address, Date-due-back)
PERSON (<u>Name</u> , <u>Address</u> , Status)
LOAN-STATUS (<u>Status</u> , Loan-period, Max-num-books)

Figure 2.13 The Library Example — 3NF Relations

A data model diagram can now be drawn using a modified notation as compared with that used in the previous section. This is shown in Figure 2.14. Relations are represented diagrammatically by rectangular entity boxes, and relationships between them are represented by dotted lines linking appropriate attributes in the different relations. In each relationship, the linking attribute is the primary key of one of the entities (e.g. Isbn links Catalogued-Book, Book, and Reservation, and is the primary key of Catalogued-Book, and Status links Loan-Status and Person, and is the primary key of Loan-Status).

2.6.3 Comments on the Normalisation Approach

The notation in the relational diagram of Figure 2.14 reflects the limited semantics of the normalisation approach. There is no distinction between entity set and relationship set, and no type and existence characteristics of relationships are shown. Such information can be added to the relational diagram by incorporating an additional stage in data modelling after the normalisation methodology has been applied; this stage would concentrate on analysing the relationships in the model.

A further difference between the normalisation approach and the top-down approach relates to the way in which relationships are represented. In the normalisation approach entities are linked by means of attributes, while in the top-down approach entities are linked directly. Hence attributes, such as Isbn in the Book-Loan relation, which are required purely to maintain a link (association, relationship) with some other relation, do not exist in the top-down model.

The most significant difference between this model (Figure 2.14) and the one in the previous section (Figure 2.12) is the absence of the Loan relationship set. The loan relationship is combined with book data in Book-Loan. This is primarily due to the fact that the normalisation approach is implicitly based on the notion that one-to-one relationships between objects are represented by means of entity sets (relations) while

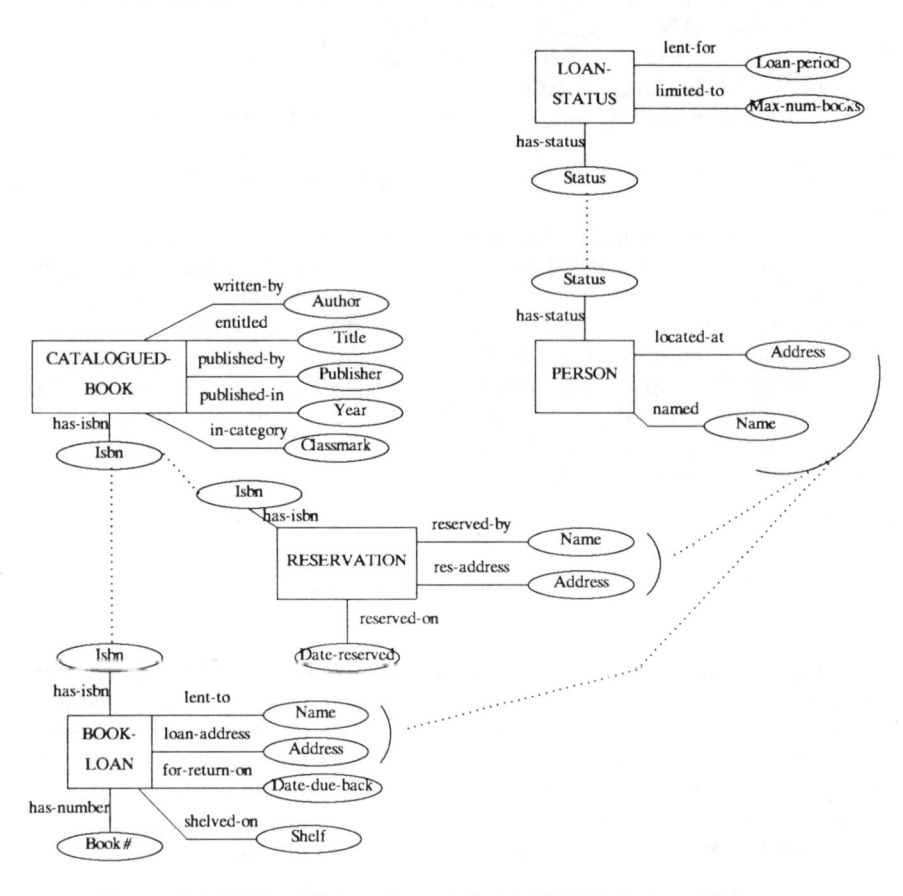

Figure 2.14 The Library Data Model 3NF Relational Diagram
derived using the Normalisation Approach

one-to-many relationships are represented implicitly by attributes in different relations which are drawn from a common domain (as in the case of Isbn in Book-Loan and Reservation which implicitly represent respectively the 'has-copy' and 'reserved-by' relationships with Catalogued-Book). Hence the one-to-one relationship between a book and a loan is 'hidden' in the Book-Loan relation. The main disadvantage of this is the existence of null values for the name, address, and date due back attributes of Book-Loan when a book is not currently on loan, since the relationship between a book and a loan is actually contingent. If the relationship were mandatory there would be no null value problem. Null values have been the subject of some controversy as to whether they should be catered for in a DBMS and if so how they should be handled, and they will be referred to again in the next section.

To complete this section on the normalisation methodology, it will be useful to give some indication of the undesirable update dependencies which can be eliminated by normalisation, since it was indicated at the beginning of this section that the highlighting of constraints and dependencies, and the elimination of undesirable dependencies are important advantages of the normalisation methodology. Basically, a database consisting of relations which are not at least in 3NF may contain dependencies which make updates to the database difficult and may render the database liable to inconsistencies thus reducing the integrity of the database.

To illustrate this point some examples will be provided. Firstly, consider the 1NF Book-Loan-Data and Book-Reserved-Data relations. Suppose it is required to change a particular person's status or address; it is likely that many records will need to be updated in both relations although logically only a single change is required. Furthermore, great care would need to be taken in carrying out the updates to ensure that either all or none of the relevant records are updated, otherwise the data in the database will be inconsistent. The above-mentioned 1NF relations also exhibit an insertion dependency. A person cannot be added to the database unless that person borrows or reserves a book. Hence, 1NF relations do not produce well-designed databases.

Even the 2NF relations exhibit dependencies. For example, there is a deletion dependency in the 2NF Person-Data relation. If a particular status exists which is associated with only one person at a particular point in time and that person is deleted from the database, the information about loan period and maximum number of books associated with that status is lost in the deletion. All these undesirable dependencies do not exist in 3NF and higher NF relations.

Before leaving this section it should be stressed that the top-down approach of the previous section is an informal intuitive approach, whereas the normalisation approach introduced in this section is a formal approach. The former cannot be guaranteed to result in good models — so much depends on the modeller's skill in determining what objects are entities, attributes and relationships; the latter, however, can be guaranteed to result in good models (though not necessarily the best) so long as the modeller applies the normalisation rules rigorously. A good model may be defined as one which is devoid of update dependencies as far as possible, and which remains structurally relatively stable over time despite environmental changes. It should be noted, however, that some update dependencies may be allowed to remain in a model in order to accommodate anticipated future changes, but the modeller will be aware of their existence.

The best approach to data modelling is probably to use top-down analysis initially, and then apply the normalisation rules to the attributes in the resulting entity and relationship sets, to ensure that the design is good. A skilled modeller will find that his model is in 3NF or a higher normal form before he applies any normalisation rules. Normalisation will however serve to verify that his model is a good one. The reader can verify that the data model in Figure 2.12 is in 3NF.

2.7 Further Semantic Aspects of Conceptual Models

Early approaches to data modelling, notably the Bachman diagram and relation normalisation, were oriented towards specific DBMSs and these tended to result in data models which were semantically weak in content. During the past decade however much effort has been devoted towards the objective of devising the best notation and methodology for describing the rich semantic aspects of data models, independent of any specific DBMS. The advantages of this include:
1. generality: due to its independence from specific DBMSs, the best methodology could become a standard for data modelling;
2. flexibility: a semantically rich data model can be mapped into a number of different DBMS data models and hence would be suitable for use as a global model in a distributed database system (see Chapter 6);
3. database integrity: the semantic constraints and rules could be used as a basis for developing application programs which maintain the integrity of the database, by ensuring that integrity constraints and rules in the data model are not violated by the program (this aspect will be discussed further at the end of Chapter 3).

Amongst the various approaches which have been devised are the Entity-Relationship (E-R) appproach of Chen (1976), various approaches based on entity analysis including those of Rock-Evans (1981), Robinson (1981), and others, the Semantic Data Model (SDM) of Hammer (1981), extending the relational approach (Codd 1979), and the functional dependency approach of Bernstein (1976), and Vetter (1981). Chen, Rock-Evans and Robinson utilise a diagrammatic notation; they each have their good points but they also exclude some types of semantic information. Chen's model has gained a great deal of attention and extensions to it have been suggested to enable more semantic information to be incorporated into the model (Scheuermann 1980, Bussolati 1983).

All the above approaches are entity-based and therefore most suited to mapping into entity-based DBMSs. SDM is the most comprehensive and flexible but is complex and purely descriptive.

In this section further aspects of conceptual models will be discussed, together with ways in which they may be represented diagrammatically. The following additional semantic aspects will be briefly discussed: *categorization* (or subsetting), *generalization* (or classification), *aggregation*, and set attributes. These add another dimension to the data models, deriving lower or higher level objects from existing objects. A further 'dimension' of data models — the temporal dimension: time — is also introduced, and the section ends with a discussion of the semantics of null or missing values, and the problems of connection traps.

2.7.1 Categorization and Generalization

Some of the derivation and inference rules referred to in section 2.2 may relate to the types of higher and lower level objects mentioned above. For example, the rule used as an illustration in that section:
. if date due back of loan is less than current date
then loan is overdue
defines a lower level relationship set — overdue loans — which is a *category* or *subset* of the loan relationship set. If, to the above rule, 'else loan is not overdue' is added, then loans are divided into two mutually exclusive subsets — overdue and not overdue.

One of the important types of higher level object is the *generic object*. The generic object represents a *generalization* of different objects which have something in common. Generalization is also referred to as a type hierarchy and it may go down to many levels. As an example of a single level generalization, car, bus and lorry may be represented as different entities in a particular data model but a single higher level generic object — road vehicle — may be defined to represent those aspects which cars, buses and lorries have in common. A further higher level generic object — vehicle — might also be introduced as a generalization of road vehicle, sea vehicle, and air vehicle. There are distinct similarities between categorization and generalization. At first sight it might be thought that one is the inverse of the other. However, the difference is that a category or subset is derived from a single type of object by means of a rule based on the values of an attribute (or attributes) of the object, while a generic object defines a classification of different types of object. This difference is significant and hence the diagrammatic notation used to represent the semantics of categorization and generalization will be different. The example in Figure 2.15 shows University Member as a generic object which provides a single classification of a Student or a Staff member.

Student and Staff are different entities as they have different associated attributes. The relationship between the generic object and the associated entities is always one-to-one. The example also shows undergraduate (U/G), postgraduate (P/G), and short term (S/T) students as categories of the Student entity distinguished by a status attribute within the entity, and administrative (Admin) and academic (Acad) staff as categories of the Staff entity, also distinguished by a status attribute.

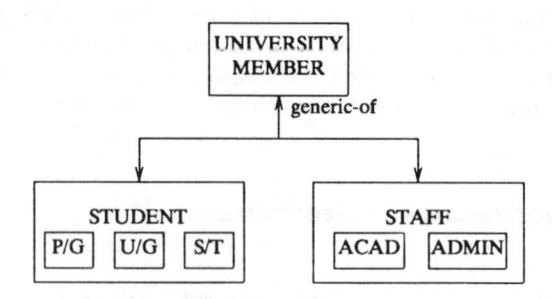

Figure 2.15 Generalization and Categorization

It should be noted that an important characteristic of generalization is that both the higher and lower level objects involved in the generalization possess the same identifier; thus if Person# is the identifier for Staff, it must also be the identifier for University Member. Furthermore, the inheritance of attributes is implied by a generalization; i.e. by referring to a particular student or staff, one not only has access to the appropriate attributes for those entities, but also to the attributes of the related University Member object.

2.7.2 Aggregation and Other Higher Level Objects

Cover aggregation

Many different types of aggregation have been introduced by various authors. In this subsection, *cover aggregation* will be discussed; this type of aggregate was introduced by Codd (1979), and is represented in Hammer & McLeod's Semantic Data Model by a 'grouping class' option (Hammer 1981).

Cover aggregation, like generalization mentioned above, is an important type of higher level object. It is similar to the generic object in that it represents a classification of different types of object, but the difference is in the nature of the classification — it is a grouping of objects. Whereas there is always a one-to-one relationship between a generic object and the objects for which it is a generalization, there is in general a one-to-many or many-to-many relationship between an aggregate object and the objects which are grouped together by the aggregate. Figure 2.16 provides two examples of aggregate objects.

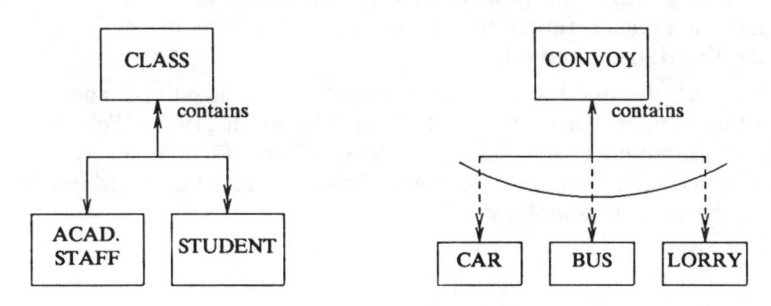

Figure 2.16 Cover Aggregation

The first shows a Class object which contains one academic staff and many students as members, and since there is a 'many' arrow in the direction of Class, the implication is that a specific staff member or student may at any point in time be a member of more than one class. The second example shows a Convoy object which may contain either cars as members or buses as members or lorries as members, but not all at the same time in one convoy. Note that the relationship is contingent; a car, bus, or lorry may exist in the database without it being a member of a convoy. The arc associated with the members of the Convoy aggregate is a mechanism for representing *exclusivity* and can be used in other contexts where relevant. Note that since there is no exclusivity arc in Figure 2.15, the implication is that a university member may be both student and staff at the same time. This is realistic since some members of staff can be registered for postgraduate degrees. An exclusivity arc through the student and staff arrows in Figure 2.15 would indicate that staff members are not permitted to be students and vice versa.

Set attributes and aggregate functions

Two final types of higher level object to be discussed in this section are the set attribute and aggregate function. Both involve a single-valued object associated in some way with a set of objects (entity set, relationship set, attribute set). The *set attribute* is a single-valued attribute which applies to all members of the set associated with that attribute. For example, consider a car entity set. A single road tax value is associated with every member of the set; all cars are charged the same tax. Road tax can thus be represented as a set attribute, rather than as an entity attribute, the former implying a single value for a complete entity set and the latter implying many values — one for each entity in the entity set, though not all values will necessarily be distinct.

The *aggregate function* is a function which is applied to the values of an attribute and which produces a single value as a result. For example, a 'count' function applied to the Isbn attribute of Catalogued Book would produce as a result the number of different books in the library. Other common aggregate functions are maximum, minimum, sum, average, standard deviation, and others.

Further discussions of categorization, generalization, aggregation, and other semantic aspects may be found in Smith (1977), Scheuermann (1980), Hammer (1981), Codd (1979), Kent (1979), Gray (1984), Bussolati (1983). It should be noted, however, that these authors do not all use the same terminology.

2.7.3 The Time Dimension

Time logically adds another dimension to a data model, but in many databases it is not a major aspect and is modelled as an attribute. In the library model, for example, date due back and date reserved are both time-oriented objects which have been modelled as attributes. In some application areas, however, time — the temporal dimension — is a significant aspect and the semantics of time are important.

One aspect of time relates to events. In general, an update is carried out when an event occurs, and it is a destructive update, i.e. once an update has been successfully completed the previous situation is no longer part of the database (the previous situation may be recoverable though, via a backup or transaction log file). An example of a situation in which updates must not be allowed to 'wipe out' the previous position is the case of an employee's job history. Job history is generally therefore modelled as an entity set, with a one-to-many relationship between the employee and job history entity sets:

Employee <————————>> Job-History

and each job history entity will have a date attribute.

An alternative means of reflecting the time dimension is via *snapshots*. Using this mechanism, when an event gives rise to an update or updates, a 'snapshot' is taken of the part of the database to be updated; this is then dated and stored, and the update is carried out on the current database. The database therefore contains a set of dated 'snapshots' which reflect past history, as well as the current database. (These history snapshots should not be confused with view snapshots, which represent user views and are briefly discussed in section 4.8; history and view snapshots are actually very similar but serve a different purpose.)

However, it should be mentioned that the snapshot alternative is not in general feasible due to the increased storage space requirement and the relatively high cost of fast access storage for large volumes of data. Hence, in general the 'employee<———>>job history' type of solution to the time dimension problem is adopted.

Another aspect of time is the time period or duration. A particular situation may be valid for a particular time period and it may be important for an event to be triggered by the expiry of that period of time. Kowalski (1984) illustrates how time periods can be modelled in a logic language such as Prolog, using binary relations to record the start and end of each time period, and rules to automatically update the time period data when an event occurs. However, duration is generally modelled as an attribute, due to the lack of provision in database systems for handling time as a semantic object in its own right. For example, the Date-due-dack attribute in the library model in reality represents the expiry of the loan period.

Readers interested in the subject of the time dimension in databases may like to refer to Lum (1984), Clifford (1983), Lundberg (1983), Anderson (1983), as well as Kowalski (1984).

2.7.4 Null Values

The final semantic aspect to be considered in this section is the semantics of *null* or *missing values*. There are two possible causes of null values. Firstly, a null value may be due to missing data — the 'not known' situation; a value for a particular attribute of a particular entity may exist in the real world but the value is not known to those responsible for creating, maintaining, and using the database, or is not known at a particular point in time. The second cause is the 'not applicable' situation; this arises when a particular attribute is not relevant to a particular entity at some point in time, although it may be relevant to some other entities of the same type and may also be relevant to this particular entity at some other time. An example of a possible 'not known' situation is when a copy of a book is being recorded in the database and it is not yet known what shelf it is to be placed on. An example of a 'not applicable' situation is in the Book-Loan relation of Figure 2.13 in the previous section; when a particular copy of a book is not currently on loan, the name, address and date due back attributes are not applicable.

There has been much debate about null values, whether they should be allowed to exist, what values should represent null, what the results of operations involving null values should be, etc. Clearly the 'not applicable' situation can be avoided by treating such groups of attributes as a separate entity related to the original entity. For example, in the 3NF relational model produced using the normalisation approach, the loan attributes of the Book-Loan relation can be separated from the other book details, producing separate Book and Loan relations as a refinement of the model. (This would also incidentally produce a normalised model more similar to the conceptual model derived from the top-down approach.) The 'not known' situation is not so easy to avoid though, and some systems have adopted special null values and rules for handling nulls, including 3-valued logic (true, false, and unknown) for the evaluation of conditional expressions.

The importance of being able to represent the existence characteristic of entity-attribute relationships in the data model can clearly be seen. It enables the possible presence of null values in the database to be identified (when an entity-attribute relationship is not mandatory), and hence assist the data modeller in producing a well designed data model by drawing his attention to possible 'not applicable' situations which can be avoided in the final version of the model. Most data modelling methodologies concentrate on analysing the relationships between entity and relationship sets, but it is as important to analyse the entity-attribute relationships, even when an entity-based DBMS is to be used. Further discussion of null values may be found in Codd (1979), Babad (1984), Date(1983b).

2.7.5 Connection Traps

Before leaving this section on further semantic aspects of conceptual models, the importance of carefully analysing all the relationships in the data model, both direct and indirect, will be mentioned. If attention is focussed only on the direct relationships between objects, some indirect relationships implied by the data model may inadvertently give rise to the incorrect interpretation of the underlying semantics.

The incorrect interpretation of an indirect relationship is referred to as a *connection trap*. An indirect relationship exists between two objects if they are not directly related but an *access path* exists between them (see section 2.5). For example, an indirect relationship connects A and B in the diagram below:

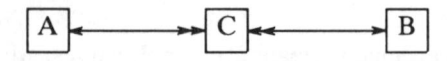

$$A \longleftarrow \longrightarrow C \longleftarrow \longrightarrow B$$

Two examples will be used to illustrate how a connection trap can exist. In each case the data model is shown first, followed by example occurrences of part of the model (selected attributes only).

Example 1: no connection trap

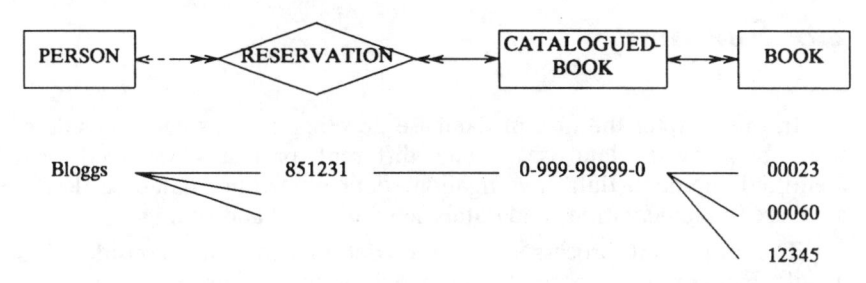

```
PERSON <--->> RESERVATION >><-- CATALOGUED-BOOK <-->> BOOK
```

Bloggs —— 851231 —— 0-999-99999-0 —— 00023
                                        00060
                                        12345

Example 2: a connection trap exists

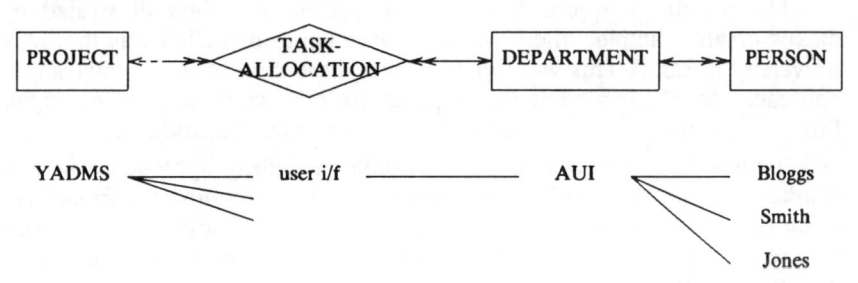

```
PROJECT <--->> TASK-ALLOCATION >>--> DEPARTMENT <-->> PERSON
```

YADMS —— user i/f —— AUI —— Bloggs
                              Smith
                              Jones

The two examples above have the same basic structure, but only in the second does a connection trap exist. In the first, one can deduce, by following the access path from Person to Book via Reservation, that Bloggs has a reservation which applies to Book numbers 00023, 00060, and 12345; this is a valid interpretation since although Bloggs only wants to borrow one of these books, any one of the three will do (they are all relevant to that particular reservation). In the second example, though, one cannot deduce that the project YADMS has the 'user i/f' task allocated to Bloggs, Smith and Jones; one or more of them may be working on that task, but this is not necessarily the case. One can only deduce that the AUI department has that particular YADMS task allocated to it. This suggests that the data model of the second example is really incomplete, i.e. it does not reflect the full semantics; it is necessary to add a direct relationship between Person and Task-Allocation, if the true semantics are to be reflected in the model.

Further examples, and a fuller discussion of connection traps, may be found in Howe (1983).

2.8 Summary

In this chapter the task of database development has been considered (i.e. building a database). The different processes involved were identified, namely, data investigation, data modelling, database design, database implementation, and database monitoring and tuning.

The important process of data modelling was then considered in detail. Firstly, the purpose of data modelling was discussed, and then the different components: relationships, entities and attributes, were described.

The top-down approach to data modelling was then illustrated by means of an example; the application area being modelled was that of a university library. This was followed by a discussion of the normalisation approach to data modelling, applied to the same library example. Finally, further semantic aspects of data models were introduced.

It must be stressed that the two data modelling approaches in this chapter are not the only ones available. The top-down approach as discussed in this chapter has in fact combined techniques from various different approaches. References to other approaches have been provided where relevant.

In the next chapter, the data models provided by some actual database systems are discussed, including the relational model, the binary relationship model, the network model, and the hierarchical model. The process of mapping from the conceptual model to the DBMS-specific models will be illustrated, and similarities and differences will be discussed.

CHAPTER THREE

Database Design: Mapping from the Conceptual Model to the Database Schema

3.1 Introduction

The conceptual model discussed in the last chapter can be referred to as a *generalised* model. It is generalised since it is independent of any specific DBMSs. It is an abstraction from reality, and is a limited view of reality in the sense that only those aspects which are relevant to the application area are reflected in the model. Such a model is a very useful tool in its own right. It is of course essential for the development of an efficient and effective database, but it also provides an insight into the actual structure and operation of a company, highlighting interrelationships, dependencies and constraints; in this respect, it could be considered as a useful tool for management.

Returning, though, to consider the conceptual model as an intermediate product in the process of database development, its main purpose is to provide sufficient information for deriving a DBMS-specific data model. This is carried out at the database design stage. There are various different types of DBMS and each has its own rules and restrictions. Most of the currently existing DBMSs, however, are based on one of the following approaches: *relational, network, hierarchical*, while in recent years the *binary relationship* approach has been gaining in importance and much research effort has been devoted to systems based on this approach (including fact/logic-based and functional systems).

The relational, network, and hierarchical approaches are all entity based. A brief background to these approaches is relevant here. Relations were described briefly in Chapter 2. A hierarchy is an inverted tree type of structure, with a single root object at the top and branch objects hanging from the root. At each branch level, a particular object may only be connected to one object at a higher level, though it may be connected to many objects at a lower level. A network structure is one in which a branch object may be connected to many objects at a higher, as well as a lower, level.

From well before the era of databases, Cobol has provided two hierarchical data structure facilities. Firstly, a simple hierarchical facility by means of the 'occurs' clause, enabling one-to-many relationships between two entities to be represented in a single Cobol record type. The second alternative, for more complex hierarchies, is a file containing multiple record types; in this case each 'master' record (i.e. the record representing the entity in the 'one' direction) is followed by a set of related 'detail' records (representing the entities in the 'many' direction). However, what is lacking in Cobol is the higher-level language facility to manipulate this logical hierarchy; the Cobol programmer has to carry out the hierarchical data storage and manipulation himself at the physical level.

With the increase in electronic data processing in the 1960's came the recognition that many real world structures are hierarchical in nature; for example, an order form consists of many ordered items, a student studies many courses, a company consists of many departments, a department contains many employees, and so on. This factor, together with the limitations of Cobol led to the development of the first hierarchical database systems. But as expertise in the database field increased, there was a growing awareness that not all real world structures are hierarchies, and network and relational systems were developed to overcome the limitations of hierarchical systems.

In this chapter, these three entity based approaches will be discussed first, followed by the binary relationship approach. The main features of the data models associated with these approaches are introduced, and the library example of Chapter 2 is used to illustrate the mapping of the generalised conceptual data model into the data models of these approaches. The data model derived using the top-down approach in section 2.5 will be used as the basis for the mappings. Sample schema are defined for the DBMS data models using an appropriate data description language (DDL).

In the mapping process it will be found that in most cases not all the information contained in the generalised model can be mapped into the

DBMS-specific model since most systems do not enable models to be built which are as rich in semantic concepts as the model developed in the last chapter. This point will be discussed later in the chapter.

In the final main section of the chapter, user views and external schema will be put into context and discussed.

The conventions to be used in the examples are designed to be consistent with notation used in examples in the previous chapter. Names of objects at the entity level (e.g. entity and relationship sets, relations, record types) are in upper case, attributes are in lower case except for the initial letter, and relationship names are all in lower case. In addition, where a specific language is used in an example, keywords of the language are in bold upper case. It should be noted that these conventions are not necessarily valid in actual DBMS implementations, and they apply only to the examples, not to the text.

Before introducing the different DBMS approaches, two related terms — the *intensional database* and the *extensional database* — will be introduced and briefly explained. The DBMS data model and associated conceptual schema, which describes the DBMS representation of the conceptual model, may be referred to as the *intensional database*; that is, it describes what the data in the database is intended to represent by defining the object types (entities and attributes), relationships, and constraints. The actual data in the database comprises the *extensional database* and consists of various occurrences of object types and relationships declared in the schema or intensional database (Date 1983a). It is important to appreciate the difference between the intensional database and the data model (type) diagram on the one hand, and the extensional database and occurrence diagrams on the other hand.

3.2 The Relational Model

3.2.1 Introduction to Relations

Relations were briefly introduced in the last chapter as a basis for discussing the normalisation approach to data modelling, but a detailed discussion of relations and relational databases was not appropriate at that stage. In this subsection relational concepts are introduced, and in the next subsection, the conceptual model of section 2.5 is mapped into a relational model.

The relational approach to data modelling was introduced by E.F. Codd in the late 1960's (Codd 1970). It is based on the mathematical concepts of relations and sets. A *relation* represents an entity set or some aspect of an entity set, and the attributes of a relation are attributes associated with the entity set which it represents. ('Entity set' is used loosely here to include relationship sets.) Thus, the relational model is an entity-based model.

A relation may be described by its name and its associated attributes; an example description of the relation representing the catalogued book entity from the library model is as follows:

CATALOGUED-BOOK (Isbn , Publisher, Author, Title, Year, Classmark)

The underlined attribute — Isbn — is the identifier (primary key) of the relation.

Figure 3.1 is an example of a possible occurrence of the Catalogued-Book relation. The actual record occurrences in a relation are referred to as *tuples*, or more explicitly, *n-tuples* where n is the number of attributes in the relation (i.e. the degree of the relation). Relations themselves are sometimes referred to as *n-ary relations*. This is to distinguish Codd's relational approach from the binary relationship approach which will be discussed in a later section. However, it is now accepted that the term *relation* is used to refer specifically to the n-ary relation approach.

Isbn	Author	Title	Publisher	Year	Classmark
0-999-99999-0	Bloggs C.J.	Data Models	Ackson-Bull	1980	QA264
0-12345-123-X	Smith W.F.	Relational Systems	Wilkinson	1984	QA264
0-33333-333-0	Hicks S.A.	Intro to DBMS	Porter	1983	QA76
0-5656-5656-2	Roberts H.	Data Models	Ackson-Bull	1984	QA264
1-222-44444-5	Jones B.	Query Languages	Clarkson	1978	QA264
1-987-65432-3	Bloggs C.J.	Database Systems	Clarkson	1985	QA76
.....	.....	.....	.....	.....	.....
.....	.....	.....	.....	.....	.....

Figure 3.1 An Example of a Catalogued-Book Relation Occurrence

The relation, then, is a simple construct. It is similar to a simple file or table, with each tuple corresponding to a record in traditional file terminology, and each attribute to a field.

The formal definition of a relation is as follows:

Given sets D1, D2, ..., Dn (not necessarily distinct), R is a relation on these n sets if it is a set of n-tuples <d1, d2, ..., dn> such that d1 belongs to D1, d2 belongs to D2, and so on.

Sets D1, D2, ..., Dn are called the *domains* of R.
The value n is called the *degree* of R.
(Note: R is a subset of the Cartesian product: D1 x D2 x ..... x Dn.)

Two important characteristics of relations are: firstly, each attribute value must be atomic (i.e. each attribute in each tuple must be represented by a single value, not a set of values — a relation which satisfies this condition is said to be normalised); and secondly, all tuples (record occurrences) in a relation must be distinct (i.e. no two tuples in a relation should be exactly equal). This second characteristic means that each tuple in a relation may be uniquely identified, by means of one or more attributes in the relation; the attribute(s) selected as the unique identifier are referred to as the *primary key*. (Candidate, primary, and alternate keys were discussed in section 2.6).

There are also two basic integrity rules associated with relations: *entity integrity* and *referential integrity*. Entity integrity is concerned with the primary key of a relation; the rule states that no primary key and no part of a multi-attribute primary key may have a null value. Referential integrity is concerned with foreign keys (i.e. attributes in one relation which are primary keys of some other associated relation); this rule states that the value of each foreign key in a relation must either be null or correspond to an existing primary key value in an associated relation.

A full discussion of the relational approach may be found in Codd (1970), with a summary in Codd (1979) together with some suggested extensions.

3.2.2 Relations and the Mapping Process

In this subsection, the generalised conceptual model derived using the top-down approach in section 2.5 will be mapped into a relational data model. It should be noted that if the relation normalisation approach to data modelling is used, the result is, of course, a relational data model so no mapping is necessary in this case.

The mapping takes place in three stages:

Stage 1: Create relations for each entity and relationship set.
Stage 2: Map the relationships, using appropriate rules.
Stage 3: Complete the relations, by adding identifiers (primary keys) where these do not currently exist.

These three stages are discussed in turn.

Stage 1: Creating relations for each entity and relationship set

The first stage in mapping from the conceptual model to the relational model is to create one relation for each entity set and relationship set, containing the attributes which are associated with that entity or relationship set. The entity identifier where it exists becomes the *primary key* of the relation and it appears in the relational model as an underlined attribute (as illustrated below).

The result of the first stage of mapping into relations produces:

CATALOGUED-BOOK (<u>Isbn</u> , Author, Title, Publisher, Year, Classmark)

PERSON (<u>#</u> , Name, Address)

BOOK (<u>Book#</u> , Shelf)

LOAN (Date-due-back)

RESERVATION (Date-reserved)

LOAN-STATUS (<u>Status</u> , Loan-period, Max-num-books)

Note: # in Person is the ghost identifier referred to in section 2.5 (step 4).

At present these relations are incomplete; only a ghost identifier exists as the primary key for Person and no identifiers exist for Loan and Reservation. Primary keys will be filled in where missing, in stage 3 of the mapping process.

Stage 2: Mapping the relationships

It should by now be clear how entities and attributes are represented in a relational model, but how, one might ask, are the relationships between entities represented? Relations are linked together *implicitly* by means of their attributes. But stage 1 in the mapping process has produced a set of relations which, as well as being incomplete as far as primary keys are concerned, contain no linking attributes — the relationships between the entities are missing from the relational model at present. The second stage in the mapping process is concerned with the mapping of relationships. There are two main approaches to mapping relationships; these are:

(1) the *relationship relation* approach: one relation is created for each relationship, with attributes consisting of the primary keys of the related entities;

(2) the *foreign key* approach: for each set of related entities, the primary key(s) are placed in one of the entities as foreign keys, where such action does not conflict with the semantics of the conceptual model (this may be referred to as the 'posting' of attributes (Howe 1983)).

Some authors (Chen 1976, Wilmot 1984) advocate that the relationship relation approach should be the only approach used, to ensure full data independence. The advantage of this is that all relationships are represented by independent relations — no relationships are hidden inside entity relations; thus, in a particular database over time, if a simple relationship evolves into a relationship set the structure of the relational model in terms of relations will remain unchanged; only new attributes will need to be added to the appropriate relationship relation. A further advantage is that many-to-many relationships always have to be represented as relationship relations — the foreign key approach cannot be used for these cases; the relationship relation approach therefore provides a single standard mechanism for representing relationships. The disadvantage of this approach though is that it can result in a very large number of relations in the database, which may not be desirable for implementation efficiency reasons. Hence, other authors (e.g. Howe) advocate using the relationship relation approach followed by a relation synthesis technique where possible (using foreign keys) to reduce the number of relations in the resulting model. A similar approach is adopted by Vetter & Maddison (Vetter 1981, ch.4); they show how to analyse functional dependencies to determine elementary relations which represent 'irreducible units', and then describe an algorithm to reduce the number of relations and produce a minimal cover. In this book, the two approaches are combined, and rules are given for determining under what circumstances the approaches should be used.

The separate cases will now be dealt with by considering the types of relationship which can exist between two entities in a conceptual model (which will be referred to as A and B).

(1) Many-to-many relationships

In the relational approach, many-to-many relationships are represented by creating a new relation — a relationship relation — with no attributes apart from the primary key which is formed from the primary keys of the entities which are related. This relation therefore only contains foreign keys which represent the relationship. For example, suppose we have relation A with primary key A# and relation B with primary key B#, and suppose also that there is a many-to-many relationship between them. This relationship is represented by the following new relation:

A-B (A# , B#)

It should be noted that this new relation creates a one-to-many relationship between each of the two original relations and the relationship relation (e.g. the relationship between A and A-B is one-to-many, as is that between B and A-B).

(2) One-to-many relationships

One-to-many relationships may be split into two groups:

(a) mandatory in the 'many' direction

i.e. A <————————>> B   or   A <----————>> B

In both these cases an entity of type B can only exist if it is related to an entity of type A. The primary key of A can be placed in B as an additional (foreign key) attribute. Thus B becomes:

B (**B#** , ..., A#)

where A# is the primary key of A and is a foreign key in the B relation.

(b) optional in the 'many' direction

i.e. A <————————---->> B   or   A <----------->>B

In these two cases an entity of type B can exist without being related to an entity of type A. Hence if the primary key of A were to be added to the B relation (as in (a) above), then the A# attribute in B would have a null value in those cases where a particular B entity was not related to an A entity. As indicated in Chapter 2, it is generally considered desirable to avoid null values wherever possible, so this type of relationship will be represented by a relationship relation with B# as the primary key, e.g.:

A-B (A#, **B#**)

An occurrence of A-B will only exist for those B entities which are related to an A entity.

(3) One-to-one relationships

One-to-one relationships may be split into three groups:

(a) mandatory

Either the primary key of A may be placed as a foreign key in B, or vice versa.

(b) optional

A relationship relation is created containing the primary keys of A and B, and either one of these may form the primary key of the new relation. For e.g.:

A-B (**A#** , B#)

(c) contingent

The primary key of the entity in the optional direction is placed in the relation representing the entity in the mandatory direction. For e.g.:

in the case of   A <----————> B

A# is placed in the B relation as in (2a) above.

Using the above mapping rules, under rule (2a) Isbn will be placed as a foreign key in the Book relation to represent the relationship between Catalogued-Book and Book, and Status will be placed as a foreign key in Person representing the relationship between Loan-Status and Person. Again under rule (2a) both Isbn and the Person identifier will be foreign keys in Reservation. Only the relationships with Loan now remain; under rule (2a) the Person identifier will be placed in Loan and under rule (3c) Book# will be placed in Loan.

After stage 2 we have the following (still incomplete) relations:

CATALOGUED-BOOK   (Isbn , Author, Title, Publisher,
                    Year,   Classmark)
PERSON (# , Name, Address, Status)
BOOK   (Book# , Shelf, Isbn)
LOAN   (Date-due-back, Book#, #-of-Person)
RESERVATION (Date-reserved, Isbn, #-of-Person)
LOAN-STATUS (Status , Loan-period, Max-num-books)

Stage 3: Completing the relations

To complete the relations — stage 3 — identifiers (primary keys) must be provided for Person, Loan and Reservation. It was noted in the last chapter that name and address together could be used to identify person entities in a 'natural' way, while the less natural alternative of devising a coding scheme has the advantage of conciseness. The choice between the alternatives is left to the designer of the database who needs to take into account such factors as storage minimisation and retrieval efficiency. Observing the above relations, it will be noted that the identifier for Person occurs in two relations as a foreign key. This would suggest that for efficiency reasons a coding scheme — Person# — should be devised for identifying Person.

As far as Reservation is concerned, a coding scheme could be used for the primary key of this relation, but since it represents a relationship set derived originally from a many-to-many relationship, it is similar to the relationship relation produced under mapping rule 1 above. Hence the same approach will be used, i.e. the foreign keys will form the primary key — Isbn, Person#.

Finally, Loan also represents a relationship set but was derived originally from a one-to-many relationship. A similar approach to Reservation can be used, but since a book can only be on loan to one person at a time, Book# on its own is sufficient to identify a particular loan and hence it can be used as the primary key for Loan.

The resulting relational model is given in Figure 3.2. It could also be represented in diagrammatic form as in the section on normalisation in the previous chapter (see section 2.6 and Figure 2.14).

CATALOGUED-BOOK (<u>Isbn</u> , Author, Title, Publisher, Year, Classmark)
PERSON (<u>Person#</u> , Name, Address, Status)
BOOK (<u>Book#</u> , Shelf, Isbn)
LOAN (Date-due-back, <u>Book#</u> , Person#)
RESERVATION (Date-reserved, <u>Isbn</u> , <u>Person#</u>)
LOAN-STATUS (<u>Status</u> , Loan-period, Max-num-books)

Figure 3.2 The Relational Representation of the Conceptual Model of Figure 2.12

This relational model contains much of the information in Figure 2.12, some of it explicit and some implicit; the missing aspects are the degree and existence characteristics of the relationships. This limitation of the relational model was mentioned in section 2.6 during the discussion of the normalisation methodology for data modelling. In addition, since the relation construct is very simple, it does not support the additional semantic aspects introduced in section 2.7, such as categorization, generalization, aggregation, and set attributes, although extensions to the relational model to support these aspects have been suggested by Codd (1979). In section 3.6, these limitations, together with those of the other models to be introduced in this chapter, will be reconsidered.

3.2.3 The Relational Schema — An Example

The end result of the database design stage is the DBMS-specific conceptual schema and associated external schema. The latter will be discussed in section 3.7. The DBMS conceptual schema is a description of the DBMS data model written in the relevant data description language (DDL). Each relational DBMS will provide a different DDL but they will be very similar in most respects as they will all have the same conceptual basis — relations. In this subsection, part of the library schema will be used to illustrate a relational DDL. The language to be used is SQL (which also provides query and update facilities). SQL was originally known as Sequel (Chamberlin 1976); it is used in IBM's SQL/DS and Database 2 (DB2) systems and in Oracle UK's Oracle system.

```
CREATE TABLE   CATALOGUED-BOOK
         (Isbn      CHAR(13) NONULL,
          Author    CHAR(20) VAR NONULL,
          Title     CHAR(40) VAR NONULL,
          Publisher CHAR(20) VAR,
          Year      CHAR(4),
          Classmark CHAR(10) NONULL )

CREATE TABLE   BOOK
         (Book#  CHAR(5) NONULL,
          Shelf  SMALLINT,
          Isbn   CHAR(13) )

CREATE TABLE   PERSON
         (Person#  CHAR(5) NONULL,
          Name     CHAR(20) VAR NONULL,
          Address  CHAR(40) VAR NONULL,
          Status   CHAR(5) )

CREATE TABLE   LOAN
         (Book#         CHAR(6) NONULL,
          Person#       CHAR(5) NONULL,
          Date-due-back CHAR(6) NONULL )
```

Figure 3.3 Part of the Library Relational Schema
in the SQL DDL

As indicated earlier, there are a number of variations on a theme as far as relation definition is concerned, but in all relational DDLs each relation or table is defined independently by specifying the name of the relation followed by the attributes associated with the relation. For each attribute the type and size (where relevant) must be specified. In the example, Book# is defined as a 5-character field, while Shelf is defined as a small integer. Other possible types are integer, decimal, and float. The keyword VAR following a character field description indicates that the field is variable length. SQL permits null values by default, but it should be noted that not all relational systems have this facility. In cases where an attribute must not be null (e.g. a primary key attribute) the attribute definition is qualified by the NONULL keyword.

Other data definition facilities which are provided by some relational DDLs are: primary key definition, domain specification, date datatype, boolean datatype, and simple constraint specification.

3.3 The Network Model

3.3.1 Introduction

The network approach is based on the idea of explicit links between related entities. The most well-known network model is the Codasyl (or DBTG) model. Another quite widely used system based on the network approach is Total but it only supports a restricted network model. Hence, the Codasyl network model will be used here to illustrate the approach.

Codasyl stands for
COmmittee on DAta SYstems Languages.
This Committee is composed of a number of sub-committees and groups, some of which specialise in databases. It has produced a series of proposals over the years for a Data Description Language (DDL) and a Data Manipulation Language (DML) to support a network database. The first of these was produced in 1969 by a group under Codasyl known as the Data Base Task Group (DBTG). The various revisions since 1969 have been designed to remove inadequacies from the languages in the light of experience and provide enhancements as relevant, but all have been based on the same underlying data model. (References to the various Codasyl reports may be found in Olle (1978); the most recent DDL and Cobol DML proposals may be found in Codasyl (1981a and 1981b)). Many implementations of the Codasyl proposals currently exist, the most well known being IDMS. Codasyl-based systems have been particularly successful in large database environments, since the explicit links can provide fast access to related data (more about this in a later chapter).

The most important construct of the Codasyl model is the 'set'. The term has been placed in inverted commas as it is not the mathematical concept of a set. For this reason, it is often referred to as a *coset* and this terminology will be used here. The coset is the means by which two or more related record types (representing entity or relationship sets) may be linked together. Thus the coset is the network representation for a relationship.

Diagrammatically, a coset consists of an *owner* record type linked by means of a named and directed arrow to one or more *member* record types. This is illustrated in the following diagram (known as a Bachman diagram) which represents a relationship named A-B between two record types: A and B (cf. notation (ii) Figure 2.2 in Chapter 2).

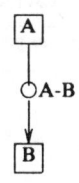

```
    [A]
     |
     ○ A-B
     ↓
    [B]
```

In this diagram A is the owner record type of the A-B coset and B is the member. The relationship is implicitly one-to-many in the direction of the arrow. One-to-one relationships are modelled in the same way, while many-to-many relationships have to be broken down into one-to-many relationships as in the relational model. This will be discussed in more detail later.

A coset is represented in the database by a group of coset occurrences, each consisting of one owner record linked to a set of related member records. A logical representation of a set occurrence is shown in Figure 3.4. This shows an occurrence of the 'has-copy' coset, with Catalogued-Book as the owner of the coset and Book as the member. This particular occurrence relates to a Catalogued-Book record for the book with Isbn 0-999-99999-0; there are three copies of it in the database, represented by Book records with Book# 00023, 00060, and 12345, which are all linked together. In a later chapter the ways in which coset occurrences may be physically represented will be discussed; here it is the logical representation, with explicit links between owner and member records, which is of interest.

With regard to the existence characteristic of relationships in the Codasyl network model, limited facilities exist for supporting this characteristic. In the DDL (as will be seen later) the member of a particular coset type may be classified as fixed, mandatory or optional. That is, a record which is a *fixed* member must remain linked to the same owner throughout its life, a record which is a *mandatory* member must always be a member of that particular coset type but its owner within the coset may change, and finally, a record which is an *optional* member may exist in the database without being linked into that particular coset type. It should be noted that this classification only applies in one direction of the relationship — to the members of cosets and not to the owners, whereas the existence characteristic of the conceptual model applies in both directions of the relationship.

Examples will illustrate these different membership classes. First consider the 'has-copy' coset referred to above. Book is obviously a fixed 'has-copy' coset

'owner' record

CATALOGUED-BOOK

| 0-999-99999-0 | ..... |

'member' records

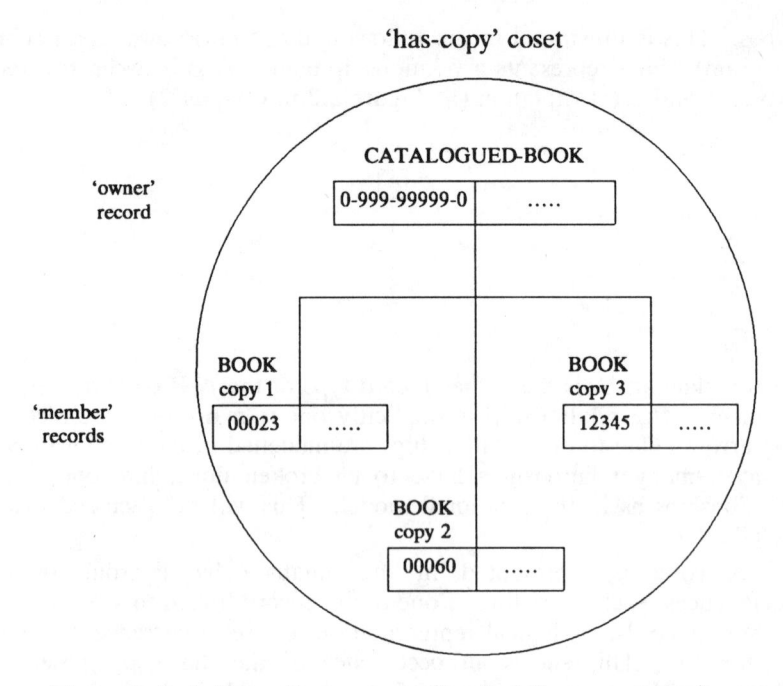

| BOOK copy 1 |
| 00023 | ..... |

| BOOK copy 3 |
| 12345 | ..... |

| BOOK copy 2 |
| 00060 | ..... |

Figure 3.4 A Coset Occurrence (Logical Representation)

member in this coset since once it has been linked to a particular Catalogued-Book, it cannot be linked to any other; it is always associated with the same catalogue entry (Isbn). Next consider a coset named 'status-of' linking Loan-Status and Person, with Loan-Status as the owner and Person as the member. Person is clearly a mandatory member of this coset. A person must always have a status, but his status may change (e.g. he may change from a postgraduate to a member of staff); hence although a person will always be a member of a 'status-of' coset, he may be linked to different owners over time.

All the membership classes in the library data model are either fixed or mandatory so it is necessary to consider an example from another database to illustrate the optional class. Consider the case of a coset in a personnel database representing trade union membership, with trade union as the owner and employee as the member record types. If there is no closed shop in the company then membership of a trade union is optional and an employee may exist in the database without being linked to a trade union in the union-membership coset; hence employee is an optional member in this coset.

The coset is a powerful building block with which complex network structures can be built. A record type which is a member in one coset type may be a member of other coset types, and may also be an owner of other coset types. Figure 3.5 provides some examples of different types of data structure which can be created by means of the coset; these data structures can be combined together as relevant to the data model.

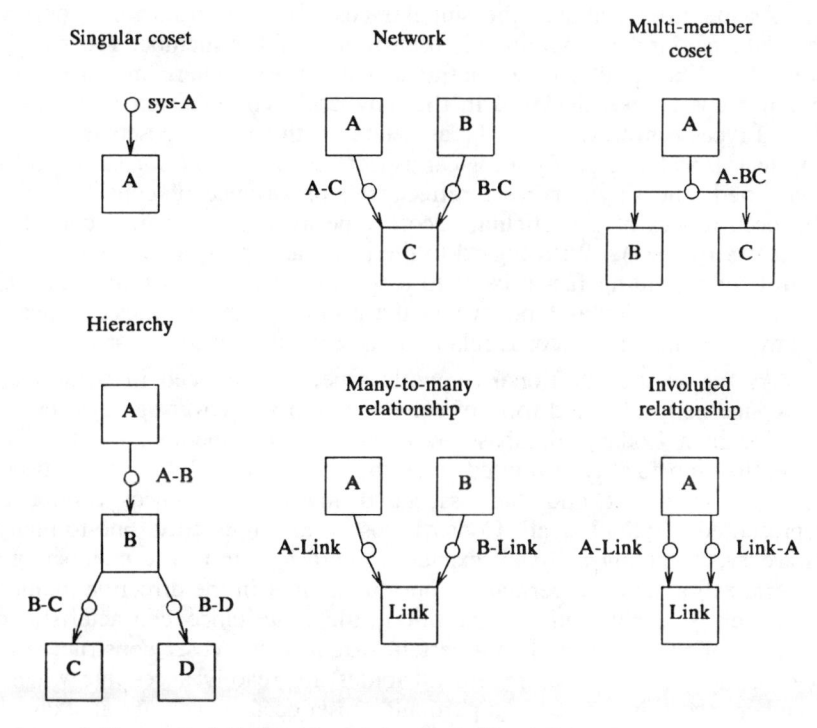

Figure 3.5 Examples of Some Codasyl Data Structures

A 'singular coset' (also known as the 'system-owned' set) has one occurrence only in the database; it is owned by the DBMS and contains all occurrences of the member record type. The significance of the singular set will be discussed below. The 'network' structure shows the record type C as a member in both the A-C and the B-C cosets; it has two owners. The 'multi-member coset' has two different record types: B and C as members of the same coset. In the 'hierarchy', the coset A-B represents a single level hierarchy, while the complete structure represents a multi-level hierarchy. The 'many-to-many relationship' shows a Link record type linking A and B; the Link record type performs a similar function to the relationship relation of the relational model. The 'involuted relationship' shows a record type A for which there is a relationship between different records of the same type, i.e. an A record may own other A records. Codasyl does not permit this type of relationship to be represented directly but it can be represented using a Link record type. The A-Link coset in the example links an owner record A with its members, while the Link-A coset links a member record A with its owner(s). Although link record types have been named 'Link' in the examples, they may be given any name.

As mentioned above, the singular coset has one occurrence only in the database and it contains all occurrences of the member record type (i.e. it is like a set in the mathematical sense). There may be many singular coset types declared in the database. The decision as to which record types (entities) should be associated with singular cosets is partly a physical aspect and partly a logical aspect. As far as the logical aspect is concerned, the singular coset reflects the importance of considering all the occurrences of a particular record type as a single logical collection (i.e. as a true set). With regard to the physical aspect, a singular coset is useful for providing fast accesss to a specific record occurrence or to all records of a particular type, while the normal coset provides fast access to any or all member records related to a particular owner record.

As far as the additional semantic aspects introduced in section 2.7 are concerned, a limited form of generalization and cover aggregation are possible in a Codasyl database by means of multi-member cosets. The generalization facility is limited since the one-to-one relationship between the generic object and the associated lower level object cannot be represented explicitly; all Codasyl cosets are implicitly one-to-many. However, by giving a 'fixed' existence characteristic to the member of a generalization coset, a permanent one-to-one link in the direction member to owner is established. In addition, the inheritance characteristic of generalization is reflected to a certain extent in the coset construct since both owner and member record attributes are readily accessible when a member record is located in a particular coset occurrence. As an example of generalization, in the multi-member coset of Figure 3.5, A, B, and C might represent University Member (as the generic object), Student, and Staff respectively (as in Figure 2.15 without the categorization features).

The cover aggregation facility is limited since only one-to-many relationships can be represented (the Convoy example of Figure 2.16 could be represented, but not the Class example since there is a many-to-many relationship between Class and Student).

3.3.2 Mapping from the Conceptual Model to the Codasyl Network

To map from the generalised conceptual model to the Codasyl network the following stages are carried out.

In stage 1, the entity-relationship model of Chapter 2 is mapped into a Bachman diagram. Firstly, the entity sets and relationships sets are mapped into record types (which will be represented by rectangular boxes in the diagram). Then, for one-to-one and one-to-many relationships between the entity and relationship sets, the relationships are mapped into cosets (with the arrows directed towards the 'many' end of a one-to-many relationship, or towards the most appropriate record type to represent the member of the coset in the case of a one-to-one relationship). Many-to-many relationships are broken down into one-to-many relationships by means of a link record type as illustrated in Figure 3.5 above. Each record type participating in a particular many-to-many relationship becomes the owner of a coset which has the link record type as a member.

To complete stage 1 the cosets may be labelled (F), (M) or (O), depending on whether membership is fixed, mandatory or optional, and singular cosets are added where relevant. Figure 3.6 shows the Bachman diagram resulting from the mapping of the entity-relationship diagram in Figure 2.10 into a Codasyl network model.

Stage 2 of the mapping process involves associating attributes with record types. There is no specific diagrammatic representation for this stage, and hence the entity-attribute diagrammatic representation introduced in Chapter 2 can be used. The network entity-attribute diagram may be the same as that of the conceptual model derived in section 2.5, except that 'ghost' identifiers (e.g. # in the Person entity) are replaced by actual identifiers (e.g. Person# as in the relational model in the previous section). Since entities are linked explicitly by means of the coset, it is not necessary to place linking attributes (foreign keys) into related entities. The resulting network model is very similar to the conceptual model of section 2.5, except that the representation of the degree and existence characteristics of relations is more limited.

However, to aid integrity checking and for physical efficiency reasons, it may be considered desirable in some applications to redundantly include owner key attributes (as foreign keys) in member entities in certain cosets. If all relevant foreign keys are included in member entities, the resulting network model is very similar to the relational model, except that the relationships are then both explicitly and

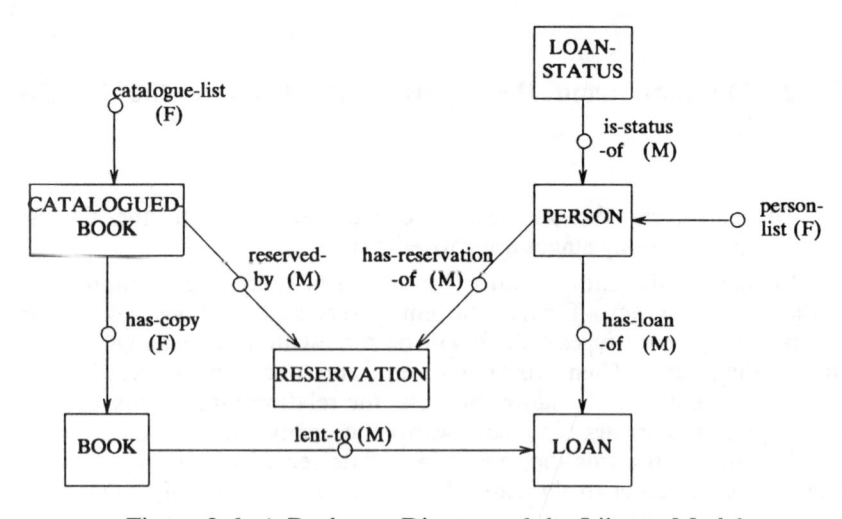

Figure 3.6 A Bachman Diagram of the Library Model

implicitly represented in the model.

3.3.3 The Codasyl Network Schema — An Example

As in the case of the relational model, part of the library schema will be used to illustrate the Codasyl DDL. As mentioned at the introduction to this section on the network model, a number of Codasyl proposals exist, the later ones representing improvements and enhancements to earlier versions. Codasyl schema definitions will therefore vary slightly from one implementation to another, since they are not all based on the same proposals; in addition, some may have implementation-dependent enhancements or may only be subsets of the full proposals. However, the basic facilities and concepts are the same. One major difference between most implementations and the more recent proposals, though, is the omission in recent proposals of some clauses which relate to purely physical aspects; most implementations have not yet been modified in the light of these changes. When they have been, they will provide schema definitions which are more purely conceptual-model oriented.

The example schema in Figure 3.7 is based on the 1981 Codasyl proposals (Codasyl 1981a), with physical aspects omitted from the schema.

```
SCHEMA NAME IS    LIBRARY.
........
RECORD NAME IS    CATALOGUED-BOOK
     KEY Cat-key IS Isbn DUPLICATES NOT ALLOWED.
     Isbn      TYPE IS CHARACTER 13.
     Author    TYPE IS CHARACTER 20.
     Title     TYPE IS CHARACTER 40.
     Publisher TYPE IS CHARACTER 20.
     Year      TYPE IS CHARACTER 4.
     Classmark TYPE IS CHARACTER 10.
RECORD NAME IS    BOOK.
     Book#     TYPE IS CHARACTER 5.
     Shelf     TYPE IS FIXED 1.
RECORD NAME IS    PERSON
     KEY Person-key IS Person# DUPLICATES NOT ALLOWED.
     Person#   TYPE IS CHARACTER 5.
     Name      TYPE IS CHARACTER 20.
     Address   TYPE IS CHARACTER 40.
RECORD NAME IS    LOAN.
     Date-due-back   TYPE IS CHARACTER 6.
........
SET NAME IS    catalogue-list.
     OWNER IS SYSTEM
          ORDER IS SORTED BY DEFINED KEYS.
     MEMBER IS    CATALOGUED-BOOK
          INSERTION IS AUTOMATIC     RETENTION IS FIXED
          KEY IS ASCENDING    Isbn
               DUPLICATES ARE NOT ALLOWED.
SET NAME IS    person-list.
     OWNER IS SYSTEM
          ORDER IS SORTED BY DEFINED KEYS.
     MEMBER IS    PERSON
          INSERTION IS AUTOMATIC     RETENTION IS FIXED
          KEY IS ASCENDING    Person#
               DUPLICATES ARE NOT ALLOWED.
SET NAME IS    has-copy.
     OWNER IS    CATALOGUED-BOOK
          ORDER IS LAST.
     MEMBER IS    BOOK
          INSERTION IS AUTOMATIC     RETENTION IS FIXED.
SET NAME IS    lent-to.
     OWNER IS    BOOK
          ORDER IS DEFAULT.
     MEMBER IS    LOAN
          INSERTION IS AUTOMATIC     RETENTION IS MANDATORY.
SET NAME IS    has-loan-of.
     OWNER IS    PERSON
          ORDER IS LAST.
     MEMBER IS    LOAN
          INSERTION IS AUTOMATIC     RETENTION IS MANDATORY.
........
END SCHEMA.
```

Figure 3.7 Part of the Library Network Schema
in the Codasyl DDL

The example shows the important clauses in a Codasyl schema. A number of other optional clauses are also available, including the ability to specify privacy locks at each level (schema, record, attribute, set) and also procedures which are to be carried out if an error occurs at a particular level; these optional clauses have not been included in the example.

Looking at the example in Figure 3.7, it will be seen that a Codasyl schema commences with a schema clause naming the schema. This is followed by a set of record type definitions, one for each record type (entity or relationship set) in the database. Record type definitions consist of at least a clause naming the record type, and one clause for each attribute in the record type giving its name and type. The Catalogued-Book and Person definitions also include a key clause; this is an optional clause which, if included, indicates which attribute(s) in the record provide the unique key (identifier) for that record. A name for the key is first declared (i.e. Cat-key and Person-key in the example), followed by the name of the attribute to be used as the identifier (or list of names, in the case of multi-attribute keys).

After all the record types have been declared, the coset types are defined. These definitions consist of at least a clause naming the coset type, an owner clause naming the record type which is the owner of the coset (or SYSTEM if it is a singular coset), an order clause indicating the logical order of members in the set (discussed below), and a member clause naming the record type which is the member of the coset (or record types, if a multi-member coset). The member clause also includes the 'retention' (existence) characteristic of the member record (retention may be fixed, mandatory, or optional, as discussed in subsection 3.3.1), and an 'insertion' characteristic which may have the value automatic or manual. The significance of the insertion characteristic relates to the manipulation of data in the database (input and updates) and is discussed briefly below.

The order clause enables a 'logical' ordering of members in a coset to be specified. Note that this clause does not necessarily imply any physical ordering. Order options include sorted, first (LIFO), last (LILO), and default. Sorted order requires a sort key to be specified in the member clause. For example, the 'catalogue-list' coset, which is singular, is sorted by Isbn in ascending order and duplicate Isbn's are not allowed. Order has been specified as 'last' in the 'has-copy' and 'has-loan-of' cosets. This means that the member records in both of these cosets will be kept in the order in which they are inserted (chronological order) — the last inserted will the the last in the set (hence LILO — last in, last out). Order is specified as 'default' when any logical order is acceptable; the 'lent-to' relationship is one-to-one so the order in this coset is immaterial as there will only ever be one member record in each coset occurrence.

The insertion and retention clauses provide six possible combinations, since insertion can be automatic or manual, and retention can be fixed, mandatory or optional. However, in practice not all these combinations are important. If insertion is specified as automatic in a particular coset type, the system automatically links a member record into the current occurrence of that coset type (or to the occurrence defined in a 'set selection' clause, which is not discussed here), when that record is stored in the database; if insertion is manual, the user must explicitly link a member record into a coset occurrence at an appropriate time. Fixed and mandatory retention are normally (though not necessarily) associated with automatic insertion, while optional retention is normally associated with manual insertion.

Two other important optional clauses are the 'SET IS PRIOR processable' and the 'member LINKED TO OWNER' clauses. These are concerned with retrieval efficiency and are not discussed until Chapter 5 in the section on implementation aspects.

3.4 The Hierarchical Model

A hierarchy is a restricted form of a network; it is one in which no object can be connected to (owned by) more than one object higher up in the hierarchy, although it can be connected to (own) many objects at a lower level. Due to the limitations of hierarchical structures, the hierarchical model will not be dealt with in as much detail as the other types of model, but a book of this nature would not be complete without a discussion of hierarchical models.

Since an object cannot be 'owned' by more than one object in a hierarchical structure, there is only one object type at the top (or root) level of a hierarchy, but there may be many branches, each of which can itself be a hierarchy. At each branch of the hierarchy, there can only be a one-to-one or one-to-many relationship with the next branch; there cannot be a many-to-one relationship as this would create a network structure.

The library data model is not a hierarchical structure, but a network one. For example, Reservation objects are owned by more than one object type — Catalogued-Book and Person; and although Catalogued-Book to Reservation is a one-to-many relationship, Reservation to Person is many-to-one. The model can however be represented as a hierarchy, but only by introducing duplication into the model. Figure 3.8 is an example of a hierarchical version of the library model with Catalogued-Book at the root of the hierarchy. For each catalogued book there will be information relating to each copy of the book and each reservation at the

```
              CATALOGUED-
                BOOK
         ┌───────┴───────┐
       BOOK           RESERVATION
         │                │
       LOAN            PERSON *
         │
      PERSON *
```

          * includes
         loan-status data

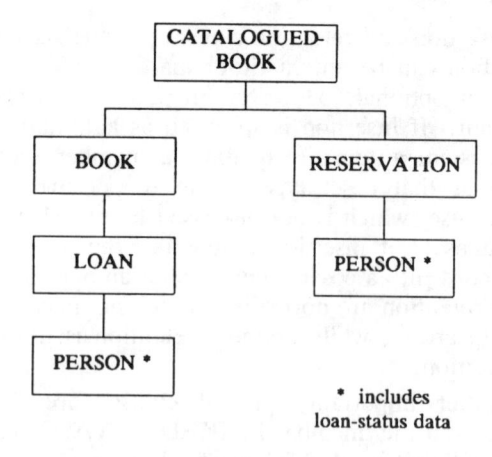

Figure 3.8   A Single Hierarchy Version of the
Library Data Model

first level of the hierarchy. For each copy of the book there will be loan information and also information about the person to whom the book is lent, which will include loan-status information. For each reservation there will be information about the person who has made the reservation, again including loan-status information. Figure 3.9 shows a possible occurrence of this hierarchy (note that there are currently no reservations for the book in question).

  There are two major problems with such a model. Firstly, duplication. Person information may be repeated in different occurrences of the hierarchy since a person may have many copies of books on loan and may have reservations for many others. Also, the loan-status information must be duplicated for each person with the same status. The second major problem is that of access to data. In a hierarchical model, access to specific objects is via the appropriate root object occurrence. Hence, to find a particular person for example, it may be necessary to scan the database from the first catalogued-book until one is found with a loan or reservation associated with the required person.

  The similarities between the model represented by Figures 3.8 and 3.9, and the unnormalised universal Book-Data relation (section 2.6 in Chapter 2) should be noted. Readers should satisfy themselves that they recognise the fundamental similarities. Due to these similarities, the hierarchical model of Figure 3.8 possesses all the undesirable dependencies of an unnormalised relation.

  An alternative to a single hierarchy database as in Figure 3.8, is a multiple hierarchy database version as illustrated in Figure 3.10. In this version, the problem of access to data relating to particular persons has

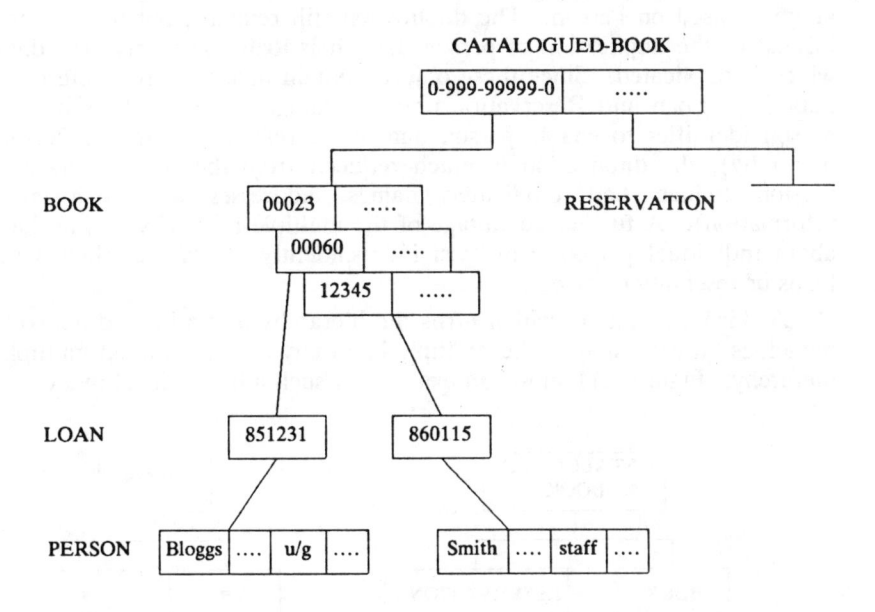

Figure 3.9 An Occurrence of a Hierarchical Database Record

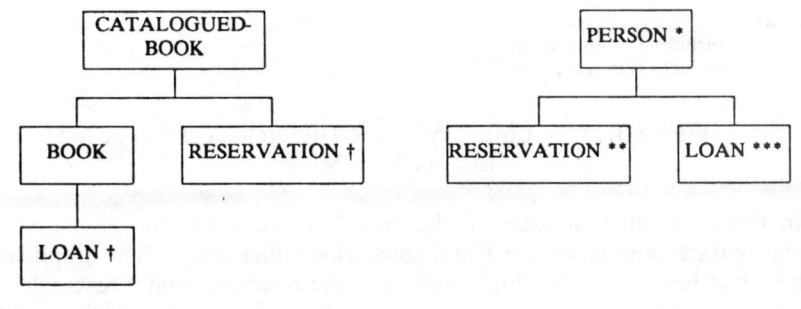

Notes:
- * includes Loan-Status data
- ** includes Isbn
- *** includes Isbn and Book#
- † includes Person identifier

Figure 3.10 A Multiple Hierarchy Version of the Library Data Model

been eliminated by having one hierarchy based on Catalogued-Book and another based on Person. The duplication still remains, but in this case instead of the duplication of person data, it is loan and reservation data which is duplicated. Since these objects contain date and cross-reference data (e.g. Loan and Reservation under Catalogued-Book will contain a person identifier to enable person data to be retrieved from the Person hierarchy), the duplication is much reduced from the single hierarchy version (which had duplicated names, addresses and loan-status information). A further advantage of the multiple hierarchy is that data about individual persons can exist independently of whether they have loans or reservations or not.

A third alternative, which turns the hierarchy into a limited network model, is an extension of the multiple hierarchy and is a linked multiple hierarchy. Figure 3.11 shows an example of such a hierarchical model.

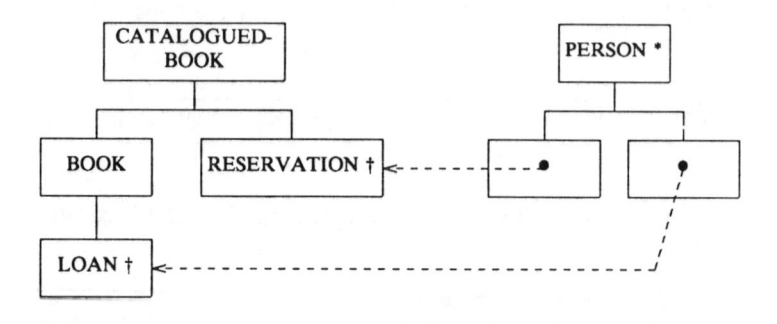

Notes:
* includes Loan-Status data
† includes Person identifier

Figure 3.11 A Linked Multiple Hierarchy Version of the Library Data Model

In this case, all that exists at the branches below Person are pointers to appropriate objects in the Catalogued-Book hierarchy. The duplication has thus been virtually eliminated, and the resulting model resembles the network model, except in relation to the loan-status data which is part of Person in the hierarchical model. (The reader might like to consider the implications of separating the loan-status data from the person data.)

The most comprehensive hierarchical system is IBM's IMS, which has been particularly successful in certain large database environments, though other hierarchical systems also exist and are widely used (such as System 2000 and Delta which is a micro DBMS). It is worth noting that IMS was enhanced some time back to support network structures by means of linked hierarchies.

This discussion of hierarchical models should be sufficient to provide an insight into the nature of such models and into the similarities and differences as compared with other types of model. More complete discussions of the hierarchical approach and of the data model aspects of the IMS system may be found in Date (1981).

3.5 The Binary Relationship Model

3.5.1 Introduction

The *binary relationship* approach is an approach which is appropriate to logic-based and fact-based systems, as well as to functional database systems. All relationships are represented at the lowest level, with no distinction made between entities and attributes — all are considered as basic objects or entities. This approach provides the basis for various different systems related only by the level at which the relationships are represented. It should not be taken to be representative of any particular system.

Interest in a binary approach arose from an awareness of the inadequacies of the entity or record oriented approach, which are summarised in Kent (1979). Limitations include the following three points. Firstly, the record oriented approach attempts to represent non-homogeneous objects (e.g. entity sets and relationship sets) in a homogeneous structure — the record or relation. Secondly, the relational approach represents a single type of object — the relationship — in various ways, e.g. as an attribute, as a relation, and as a foreign key. Thirdly, a particular object may be represented in one way (e.g. as an attribute) in one context, and in another way (e.g. as an entity) in some other context. The binary relationship approach does not have these limitations; its primary advantage is its generality and flexibility. The main disadvantage with this approach, though, is the difficulty of implementing efficient systems to manage data represented in this way; this will also be discussed in a later chapter.

The binary relationship approach owes much to a paper by Abrial entitled 'Data Semantics' (Abrial 1974), but research in the mid 70's by Senko on the Diam system (Senko 1975, 1976a), by Falkenberg on binary association and role concepts (Falkenberg 1976), by Bracchi et al on binary logical associations (Bracchi 1976), and others, stimulated more recent interest in the approach, e.g. Daplex (Shipman 1981) and Adaplex (based on a Functional Data Model), Asdas (Frost 1981), Nijssen's Niam (Verheijen 1982), and others. It is interesting to note that parallel research efforts in the broad area of binary relationships have been undertaken for a number of years by artificial intelligence (AI) researchers, and it is only in recent years that database and AI researchers have come together to pool their knowledge and expertise.

The binary relationship approach has its roots in the mathematical concepts of sets, functions and relations. Abrial defines a binary relation as "an atomic link between pairs of objects belonging to certain categories". Abrial initially names the relationships in both directions with one direction identified as the primary direction and the other as the inverse, and later introduces a special operator 'inv' to eliminate the need for naming the inverse relation. Each binary relation has an associated degree characteristic, one-to-one or one-to-many, when viewed from either the primary or the inverse direction. Combining the primary and inverse relationships of a binary relation, the overall relationship may be one-to-one, many-to-one, one-to-many, or many-to-many (cf. discussion of relationships in section 2.4.1). When a relation has an overall degree of one-to-one or many-to-one it represents a function in the mathematical sense (Vetter 1981, ch.2). Functions may be *total* or *partial*. A total function from A to B is such that all members of the set of A objects are associated with exactly one member of the set of B objects. A partial function from A to B is such that all members of the set of A objects are associated with either zero or one member of the set of B objects (i.e. some A's may not be associated with any B). Various combinations of total and partial, primary function and inverse are equivalent to the mandatory, optional and contingent existence characteristics introduced in Chapter 2. This correspondence is represented below.

primary function	inverse	existence
total	total	mandatory
total	partial	contingent
partial	total	contingent
partial	partial	optional

It is beyond the scope of this book to discuss the many different approaches which may loosely be classified as binary relationship based. Comprehensive coverage of the mathematical concepts underlying this approach may be found in Vetter (1981), and a general discussion of binary relations, and functional and logic systems, including Daplex, Adaplex, and Prolog, may be found in Gray (1984). References to specific systems were given above. In the next two subsections, a general binary relationship model will be developed, and Prolog, a logic-based system (Clocksin 1981), will be used for illustrative purposes.

3.5.2 Mapping to a Binary Relationship Model

It will be remembered that the final step in the top-down approach to designing the conceptual model in the previous chapter was to combine the entity-relationship and entity-attribute diagrams into one data model diagram. This data model diagram (Figure 2.12) provides all the information necessary for mapping to the binary relationship model (except that the inverse relationships are not named).

Binary models are frequently drawn using the diagrammatic notation below in which the arrow represents the direction of the primary relationship.

$$ A \longrightarrow B $$

However, such notation is limited in its semantic content, and while some binary approaches are similarly limited, others are semantically richer. For this reason, relationships will contain existence and degree information as in the conceptual model.

The mapping from conceptual model to binary relationship model is carried out in two stages. Firstly all objects — entity sets, relationship sets, and attributes — are represented in the same way; an ellipse will be used for this purpose. Secondly, related pairs of objects are linked together by means of arrows representing the relationship, and these can be named in both directions but are named in one direction only in Figure 3.12 below (generally the primary or major direction, which is obvious from the name and context). Figure 3.12 shows the binary relationship model resulting from the application of these two stages. This diagram contains the degree and existence characteristics of the relationships, as in the conceptual model, although not all current systems based on this approach provide facilities for expressing this information.

An important feature of the binary relationship approach is that, unlike the entity-based approaches, many-to-many relationships do not require any special mappings, since atomic items are always represented in the relationships. The special mappings necessitated by the entity-based models are due to the fact that entity sets represent composite objects — the entity plus its associated attributes. In the library model there are no direct many-to-many relationships. The reservation relationship was originally many-to-many but was converted into a relationship set in step 3 of the modelling process in section 2.5. However, in the discussion on entity-attribute relationships (step 2), it was assumed that only one author would be recorded for each book in the

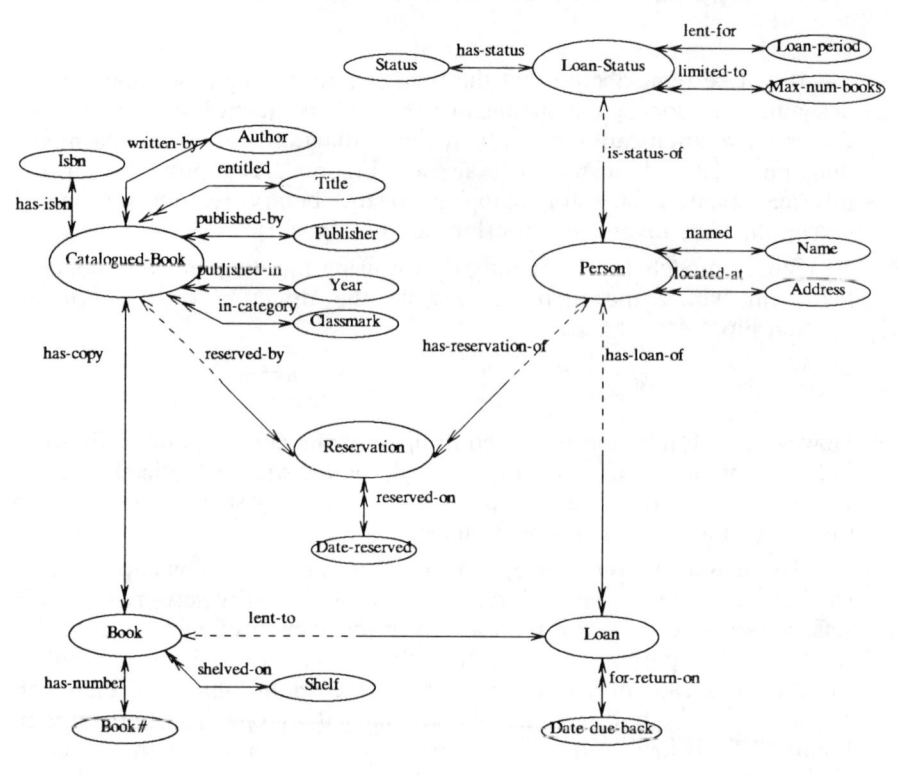

Figure 3.12 A Binary Relationship Version of the Library Model

library catalogue, and it was left to the reader to consider how the recording of multiple authors could be handled. In the conceptual model the relationship would be represented as:

which would simply be mapped into the binary relationship:

The reader should by now appreciate that such a simple mapping is not possible in the entity-based approaches, and should return at the end of this chapter to consider this problem.

The naming of relationships in the binary approach deserves some comment. Relationship names in the conceptual model of Chapter 2 were

chosen to be meaningful when an infix (fact) notation is used; for example:
>> Book shelved-on Shelf
>> Person named Name
>> Loan-Status is-status-of Person

with corresponding inverse relationships which have been omitted from the diagrams:
>> Shelf is-shelf-of Book
>> Name is-name-of Person
>> Person has-status Loan-Status

In prefix (binary relation) notation these relationships would be represented as:
>> shelved-on (Book, Shelf)
>> named (Person, Name)
>> etc.

In functional notation on the other hand, the relationship names might be changed so that they are more meaningful in this notation; for example:
>> shelf-of (Book) —> Shelf
>> name-of (Person) —> Name
>> etc.

(The arrow (—>) may be read as the word 'is'; e.g. name-of Person is Name.)

In all these cases, we are dealing with 2 objects which are connected by means of a relationship or function. Thus despite the existence of many 'variations on a theme', we refer to this approach as the binary relationship approach.

3.5.3 Representing Facts in Prolog

To illustrate the description of binary relationship models, the Prolog language will be used. It should be remembered though that a number of different types of system are based on the binary relationship model and so Prolog should be considered only as an example system and not necessarily as representative of all systems based on, or related to, the binary relationship approach.

Prolog is a logic-based system in which the data description, the actual data (facts), and the rules (implications) are combined together to form a single unit — the Prolog database. A *fact* consists of a predicate or relationship, with one or more arguments in parentheses. The arguments represent objects which may be considered as entity values or attribute values, but as far as Prolog is concerned they are all just values. Clocksin & Mellish define a *rule* as "a general statement about objects and their relationships" (Clocksin 1981, p.14). A rule is a means by which a set of unary, binary or n-ary facts can be derived from other facts in the database. Facts and rules will be discussed in more detail below and in the next chapter; a comprehensive description of the language may be found in Clocksin (1981).

A fact may actually be unary, binary, or n-ary. The ability to declare n-ary facts has given rise to some research into Prolog interfaces to relational databases, and also relational interfaces (e.g. QBE) to Prolog databases (Jarke 1984a, Neves 1983). However, whereas relational systems are designed to efficiently manage a relatively small number of n-ary relation types, Prolog is designed to efficiently manage a large set of facts of varying types and of varying degrees — unary, binary, n-ary. From the binary relationship viewpoint, it is the binary facts, and the way in which reference is made to them in queries, which are of interest, but for comparative purposes the n-ary capability will also be mentioned later.

Prolog notation is important for distinguishing between actual values and variables. Hence the Prolog conventions will be used in examples, rather than those used previously. A prefix form is used to represent facts, and an example of a binary fact is:

named (p001, 'Stephens E.A.').

where 'p001' is the identifier (surrogate) for the person named E.A. Stephens. Words beginning with an uppercase letter are considered to be variables (of which more will be said in the next chapter). Any actual data values which include initial uppercase letters therefore need to be enclosed in inverted commas (as in the example above).

Figure 3.13 shows a small part of the library database declared in Prolog. Each fact is a binary fact, with surrogates (coding schemes) introduced to identify real world objects. For example, one person is known by the system as p001 and is named E.A. Stephens (there may of course be another person named E.A. Stephens in the database but the system would have a different code for him). The surrogates can be made transparent to the end-user as will be demonstrated in later examples.

N-ary facts can be set up to represent a schema if required. Users are then able to find out the structure of the database by querying the schema. Figure 3.14 shows a possible representation of such a schema; other possible representations also exist. It should be noted though that Prolog has no concept of a schema and the schema relations are therefore just additional facts as far as the system is concerned. To the user, of course, they represent metadata and can be manipulated (stored/retrieved) in the same way as other data.

has-isbn (cb001, 0-999-99999-0).
has-isbn (cb003, 0-33333-333-0).
has-isbn (cb002, 0-12345-123-x).
has-isbn (cb004, 0-5656-5656-2).
written-by (cb001, 'Bloggs C.J.').
written-by (cb003, 'Hicks S.A.').
written-by (cb002, 'Smith W.F.').
written-by (cb004, 'Roberts H.').
entitled (cb001, 'Data Models').
entitled (cb003, 'Intro to Databases').
entitled (cb002, 'Relational Systems').
entitled (cb004, 'Data Models').
published-by (cb001, 'Ackson-Bull').
published-by (cb003, 'Porter').
published-by (cb002, 'Wilkinson').
published-by (cb004, 'Ackson-Bull').
published-in (cb001, 1980).
published-in (cb003, 1983).
published-in (cb002, 1984).
published-in (cb004, 1984).
in-category (cb001, 'QA264').
in-category (cb003, 'QA76').
in-category (cb002, 'QA264').
in-category (cb004, 'QA264').
has-copy (cb001, b001).
has-copy (cb001, b003).
has-copy (cb003, b005).
has-copy (cb002, b007).
has-copy (cb004, b009).
has-copy (cb002, b002).
has-copy (cb003, b004).
has-copy (cb004, b006).
has-copy (cb003, b008).
has-number (b001, 00023).
has-number (b003, 00060).
has-number (b005, 00076).
has-number (b007, 00088).
has-number (b009, 00101).
has-number (b002, 00057).
has-number (b004, 00075).
has-number (b006, 00084).
has-number (b008, 00096).
named (p001, 'Stephens E.A.').
named (p003, 'Willis H.').
named (p005, 'Mills J.').
named (p007, 'Taylor D.').
named (p002, 'Brown A.J.').
named (p004, 'Parker M.P.').
named (p006, 'Fletcher F.J.').
lent-to (b003, lo105).
lent-to (b008, lo098).
lent-to (b005, lo113).
lent-to (b002, lo111).
has-loan-of (p001, lo105).
has-loan-of (p003, lo111).
has-loan-of (p007, lo113).
has-loan-of (p001, lo098).
for-return-on (lo105, 851231).
for-return-on (lo098, 851231).
for-return-on (lo111, 851215).
for-return-on (lo113, 860106).

Figure 3.13 Part of the Prolog Library Database

schema-template (predicate, object1, object2).
schema (has-isbn, 'CATALOGUED-BOOK', 'Isbn').
schema (written-by, 'CATALOGUED-BOOK', 'Author').
schema (entitled, 'CATALOGUED-BOOK', 'Title').
schema (published-by, 'CATALOGUED-BOOK', 'Publisher').
schema (published-in, 'CATALOGUED-BOOK', 'Year').
schema (in-category, 'CATALOGUED-BOOK', 'Classmark').
schema (has-copy, 'CATALOGUED-BOOK', 'BOOK').
schema (has-number, 'BOOK', 'Book#').
schema (named, 'PERSON', Name).
schema (lent-to, 'BOOK', 'LOAN').
schema (has-loan-of, 'PERSON', 'LOAN').
schema (for-return-on, 'LOAN', 'Date-due-back').

Figure 3.14 Schema Facts for the Library Model

An alternative to the use of surrogates to represent entities is the use of the objects which were selected as identifiers in the conceptual model. In this case, the set of binary 'has-isbn' and 'has-number' facts could be replaced by unary facts such as:

>   is-catalogued-book (0-999-99999-0).
>   is-book (00023).
>   and so on

or binary facts such as:

>   is-a (0-999-99999-0, 'CATALOGUED-BOOK').
>   is-a (00023, 'BOOK').
>   and so on

and the surrogate 'cb' numbers and 'b' numbers in other facts in the database of Figure 3.13 would be replaced by the relevant Isbn's and Book#'s respectively. Surrogates would still be needed to identify Person, Loan, and Reservation objects though.

For comparative purposes, an example of part of the library database using Prolog n-ary facts is given in Figure 3.15. The equivalent of the Catalogued-Book n-ary relation is shown. Note that in the n-ary fact version, the names of the predicates describing the relationships between pairs of objects are lost; it becomes an entity-based model.

>   catalogued-book (0-999-99999-0, 'Bloggs C.J.', 'Data Models',
>   'Ackson-Bull', 1980, 'QA264').
>   catalogued-book (0-12345-123-x, 'Smith W.F.', 'Relational Systems',
>   'Wilkinson', 1984, 'QA264').
>   catalogued-book (0-33333-333-0, 'Hicks S.A.', 'Intro to Databases',
>   'Porter', 1983, 'QA76').
>   catalogued-book (0-5656-5656-0, 'Roberts H.', 'Data Models',
>   'Ackson-Bull', 1984, 'QA264').

Figure 3.15 An N-ary Fact Version of the Catalogued-Book Entity

The similarities with the relational model of Figure 3.2 should be mentioned. For each relation, there will be a n-ary fact type in the Prolog version, and each n-ary fact will have the same attributes as the corresponding relation. The main difference between Prolog n-ary facts and a relational database is, of course, in the way the database is described and the way the data is input.

It is worth noting that Prolog rules can be used to derive the equivalent of the n-ary facts in Figure 3.15. An example is given in Figure 3.16.

```
catalogued-book ( Isbn, Author, Title, Publisher, Year, Classmark ) :-
    has-isbn ( CB, Isbn ),      written-by ( CB, Author ),
    entitled ( CB, Title ),     published-by ( CB, Publisher ),
    published-in ( CB, Year ),  in-category ( CB, Classmark ).
```

Figure 3.16 A Prolog Rule to Derive the Catalogued-Book Entity

This Prolog rule derives a new type of fact (or n-ary relation) called catalogued-book, which is the combination of the Isbn, Author, etc. objects from the relevant binary facts. The rule may be interpreted in formal English as follows:

a catalogued-book fact containing Isbn, Author, Title, Publisher, Year and Classmark is implied by the existence of the following facts: a particular CB value has-isbn Isbn and is written-by Author and is entitled Title and is published-by Publisher and is published-in Year and is in-category Classmark.

A rule consists of a 'head' and a 'body' connected by the symbol ':-' (which may be read as the word 'if' or 'is implied by'). The various components in the body have the same format as the facts with which they are associated. These components act as templates, and hence they contain variables and/or constants, instead of actual data values. The ',' separating components in the body represents the 'and' connective, while if a ';' were used this would represent 'or'. In the example, 'Isbn', 'Author', etc. are variables since they commence with an uppercase letter. 'CB' is also a variable which is used purely to link the different facts together, ensuring that when the rule is instantiated, only those Isbn, Author, etc. values which are associated with the same CB value are associated together in a particular derived catalogued-book fact.

Prolog rules are important for providing built-in navigation around a binary data model, thus enabling queries on the database to be very much simplified, as will be illustrated in the next chapter (section 4.5.4).

As can be seen, Prolog is very flexible and there are in fact other possible representations of the data model in Figure 3.12. As far as additional semantics are concerned, rules may be defined to derive such aspects as categorization and generalization, and Prolog lists may be used for aggregation. These semantic aspects will now be briefly considered.

Categorization can be effected by including a condition as a component of a rule body. For example:

    recent-book (CB, Isbn) :-
            has-isbn (CB, Isbn), published-in (CB, Year),
            Year >= 1982.
    older-book (CB, Isbn) :-
            has-isbn (CB, Isbn), published-in (CB, Year),
            Year < 1982.

These two rules would categorize the 'has-isbn' relationship of Catalogued-Books into two mutually exclusive subsets: recent-books published in 1982 onwards, and older-books published before 1982.

Generalization merely requires the use of 'or' connectives in the body of a rule to connect facts representing objects which are associated with the generic object in the head of the rule. For example, if unary facts are used to represent entities and their identifiers, and there exist facts in the database matching the following schema descriptions:

    student ('Person#').   and   staff ('Person#').

then a generic object 'university-member' may be derived by the rule:

    university-member (P) :- student (P); staff (P).

where ';' indicates the 'or' connective. This rule indicates that an object identified by P is a university-member if P is either a student or a staff (or both).

Cover aggregation can be carried out by means of the Prolog list construct. For example, a particular class for a lecture course could be declared as:

    class ('Data Management', p005, [p107, p151, ...]).

where the first object is the course title, the second is the member of staff in charge of the class, and the third is a list of students in the class.

Degree and existence characteristics can also be represented by means of rules.

This is a necessarily incomplete introduction to Prolog since the intention here is merely to demonstrate the way in which a binary relationship data model may be described. Further discussion of Prolog in relation to its use as a query language will be provided in the next chapter.

3.6 The Conceptual Model Revisited

It has been shown in this chapter how the DBMS-specific data models are generally inadequate as far as modelling real world information is concerned since they are weak in their semantic support, although binary relationship models are more adequate in this respect than the others. In this section a closer look at these inadequacies will be taken, and ways in which the full information can be reflected in the database applications will be investigated. In addition, possible future developments in database management systems will be hinted at.

The most serious limitations in the DBMS-specific data models as compared with the conceptual model of Figure 2.12 concern the degree and existence characteristics of relations. The degree is reflected to a certain extent. For example, in relational and network models relationships are assumed to be one-to-many; many-to-many relationships are mapped into one-to-many and one-to-one are a special case of one-to-many. However, in general the existence characteristic is not represented, except in the Codasyl model with its retention clause which indicates only the existence characteristic of the member of a coset (not the owner), and in the relational model via the referential integrity rule which again corresponds to only one direction of a relationship.

The existence characteristic is important for the integrity of the database. It indicates, for example, cases where the existence in the database of an entity of a particular type implies the existence also of an entity of some other related type. When existence characterstics cannot be represented in the DBMS model, the DBMS cannot check that such constraints are always true; updates carried out on the database could cause them to be violated.

It is possible, though, for the existence characteristic information from the conceptual model to be used to produce skeleton input and update programs which would ensure that existence constraints are not violated. Consider, for example, the 'has-copy' relationship between catalogued book and book. The existence of the relationship is mandatory, i.e. a particular catalogued book entity cannot exist without at least one book entity associated with it, and vice versa. To ensure that this constraint is never violated, the following simplified outline procedure could be used as a basis for applications which enter new books into a relational database. (Note: basic error checking has been omitted).

```
request new Book#, Shelf, and Isbn
search Catalogued-Book relation for Isbn
if not found then
    request Title, Author, etc. for Book
    add catalogue data to Catalogued-Book relation
add book data to Book relation
```

This outline procedure not only ensures that a book cannot exist without a corresponding catalogue entry, but it also ensures that two other constraints implied by the data model are not violated. These are: that a catalogue entry is only made when an actual copy of the book exists, and that there is only one catalogue entry for a particular Isbn. These constraints are implied by the one-to-many mandatory relationship between catalogued book and book. The outline procedure can be used for other mandatory relationships, modified as relevant to the particular entities involved.

As a second example, a one-to-many contingent relationship will be considered. The 'is-status-of' relationship between loan-status and person entities is contingent, with the optionality at the loan-status end of the relationship; i.e. a loan-status entity may exist without it being associated with a person entity, but not vice versa. This suggests that loan-status entities can be input to the database independently of person entities, so two procedures are relevant here, one for the input of loan-status entities and the other for the input of person entities which is similar to the procedure for books outlined earlier. The two procedures are outlined below:

Loan-Status procedure:
    request Status, Loan-period, Max-num-books
    add status data to Loan-Status relation

Person procedure:
    request Person#, Name, Address, and Status
    search Loan-Status relation for Status
    if not found then
        perform Loan-Status procedure
    add person data to Person relation

These are just two examples to illustrate the importance of representing as much semantic information as possible in the conceptual model, even when the DBMS to be used does not support such rich semantics. It provides essential information for the application system designer; it helps him to ensure that application programs maintain the integrity of the database, by highlighting the constraints which must not be violated, and the dependencies which exist in the database.

The checking of other semantic constraints, highlighted in the conceptual model, can also be built into applications. Examples are: ensuring that a one-to-one degree characteristic is not violated in those cases where one-to-many is implied by the system; checking the implied one-to-one relationship in a coset which represents a generalization relationship; and checking exclusivity in multi-member cosets where relevant, such as those representing exclusive aggregates. The reader might like to draft skeleton procedures to carry out some of these checks.

Before leaving this section it should be pointed out that the development of DBMSs supporting semantically richer data models will remove from the application designer the responsibility for ensuring the maintenance of many database integrity aspects. This point will be considered again in the final chapter.

3.7 Views and the External Schema

It is the purpose of this section to discuss *user views* and *external schema*. The different types of model and schema — external, conceptual, and internal — will be reviewed first in order to put external schema in their proper context.

The different types of model — external, conceptual and internal

In Chapter 2 and in this chapter so far, the processes involved in deriving a data model representing the view of reality relevant to the global database have been discussed. The data investigation process provides for the collection of information on the nature and use of the data; such information is used as a basis for the other processes in database development. The data modelling process derives from this information the generalised conceptual model which is a model of reality in terms of real world concepts; this model is limited to those aspects of reality which are relevant to the global application area. The database design process maps the model of reality into a data model in terms of DBMS-specific concepts, from which a conceptual schema (data model description) can be prepared using the DBMS data description language (DDL).

The conceptual schema provides the global or overall view of the database, but individual users and applications may only be interested in, or may be constrained to, particular subsets of the database. Such subsets may be referred to as user views or external models, and may be described by external schema (or subschema). The external schema would generally be derived from the DBMS data model as they must be consistent with the conceptual schema, which is also derived from this model; the fact that the external schema and conceptual schema DDLs may be different is immaterial. Each external schema relates to a specific user or application requirement, or a set of such requirements which are similar or related. Information concerning such requirements would have been obtained during data investigation. The external schema could be represented diagrammatically as DBMS external models, using a similar notation to that used for the DBMS data model.

An alternative approach suggested by Yao et al (1982) is to initially design the separate external models and then derive the overall (global) conceptual model by integrating the different external views. A related approach, LBMS-SDM, has been developed by Learmouth and Burchett (Hall, 1981); this approach starts from the user's 'views' (input and output forms) treating them as unnormalised relations, and then carries out third normal form data analysis to produce a conceptual model. However, such an approach might produce a conceptual model which is too application-dependent and not sufficiently flexible for the dynamic environment in which it will be used.

The internal schema describes the storage structure of the database; it relates conceptual schema objects to physical objects such as disc files, pages, file organisations, etc. The internal schema makes use of metadata regarding specific user and applications requirements, including statistical data concerning data volumes, access frequencies, and access relationships. The choice of physical storage structures and access mechanisms determines the efficiency of the database in relation to specific usage patterns.

The mappings between the data models and the different schema are illustrated in Figure 3.17. In summary, the conceptual model is derived from information obtained during the data investigation stage. The DBMS data model is then derived from the conceptual model. The external schema and conceptual schema (data descriptions in appropriate languages) are logical level descriptions derived from the DBMS data model. At a lower level, the internal schema is a physical level description also derived from the DBMS data model. The mappings between the schema:

external schema —> conceptual schema —> internal schema

are carried out by the DBMS automatically.

In Figure 3.17, the metadatabase is illustrated surrounding and enclosing the data models and schema. This is appropriate, as it is essential for deriving the models and schema. It contains all the relevant information and may also contain additional information, both logical (semantic) and physical.

The different schema all represent different views of the database — user or application views at the external level, the global view at the conceptual level, and the storage view at the internal level. However, the term 'view' is commonly used only in relation to the external level. In this book the term 'user view' or 'external schema' will be used to avoid any confusion.

The external schema

Having put the external schema into context they will now be discussed in a little more detail. The external schema may be described

```
                    META DATABASE
                    Conceptual
                      Model
                        ⇓
                      DBMS
                    Data Model
                        ⇓                        Logical Level
      set of         Conceptual
   External Schema →   Schema
                        ↓
                     Internal
                      Schema                     Physical Level
                    META DATABASE

                                                 ⇓ derived
                                                   models

                                                 ↓ mappings
                                                   by DBMS
```

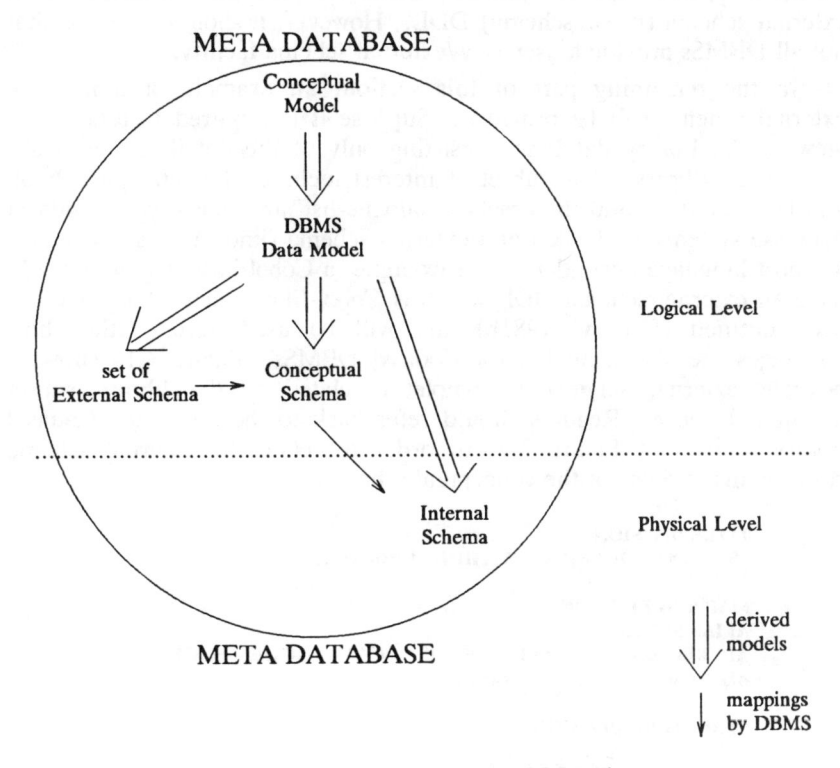

Figure 3.17 Data Models and Mappings

in various ways depending on the DBMS. An external schema DDL similar to the conceptual schema DDL may be provided, although in some cases this may be oriented towards the specific host language used for applications. Alternatively, the external schema may be expressed by means of special DBMS query/manipulation language statements, in which case 'predicates' or conditions are used to restrict the database to the required views. This alternative method will be discussed in more detail in the next chapter, after query and database manipulation languages have been discussed. It is also possible for external schema to have different conceptual bases from that of the conceptual schema; for example, it is possible to have a relational external schema supported by a Codasyl conceptual schema and DBMS. However, even in this case, the external schema would be derived by reference to the DBMS data model to ensure consistency.

In general, relational systems provide user view facilities by means of query/manipulation language statements. In Prolog, user views can also be defined in a similar way, by declaring rules which derive views.

Hierarchical and network systems provide such facilities by means of an external schema (or subschema) DDL. However, it should be noted that not all DBMSs provide a user view/external schema facility.

In the remaining part of this section, an example of a network external schema will be provided. Suppose it is required to establish a view of the library database consisting only of the details about books held in the library. The subset of interest includes the catalogued book and book entities, and the cosets 'catalogue-list' and 'has-copy'. Codasyl database systems are hosted and external schema (known as 'subschema') are host-language dependent. For example, a Cobol-hosted system would have an external schema DDL which is Cobol-like. Such a language has been defined (Codasyl 1981b) and will be used here. Other host languages are also available for Codasyl DBMSs. Figure 3.18 shows a possible external schema (incomplete) related to the library subset mentioned above. Readers should refer back to the associated Codasyl library schema of Figure 3.7, in order to relate the external schema components to those of the conceptual schema.

TITLE DIVISION.
SS BOOK-DETAILS WITHIN LIBRARY.

MAPPING DIVISION.
ALIAS SECTION.
AD RECORD CATALOGUE IS "CATALOGUED-BOOK".
AD Category **IS** "Classmark".

STRUCTURE DIVISION.

REALM SECTION.
* not discussed here.

RECORD SECTION.
1   CATALOGUE.
        2 Isbn   **PICTURE** X(13).
         ....
        2 Category   **PICTURE** X(10).
1   BOOK.
        2 Book#   **PICTURE** X(5).
         ....

SET SECTION.
SD catalogue-list.
SD has-copy.

Figure 3.18   A Skeleton Codasyl External Schema

The line starting SS (subschema) declares the external schema name within the LIBRARY schema. In the alias section, names of schema objects may be changed as required by the application or applications which will use the external schema. The example shows a change to a record name and an attribute name, but coset names may also be changed; the schema equivalents are enclosed in inverted commas. The record types are described in the record section, and if required the field sizes may be changed and attributes may be omitted completely. Finally, the cosets involved in the external schema are named. Any number of external schema may be described for a specific schema.

When external schema facilities are provided by a DBMS, a specific external schema is invoked on entry to the system and this constrains the user or application programmer to a specific subset of the database. Thus, external schema are useful for access control purposes, as well as for insulating the end-user from those parts of the database in which he is not interested.

3.8 Summary

In this chapter, the process of database design has been considered. This involves mapping from the generalised conceptual model to a DBMS-specific data model and thence using the DBMS data description language (DDL) to describe the database schema. The three main entity-based approaches — relational, network and hierarchical — were introduced, and the conceptual model derived using the top-down approach in Chapter 2 was mapped into data models based on each of these approaches. A schema for part of the library model was also provided for the relational model in the SQL DDL and for the network model in the Codasyl DDL. It should be stressed that only subsets of the DDLs were introduced. Full descriptions of these and other DDLs may be found in relevant user manuals.

The binary relationship approach was also introduced and a binary relationship version of the library model derived. An example illustrated how binary facts can be represented in Prolog, and a Prolog n-ary fact version was also introduced for comparison with the relational approach.

The objective of these sections was to highlight the similarities and differences of the different approaches, and to compare the semantic richness (or lack of it) with that of the conceptual model of Chapter 2. This latter aspect was then discussed in more detail in the section on 'The Conceptual Model Revisited'.

Finally, external schema which describe subsets of the conceptual model and represent individual user or application views were put into context and discussed.

CHAPTER FOUR

Database Query and Manipulation Languages

4.1 Introduction

So far this book has been concentrating on the actual creation of the database, and in particular on designing a data model and mapping this to the concepts specific to the particular DBMS to be used. This chapter is concerned with the process of accessing the data stored in the database, i.e. retrieving useful information from it and manipulating it as required. The chapter discusses database access from the viewpoint of the user, covering the various types of language available for this purpose. In the next chapter database access from the system viewpoint will be discussed.

There are different levels at which the database may be accessed and these are outlined in Figure 4.1. At the highest level is *natural language*. This has been placed in a dashed box as natural language interfaces are still very much at the research stage and scarcely any implementations exist, although some semi-natural interfaces exist. Next there are *query+ languages*. They are called 'query+' languages here since most of the languages at this level not only provide query facilities but also high-level facilities for updating and manipulating data in the database (they are sometimes referred to as '4th generation languages'). These include languages specifically designed for the casual end-user, i.e. the user who only occasionally wishes to access the database and who cannot therefore be expected to learn or remember a formal query language. Such languages often employ graphical techniques to assist the user. Also included at this level are languages which, although formal in nature, are

English-like, and hence are suitable for end-users who wish to access the database more frequently and are prepared to learn a simple language. At this level too are query languages which are procedural in nature and are therefore suitable only for the sophisticated end-user; such languages will be classified as 'high-level procedural' languages.

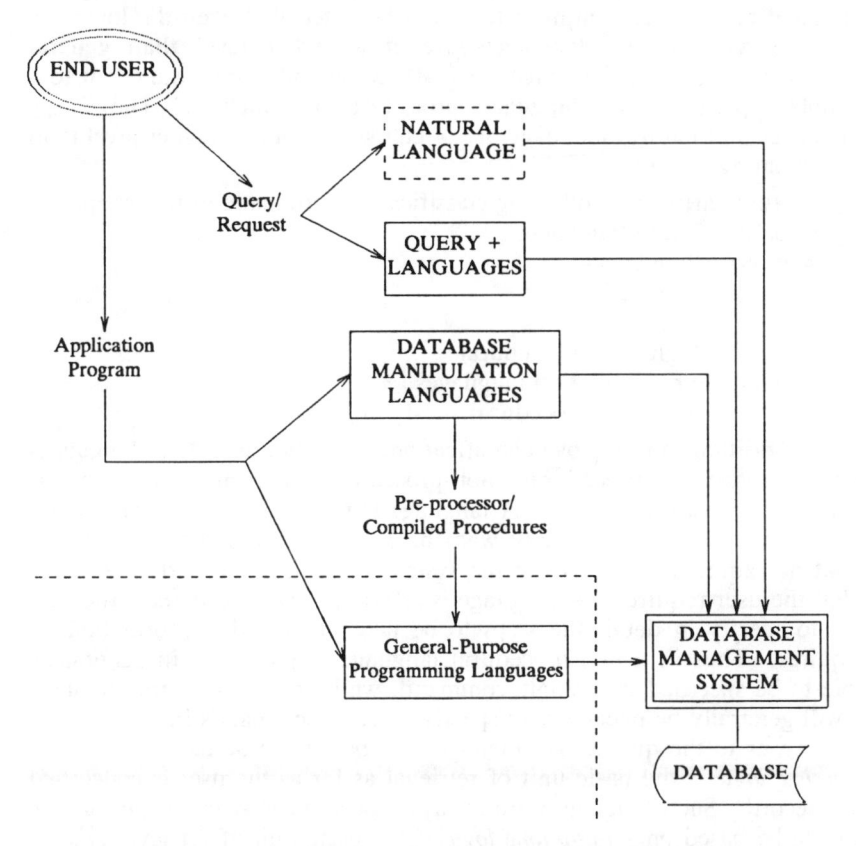

Figure 4.1 Database Languages and the End-User

At the bottom level as far as database languages are concerned are the *database manipulation languages* (DMLs). These are generally used for application programming by a database specialist, and not directly by an end-user. They will be classified as 'low-level procedural' languages. Depending on the DBMS itself, a DML interfaces with the DBMS in one of three ways: the database access commands are either built into the DBMS's own self-contained programming language, or they are inserted into a program written in a general purpose programming language (such as Pascal, Fortran, Cobol) and the program is pre-processed to convert the commands to calls to compiled procedures, or they are converted to procedure/function calls by the programmer and inserted into a program written in a general purpose programming language. In the latter two cases the DML is referred to as a 'hosted' language, it being hosted by a general purpose programming language, and the DBMS provides pre-compiled host language procedures/functions which are loaded with the compiled program at runtime. It should be noted that even the low level database manipulation languages are at a higher level than general purpose programming languages, a DML command being equivalent to a complete programming language procedure or function. The query languages and natural language are of course very much higher level than programming languages.

To summarise, the following classifications are made in this chapter:
- natural query languages
- query+ languages
    - graphic
    - formal
    - high-level procedural
- database manipulation languages
    - low-level procedural

In addition to the above classification, two other aspects of languages are of interest: the procedural / non-procedural aspect and the record-at-a-time / set-at-a-time aspect. A language is referred to as *non-procedural* if it allows the user to specify what he requires rather than how to get what he requires; in this case the system works out the best way to get what the user requires. A language is referred to as *procedural* if the user has to specify in detail the steps to be taken to get the information he requires. Thus in a non-procedural language a query will in general be able to be specified in a single command, while in a procedural language it will generally be necessary to specify a set of commands in order to get the answer to the query. A language may be said to be based on *record-at-a-time logic* if the basic unit of retrieval as far as the user is concerned is a record. Such languages are always procedural. A language may be said to be based on *set-at-a-time logic* if the basic unit of retrieval is a set (or logical collection) of records or objects. Such languages are generally, though not always, non-procedural. These aspects of languages will be returned to where relevant in the following sections.

In the sections below examples of languages in each of the classes — natural, graphic, formal, high-level procedural, low-level procedural — will be discussed. But before doing so it will be useful to look closely at the nature of queries, as this will provide a basis for discussing the similarities and differences between the languages.

4.2 The Nature of Queries

In order to compare and contrast the different types of query language, it is useful to consider the nature of queries. This will be done, firstly by taking an informal look at the basic query components and a sample query will be used for illustration. A most important query component — the *predicate* — will then be discussed.

4.2.1 Basic Query Components

A basic query consists of a *target list* and an optional *condition* which may be compound. The condition is a rule for determining which database objects are relevant and it consists of one or more predicates (or simple conditions). Predicates and predicate logic as a basis for query languages are discussed in a little more detail in the next section.

The target list specifies the objects of interest to the user and represents the answer to the query as far as the user is concerned. The condition or rule may be composed of two elements: the *selection condition* and the *linkage condition*. The selection condition is used when one wishes to restrict the scope of the query to a subset of the database based on the selection condition. For example, in a particular application one may be interested only in loans for which the date due back is before a particular date. The linkage condition is used when the query involves more than one basic object (entity, relation, etc.) in the database and the condition for linking the different objects must therefore be given. For example, it may be required to link person and loan entities, and depending on the DBMS this might be done by specifying a condition which equates the values of the person identifier in the two entity sets.

To illustrate the components of a basic query an example will be given using the SQL language. Briefly, SQL is a formal and non-procedural language designed for use with relational databases; it is discussed in detail in a later section. Consider the query:

Find the name and address of all persons with books due back on 31st December 1985, together with the number of the book.

The SQL version of this query is as follows (with conventions as in previous chapters and comments on the right hand side in italics):

    SELECT Name, Address, Book#   *the target list*
    FROM PERSON, LOAN   *the relations involved in the query*
    WHERE PERSON.Person# = LOAN.Person#   *the linkage condition*
    AND Date-due-back = "851231"   *the selection condition*

The query involves two relations: Person and Loan, hence a linkage condition is necessary; this links the Person and Loan relations on the attribute: Person#. The selection condition restricts the scope of the query to only those loans with the specified due date (dates are assumed to be stored as 6-character strings). Note that each clause in the selection condition of a query relates to a single relation, while each clause in the linkage condition relates to two relations.

The target list, selection condition and linkage condition are the basic components of a query. Other query components such as a *grouping clause* and an *order clause* are also provided by most query languages, but attention will be devoted to the basic query components in the sections which follow. In addition, most high level interfaces also provide other facilities such as updating commands, which use similar syntax to that used in queries where appropriate.

4.2.2 Predicates, Calculus and Query Languages

Before discussing the different types of language in detail, a few words need to be said about predicate logic, predicate calculus and relational calculus. A *predicate* is a relationship or function with arguments which yields a boolean result. Simple predicates may be linked to form compound predicates by means of 'and' ($\wedge$) and 'or' ($\vee$) connectives. Examples of predicates in different notations are:

    Bloggs   has-status   staff
    has-status (Bloggs, staff)
    status-of (Bloggs) —> staff
    (name = "Bloggs" and status = "staff")

These are examples of predicates which will yield the value true if Bloggs is a member of staff, and false otherwise. The first three are relevant to fact-based, logic-based, and functional systems respectively. The predicates are 'has-status' and 'status-of' and they contain the arguments 'Bloggs' and 'staff'. The fourth example is a relational representation of a predicate; it is a form which is most likely to be found in a language designed for an entity-based system (relational, network, hierarchical).

A *calculus* is a formal notation for writing expressions (or formulae) which specify what is required. Hence, *predicate calculus* provides a notation for specifying queries on a database using predicate logic. Predicate calculus includes variables, and quantifiers for specifying the range of the variables. There are two types of quantifier: *universal* and *existential*. The universal quantifier, ∀ (read as 'for all'), is used to indicate that the predicate which follows applies to all the objects over which the quantified variable ranges. The existential quantifier, ∃ (read as 'there exists'), is used to indicate that the predicate which follows must apply to at least one of the objects over which the quantified variable ranges. Two examples of quantified predicates are:

(∀x ∈ Student) (∃y ∈ Degree) registered-for-degree (x, y)

which may be read as: 'for all objects x belonging to the set of students, there exists some y belonging to the set of degrees, such that x is registered for degree y' (i.e. all students must be registered for a degree).

postgraduate (x) <—
(∃x ∈ Person) student (x) ∧ status (x, postgraduate)

which may be read as: 'x is a postgraduate if there exists a person x such that x is a student and x has the status postgraduate'.

In the above examples, x and y are variables which are always quantified in the predicates. The first example illustrates the use of a predicate to specify a constraint, and the second example illustrates the use of predicates to specify an inference rule. In this latter case, the rule will provide the answer to the query 'Who are postgraduates?' when the rule is instantiated.

Relational calculus is a special form of predicate calculus designed to operate on relational databases. Languages based on relational calculus are generally one of two types: domain-oriented or tuple-oriented (Pirotte 1978, Ullman 1980, Date 1981). With tuple-oriented relational calculus, the variables range over complete tuples (records) in a relation, while with domain-oriented relational calculus the variables range over complete domains in a relation. The example in the previous subsection illustrated a query in the language SQL which is based on tuple-oriented relational calculus. The FROM clause in the query specifies the relations involved and by implication it declares tuple variables, with the same names as the relations, which range over tuples in the relations. Also by implication, the quantifier associated with these tuple variables is the existential quantifier.

Predicate logic provides a good foundation for building non-procedural languages. A comprehensive discussion of predicate and relational calculus may be found in Gray (1984), while a discussion of the correspondence between predicate logic and relational databases may be found in Lee (1985). It will be seen that formal query languages are generally based on either predicate or relational calculus, while higher level languages can be mapped into calculus-based languages. The relationship of the languages discussed below to predicate/relational calculus will be mentioned where relevant.

4.3 Natural Language Interfaces

Natural language is by nature informal. It is also verbose and can be ambiguous. Furthermore, when we use natural language we take it for granted that the reader or listener is reasonably intelligent, understands the context in which the natural language is being used, and can therefore deduce what is meant even when some detail or fact has been omitted. It is these characteristics of the use of natural language which make communication with computers in natural language difficult. There are advantages in enabling users to communicate with computers in the most natural way (for example, they do not have to learn a special language), hence some effort has been devoted to developing natural language interfaces. It should be pointed out though that there are also disadvantages; for example, because natural language is verbose the user (who may not be able to type very well) may have to type a long query, and if the query as specified by the user is not specific enough or is ambiguous a long dialogue may be necessary before the system 'understands' the user's query. Also, Wallace states that "The description 'natural language' may be a drawback because it suggests capabilities beyond any current or forseeable implementation. It tempts the user to ask common sense questions outside the area of the database's body of information, or evaluative questions within it." (Wallace 1984, p.15).

Some prototype natural language interfaces have been developed and also a few systems, but natural language communication is still in its infancy. Examples of systems are the Rendezvous experimental system (Codd 1974, Codd 1978), the Robot natural language query system (Harris 1977), the Planes system (Waltz 1978), and the Qproc system (Wallace 1983, 1984). The characteristics of a natural language interface to a DBMS are discussed below. (Parsing and other such techniques are not discussed here as it is beyond the scope of this book; readers are referred to Waltz (1978) or Wallace (1984) for more details on natural language query processing and some useful references.)

Codd, in his paper on Rendezvous, discusses what he considers to be the important characteristics of a successful natural language interface to databases. These are:

- a simple underlying data model for the system
- an internal target language incorporating high level logic
- clarification dialogue of bounded scope
- multiple choice interrogation as a fall-back
- a facility for the system to create new definitions based

on the user's query.
. system re-statement of user's query in pseudo natural language
. query formulation separated from database access

To a large extent these characteristics have also been accepted as important by others working on natural language interfaces. For example, the Robot, Planes and Qproc systems incorporate at least some of the above characteristics. For this reason these characteristics will be discussed in more detail.

First of all it will be useful to discuss what is meant by the term 'bounded scope'. The knowledge and experience built up by an individual over the years is absolutely vast. He will refer to this accumulated knowledge at all times, although he will select information from it as appropriate to the context of the problem at hand. The DBMS has a far more restricted view of the world; it is generally limited to the information represented by the database currently in use. Although it is important that databases should be capable of storing as much semantic and contextual information as possible (and much research is currently being done in this area), it will always be the case that the computer's world will be very much more 'bounded in scope' than the user's world. Artificial intelligence (AI) research is very much devoted to extending the boundaries, in particular by designing and building systems which attempt to 'learn' with experience, but this research is not yet sufficiently developed for it to be applied generally to the field of databases. Any natural language DBMS interface must therefore communicate in a limited context — a context of bounded scope. More about this later.

The user's requirements for information will be related to his view of the real world which may not be very well structured. One of the advantages of a natural language interface is that users do not need to know anything about the structure of the database, either logical or physical. Bearing this in mind Codd suggests that the underlying data model of the database should be simple with few structural elements, and suggests that the relational model is suitable for this purpose. It is also true that a binary relationship (fact-based) model is suitable and probably more so because the user's world is more of a fact-based world than a relational (tabular) world.

A natural language interface has a difficult task. On the one hand it has to communicate with the user in an informal language, while on the other hand it must communicate with a computer system in a formal language. Programming language interfaces in general force the user to move towards the computer system, while a natural language interface is forced to move towards the user. To ease the task, the internal target language must be as high level as possible, so that it is relatively easy to translate from informal to formal and vice versa. This implies that the target must be a non-procedural language. Codd suggests his own calculus-based language Alpha as a suitable target (Codd 1974), although in the experimental system he used an already implemented language called Deduce (Codd 1978). Waltz used a special implementation of Alpha in the Planes system. Wallace's system Qproc converts natural language sentences to a formal language D&Qs which is predicate calculus based and hence close to natural language; the D&Qs query is then either interpreted as a query on a Prolog database or mapped to the formal language of the RDBMS database system for query evaluation. Other non-procedural languages would be equally suitable as the target language, for example, SQL and Quel, and also Prolog, all of which will be discussed later.

With a natural language interface the user will specify his requirements in his own phraseology. The interface must make as much sense of the different components of the request as possible. For this purpose a comprehensive data dictionary is essential, which not only contains standard metadata (as mentioned in section 2.2), but also contains additional information such as alternative natural language definitions, phrases, etc. which may be associated with elements in the database. This will help the interface to associate components in the user's request with elements in the database. It must also have a language dictionary available to enable it to accept abbreviations and to tolerate spelling and typing errors. If the interface comes across a component which it does not understand, or which is incomplete or ambiguous, the interface may commence a dialogue with the user. It is important here that the interface should not ask an open-ended question of the user, such as: "What do you mean by 'xxx'?". It was mentioned above that the interface operates in a context of bounded scope and it must therefore ensure that the user's response is also bounded in scope by asking the user a more specific question related to what it currently understands from the query and knows from the database. Clarification dialogue must be bounded in scope.

Multiple choice interrogation (or menu mode interaction) can be used as an alternative to clarification dialogue but should only be used when dialogue is inappropriate, for example in cases of ambiguity.

When a word or phrase in the user's request has required the use of clarification dialogue and/or interrogation, which has resulted in the interface being able to derive a definition of the word or phrase in terms of components understandable to it, it is important that such a definition is retained for future use — the same user would not tolerate having to go through the same clarification dialogue again on another occasion. Hence the interface must be able to add definitions, etc., to the data dictionary — it must learn from experience.

As soon as the interface is able to put together an internal version of the user's query it should convert it into pseudo natural language, and ask the user if this is what he intended. This is an area where the high level internal target language is important, as it is much easier to translate from a high level non-procedural language to pseudo natural language, than it is from a low level language. If the user does not like the system re-statement of his request, further clarification dialogue will be necessary, followed by another re-statement.

During query formulation, Codd suggests that only the metadata (data dictionary information) should be accessed, and only when the user indicates his satisfaction with the query restatement should the actual data in the database be accessed. If access were made at intermediate stages in query formulation, it could be time-consuming and might present the user with much data which he may not want. However, this particular characteristic recommended by Codd is not always desirable. There are times when a user may not know exactly what he wants and may prefer to give a 'coarse' query initially and gradually refine it after he has viewed the response to it. This can be an iterative process and is a common requirement of bibliographic information retrieval. Similarly, it may sometimes be helpful to the user if he were offered the chance to see the results of an intermediate coarse version of his query. It should be pointed out that although this approach may be desirable, it is currently only feasible with relatively small databases or dedicated information retrieval systems. Hence it is generally the case that query formulation will represent a completely independent process, and the result of this process will be a query in a formal query language which can be passed to the DBMS for processing.

A brief example of a possible dialogue between a user and a natural language interface based on the example in Codd (1978) is given in Figure 4.2 to illustrate some of the characteristics discussed above.

(Note: U = User, S = System.   Assume today is 31.12.85.)

U I want information about boks due today?
S Is the word 'boks' intended to be: 'books'?   (Yes or No)
U Yes
S With regard to 'books due today', do you mean:
     'books on loan for return on 31.12.85'?   (Yes or No)
U Yes
S What do you require about books on loan for return on 31.12.85?
     1 Book#
     2 Shelf
     3 Catalogue information
     4 None of the above
   Select one or more items.
U 3
S What do you require about catalogue information?
     1 Isbn
     2 Author
     3 Title
     4 Publisher
     5 Year
     6 Classmark
     7 None of the above

```
     Select one or more items.
U 2 3
S The system understands your query to be:
        Print the author and title from the catalogue information for all
        books which are on loan for return on 31.12.85.
     Is the system's understanding
        1 Correct and complete
        2 Not yet complete
        3 Incorrect
     Select exactly one item by number.
U 1
```

The query is then evaluated and the answer given to the user.

Figure 4.2 An Example of Dialogue in a Natural Language Query System

A major disadvantage of natural language interfaces at the present time is their 'query only' limitation. In the case of queries, it does not matter too much if a user thinks he has asked the right question but actually finds he has not got it quite right when he receives the answers; he can just modify his query as appropriate. But in an online update environment the integrity of the database is at stake. A natural language update environment may necessitate 'undoing' updates. But although that is not a trivial task, a far more critical problem is that of undetected incorrect updates. Since database updates pose far more problems than queries, most attention has so far been devoted to natural language enquiry systems.

Finally, it should be obvious from the preceding discussion that the key component in a natural language interface is the data dictionary which underlies the interface. A data dictionary supporting a formal language can be specific and concise, and far more bounded in scope than one designed to support a natural language interface. The latter must be much wider in scope, reaching out into the environment surrounding the application area, and must be much more oriented towards the real world than the formal data model which represents it.

Currently, the disadvantages of natural language interfaces to databases generally outweigh the advantages. However, it should perhaps be mentioned that interest in speech understanding and document reading systems has given an impetus to research into natural language understanding. When voice input is generally available, it is possible that natural language interfaces to databases will really 'take off'.

4.4 Graphics-oriented Interfaces

One of the disadvantages of the natural language approach for the end user is the amount of typing or dialogue necessary to construct the query, since natural language is verbose and ambiguous. For a user who cannot type well this may pose a problem unless the system in use is very 'tolerant' of typing errors. An alternative for the end user is a graphics-oriented interface. In such a system the user can build up his query gradually using building blocks provided by the system. He is able then to break down a complex query into small manageable parts in a similar manner to the way programmers use top-down programming techniques. A full-screen capability is essential for this, as the user will need to be able to move about the screen as he develops his query from a skeleton to the completed query.

In this section the main features of two graphics interfaces — QBE (Query-By-Example) and Cupid (Casual User Pictorial Interface Device) — will be discussed.

4.4.1 QBE (Query-By-Example)

QBE was designed as a very high level interface to a relational DBMS by Zloof (1975, 1977, 1978). It is based on the idea of tables representing relations which are filled in with an 'example' to represent the query; a table was considered to be a construct in widespread use and understood by most (if not all) users. Its simplicity and relative naturalness has caused it to be the subject of further research on end-user languages, and although it was designed for a relational DBMS it has also been interfaced to a Prolog database (Neves 1983). In the section on Prolog later in this chapter similarities between QBE and Prolog will be mentioned. Another related research effort is an extension to the fundamental QBE concepts; Jacobs has designed a generalised Query-By-Example language GQBE based on database logic (Jacobs 1983, 1982) which is designed to interface not only to relational database systems, but also to network and hierarchical ones. An important implementation of QBE is in IBM's DB2 system, where QBE is provided as an alternative user interface to the formal language SQL (Sordi 1984).

The important features of a QBE query are the *skeleton table*, the *example element*, the *constant element* and the *link element*. When commencing a query the user selects appropriate relations of interest from those in the database which are accessible to him. He can be provided with a menu of available relations and make his selections from the menu, rather than typing in the names of the relations. After making his selection QBE outputs skeleton tables on the screen, each one representing one of the selected relations. Figure 4.3 shows a skeleton table for Catalogued-Book.

CATALOGUED-BOOK	Isbn	Author	Title	Publisher	Year	Classmark

Figure 4.3   A Skeleton QBE Table

The user next fills in some of the columns of the tables with QBE query elements as relevant to the query. For example, suppose it is required to find the titles of all books by J. Austen, the user would fill in the table as indicated in Figure 4.4.

CATALOGUED-BOOK	Isbn	Author	Title	Publisher	Year	Classmark
		Austen J	p.xxx			

Figure 4.4   A Simple QBE Query

The entry 'Austen J' in the Author column is a QBE *constant element* and is not underlined; only those records in the Catalogued-Book relation which match this constant element will be selected in answer to the query. By default the comparison is an '=' comparison; for comparisons other than '=', the constant element must include the relevant comparative operator, e.g. '>1980'. More than one constant element may exist in a QBE query, and these are by default assumed to be connected by 'and' operators. The set of constant elements in a QBE query represents the *selection condition* as defined in section 4.2.

The p. in the Title column in Figure 4.4 indicates that whatever the titles of the selected books are, they should be printed out. A 'p.' can be placed in any number of columns; the set of attributes which are marked with a 'p.' in a QBE query represents the *target list* of the query. The xxx in the Title column is referred to as an *example element* and is underlined; it is just an example value, and such a value need not actually exist in the database. (Note: in actual implementations of QBE, e.g. DB2, example elements are often written with a single underline character preceding the example value, e.g. '_xxx'.) The example element comes into its own in multi-relation queries which will be considered below; its use in the context of the target list is purely optional.

Returning to the query used to illustrate a natural language interface in section 4.3 (Figure 4.2): 'print the title and author of all books due for return on 31.12.85', it is clear that this query involves multiple relations. Catalogued-Book is needed to obtain the titles and authors, Loan is needed to select loans which are due back on the specified date, and since Catalogued-Book and Loan are not directly related, Book is also needed to link the other two relations together. This query requires the use of the *link element*; a link element is an example element which has the same example value in the relations to be linked. The query is given in Figure 4.5.

CATALOGUED-BOOK	Isbn	Author	Title	Publisher	Year	Classmark
	isbn	p.	p.			

BOOK	Book#	Shelf	Isbn
	b#		isbn

LOAN	Book#	Person#	Date-due-back
	b#		851231

Figure 4.5 A QBE Multi-relation Query

Note that the example element under Isbn in Catalogued-Book is identical to the example element under Isbn in Book, and similarly for Book# in Book and Loan. These pairs of example elements are the link elements and together represent the *linkage condition* defined in section 4.2. Note also that no example element has been given in the Author and Title columns; examples are not necessary with the 'p.' operator, unless a link element is required in the same column.

The target list in Figure 4.5 ranges over a single relation only. If the target list ranges over more than one relation, a result table must be specified, containing all the target list items linked where relevant to the main tables in the query. Figure 4.5 could be altered to include a result table by replacing the entries under Author and Title by example elements (e.g. aaa and ttt), and specifying the following result table:

RESULT	Author	Title
	p.aaa	p.ttt

QBE is an example of a domain-oriented relational calculus. The example elements may be considered as variables which range over the domains of the relevant attributes. For example, in Figure 4.5 the example element <u>isbn</u> ranges over the *ISBN* domain both in Catalogued-Book and Book.

QBE supports many other facilities, including aggregate operators (sum, count, etc.), grouping, and an 'all' operator. It also supports data definition and database updates and is therefore not just a query language. For both data definition and updates the user uses the same tabular mechanism. Special operators 'd.', 'i.', and 'u.' are available for deletion, insertion and update respectively. For example, to delete a catalogue entry for the book with Isbn = 0-999-99999-9, all that is required is for the user to fill in the table as indicated in Figure 4.6.

CATALOGUED-BOOK	Isbn	Author	Title	Publisher	Year	Classmark
d.	0-999-99999-9					

Figure 4.6 An Example of Deletion in QBE

Subsequent to QBE, Zloof has designed a more comprehensive system which follows similar principles to QBE but extends to such office procedures as filing, letter writing, etc.; this is called OBE (Office-By-Example) (Zloof 1981, 1982).

Before leaving QBE it is worth pointing out that a study was made by Thomas and Gould of the effectiveness of QBE as compared with formal query languages, as far as end-users are concerned (Thomas 1975). The results of this study suggested that users were more likely to specify their queries correctly at the first attempt using QBE than using a formal language such as IQF (Interactive Query Facility for IBM's IMS). The results also suggested that users are able to formulate their queries quicker in QBE. A further study was made by Greenblatt and Waxman (Greenblatt (1978) in which three groups of students were trained in QBE, SQL and a relational algebra language respectively, and then examined; the results showed that the QBE group had the largest proportion of correct queries and they were more confident about the correctness of their queries than the others. A more general study of query languages, together with an assessment of the studies mentioned above, may be found in Reisner (1981).

4.4.2 Cupid (Casual User Pictorial Interface Device)

An alternative graphics interface is Cupid (McDonald 1975). Like QBE it was designed as a very high level interface to a relational DBMS. Cupid however is not tabular in form but uses symbols to represent components of a query. The user selects relevant components and builds his query from these. The amount of typing required to build a Cupid query is even smaller than for a QBE query, as it is very much a menu-oriented system.

The main symbols used by Cupid are shown in Figure 4.7.

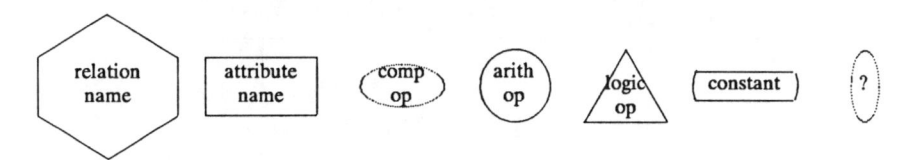

Figure 4.7 The Main Cupid Symbols

In addition to these, an arrow is used to indicate links between relations and an aggregate operator symbol is also provided.

Figure 4.8 shows a simple query involving a single relation. This query finds the titles of all books by J. Austen (cf. Figure 4.4).

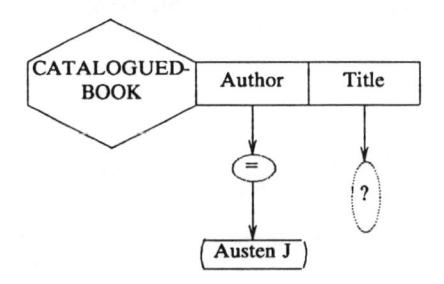

Figure 4.8 A Simple Cupid Query

This query illustrates a number of features of Cupid. Firstly, the user need only specify those attributes of relevance to his query — in this case, Author and Title. Secondly, the upright ellipse with a ? represents the *target list*, and the comparative operator "=" and constant "Austen J" linked to the Author attribute together represent the *selection condition*. Figure 4.8 would be built up by the user firstly selecting from the symbol menu and placing the symbol on the screen; if relevant, he would then be offered a menu of values appropriate to the symbol, for example, relation names in the case of the relation symbol, "=", "<", ">", etc. in the case of the comparative operator symbol, and so on. In the case of the constant symbol, the user would have to type the relevant constant value. The user would repeat the symbol selection followed by value selection procedure until the complete query has been built up.

The multi-relation query to print the title and author of all books due for return on 31.12.85 is shown in Figure 4.9. It shows how arrows and the comparative operator "=" are used to represent the *linkage condition*, and may be compared with the corresponding QBE query in Figure 4.5.

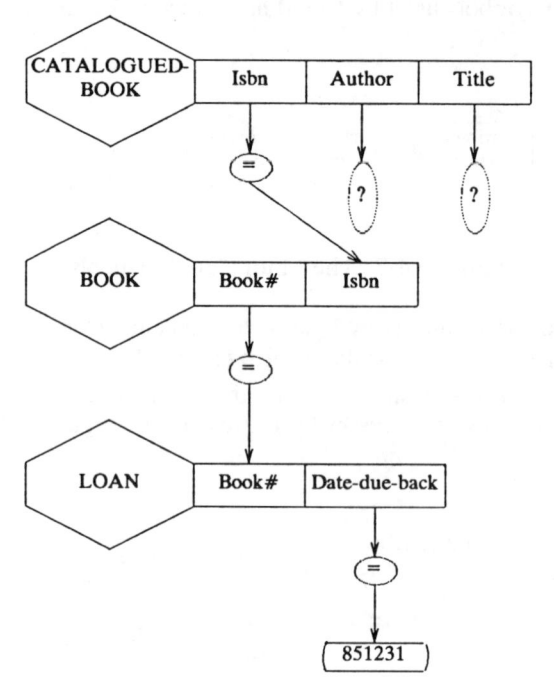

Figure 4.9 A Cupid Multi-relation Query

Cupid is based on relational algebra (discussed in a later section), although the similarities with QBE are obvious.

4.4.3 Advantages and Disadvantages of Graphics-oriented Interfaces

QBE, Cupid and similar approaches to graphical interfaces have a number of advantages as far as the casual end-user is concerned. Firstly, they minimise the amount of typing effort necessary (unlike natural language interfaces); secondly, they enable the user to build up his query by specifying the components in any order; and thirdly, the user has a 'view' of his query on the screen as it is being built up, and can add/amend query components as required until he is satisfied that the current view represents the query as intended by him. A further advantage of such systems is the possibility for making the system very user friendly by means of sophisticated pointing devices such as touch screens, light pens and mice. With such devices one can even consider the use of icons to represent relations (entities) instead of names; for example, a picture of a person could replace the entity name: Person, and a picture of a book could replace the entity name: Book, etc. Such advanced user interfaces will be considered again in the last chapter.

However, graphical interfaces such as these do have disadvantages. The user needs to understand about relations and how to link them together, and he needs to know something about the structure of the database; this is not necessary with a natural language interface. Furthermore, with graphical interfaces it can take quite a time to build up a query; the need for typing dexterity is replaced by manual dexterity. However, this is not expected to be a great disadvantage as users are becoming acquainted with sophisticated pointing devices for use with micros such as the Apple Lisa and Macintosh. A third problem is the need for a large screen, especially for Cupid. Standard-size screens are really too small for sophisticated graphics interfaces.

4.5 Formal Query Languages

Formal query languages are suited to a different class of users than those for whom natural language or graphics-oriented interfaces are suitable, although there is likely to be a fairly large overlap between the two classes of users. Natural language and graphics interfaces are most suitable for casual users who only rarely use the database and cannot be expected to remember or relearn a formal language between each use. Regular and more experienced users, however, might find such interfaces tedious and irritating to use. They are likely to know exactly what information they want to obtain from the database and how to express the relevant queries. The main advantage of a formal query language for such users is that it is precise and to the point; there is no lengthy dialogue to contend with nor is there any need to move cursors around the screen — one merely types in one's query.

In this section four formal query languages will be introduced: Quel and SQL which are designed for relational systems, QRS which is designed for a network system, and Prolog which is a logic language. Quel and SQL are based on relational calculus, and Prolog on predicate calculus.

The conventions used in the queries below are designed to be consistent with previous chapters and to highlight the different elements of the query; i.e. keywords are in bold upper case, relation names are in upper case, and attributes are in lower case except for an initial capital letter. In addition, attribute names are prefixed by the relevant relation name when they are not unique (SQL queries), and where variables are used in a specific language these are in lower case. The exception to these conventions is Prolog for the reasons indicated in the previous chapter (section 3.5.3). Where a particular command syntax is outlined, keywords are in bold upper case with variable syntax elements enclosed in angle brackets (< >). It should be noted that these conventions are not necessarily valid in actual implementations of the languages, but are used for consistency wherever possible.

4.5.1 Quel (The Ingres Query Language)

Quel is the query language of the Ingres database system (Stonebraker 1976), which was one of the first relational database systems to be available, although it was limited to UNIX† based machines. Quel is based very closely on tuple-oriented relational calculus. The basic syntax of a Quel query is:
    RETRIEVE (<target list>)
    WHERE <condition>
The WHERE clause is optional and if included the condition (or predicate) may consist of selection and linkage components. Since Quel is a relational query language the linkage condition is the means by which pairs of relations are linked together, while the selection condition is the means by which the scope of the query is restricted to specific subsets of relations.

Tuple variables are declared by means of a separate RANGE statement for each relation in the query, and at the same time the existential quantifier is implicitly declared. The RANGE syntax is:
    RANGE OF <variable> **IS** <relation-name>

A simple query requiring the retrieval of selected attributes from a single relation is shown below:
    RANGE OF cb **IS** CATALOGUED-BOOK
    RETRIEVE (cb.Author, cb.Title)
In this example, cb is declared as a tuple variable ranging over the Catalogued-Book relation and it is used as a qualifier for the attributes in the target list. Note that all the attributes in a Quel query are prefixed by a tuple variable. This query may be interpreted in a relational calculus

---
† UNIX is a trademark of AT&T Bell Laboratories.

notation as follows:

result (cb.Author, cb.Title) <— (∃ cb ∈ CATALOGUED-BOOK)

or in formal English: the result is the author and title from cb where there exists a tuple cb in the Catalogued-Book relation. (The relational calculus notation differs slightly from the predicate calculus notation since the tuple variable is a composite variable, consisting of all attributes in a tuple; it may be compared with a variable of type: record in Pascal which is a similar composite variable).

Two further queries follow. These are the same as those in section 4.4. In the first the condition contains a selection component and the query involves one relation only, while in the second the query involves three relations.

(1) Find the titles of all books by J. Austen.

RANGE OF cb **IS** CATALOGUED-BOOK
RETRIEVE (cb.Title) **WHERE** cb.Author = "Austen J"

(2) Print the title and author of all books due for return on 31.12.85.

RANGE OF cb **IS** CATALOGUED-BOOK
RANGE OF b **IS** BOOK
RANGE OF l **IS** LOAN
RETRIEVE (cb.Title, cb.Author)
   WHERE cb.Isbn = b.Isbn **AND** b.Book# = l.Book#
   AND l.Date-due-back = "851231"

In the first example the selection condition restricts the scope of the query to a subset of the Catalogued-Book relation associated with a specific author. In the second example the linkage condition consists of two clauses, one to link Catalogued-Book with Book (cb.Isbn = b.Isbn) and the other to link Book with Loan (b.Book# = l.Book#). The selection condition restricts the scope of the query only as far as Loan is concerned — to a subset associated with a specific date due back. As mentioned earlier, each clause in the selection condition of a query relates to a single relation, while each clause in the linkage condition relates to two relations. Three tuple variables are declared, one for each relation in the query, and all attributes are again prefixed by the relevant tuple variable.

The relational calculus version of the second query might be expressed as:

result (cb.Title, cb.Author) <—
   (∃ cb ∈ CATALOGUED-BOOK) (∃ b ∈ BOOK) (∃ l ∈ LOAN)
      cb.Isbn = b.Isbn ∧ b.Book# = l.Book#
         ∧ l.Date-due-back = "851231"

Having related Quel to relational calculus and shown how the example queries used previously are represented in Quel, further aspects of the language will now be considered. An extension to the RETRIEVE command enables the response to a query to be placed in a new stored relation (rather than displayed on the screen). The data description for this relation is automatically created by the system using the attribute names in the target list. Such a result relation then becomes part of the database and is indistinguishable from other relations in it. The target list may contain new attributes derived from existing attributes by means of an expression. Also, functions such count, sum, avg (average), etc. may be applied to relevant attributes in the query.

Quel provides data definition facilities similar to those of SQL presented in section 3.2.3. It also provides update facilities via append, delete and replace commands, the latter two having WHERE clauses with the same syntax as the retrieve command. There is also a version of Quel — Equel — which enables Quel commands to be embedded in a program written in the 'C' language. This provides an application program facility of the 'hosted system' type (see section 4.7 below on Database Manipulation Languages).

4.5.2 SQL (Structured Query Language)

SQL was briefly introduced in section 4.2 by means of an example to illustrate the nature of queries. It is the language adopted for IBM's System R project which was a research prototype, SQL/DS (a direct descendant of the System R project), and DB2 (Sordi 1984). SQL or an SQL-like language is also provided in other non-IBM systems, e.g. Oracle, the RaSQL interface to Rapport, and Knowledgeman (SQL-like retrieval command only).

The basic syntax of an SQL query is as follows:

SELECT <target list>
   FROM <list of relations>
   WHERE <condition>

For retrieval of selected attributes from a single relation the WHERE clause is omitted; for example:

SELECT Author, Title
   FROM CATALOGUED-BOOK

In the case of retrieval involving multiple relations, the condition will be composed of a linkage component together with a selection component if relevant. However, the linkage component may itself be a nested SQL query; for example (in outline):

```
SELECT ... FROM ...
   WHERE ... =
      (SELECT ... FROM ...
         WHERE ... )
```

Nested queries will be considered later.

The following two queries are the same as those in section 4.4 and in the Quel examples above.

(1) Find the titles of all books by J. Austen.

SELECT Title
FROM CATALOGUED-BOOK
WHERE Author = "Austen J"

(2) Print the title and author of all books due for return on 31.12.85.
This query could be written in SQL as follows:

SELECT Title, Author
FROM CATALOGUED-BOOK, BOOK, LOAN
WHERE CATALOGUED-BOOK.Isbn = BOOK.Isbn
AND BOOK.Book# = LOAN.Book#
AND Date-due-back = "851231"

(Attribute names are prefixed by the relevant relation names if they are not unique in the query.) In the second example note the use of two clauses in the linkage condition, one to link Catalogued-Book with Book and the other to link Book with Loan.

It was mentioned in section 4.2.2 that SQL is based on tuple-oriented relational calculus. Since Quel is also, it would be expected that the relational calculus version of this query would be virtually the same as that for the Quel query (see section 4.5.1). To relate SQL to relational calculus, it is necessary to consider the FROM clause, which lists the relations in the query, as the equivalent of the Quel RANGE statement, i.e. the FROM clause declares tuple variables having the same names as those of the relations over which the variables range.

The SQL statement in example (2) above is not the only way to specify the second example query in SQL; in fact this particular query provides an example to illustrate the use of nested queries in SQL. The target list only contains attributes from the Catalogued-Book relation and hence the basic (top-level) query may be considered as involving only this relation. The nested version of the query above is as follows:

(2a)
    SELECT Title, Author
    FROM CATALOGUED-BOOK
    WHERE Isbn **IN**
      (**SELECT** Isbn
       FROM BOOK
       WHERE Book# **IN**
        (**SELECT** Book#
         FROM LOAN
         WHERE Date-due-back = "851231"))

A nested SQL query incorporates relational algebra-like features, with implicit JOIN operations (discussed later) at the point of nesting. An inner subquery is processed first and returns a set of constants which are used in the outer subquery.

Amongst other facilities offered by SQL are data definition facilities (as presented in section 3.2.3), 'group by', 'order by' and standard functions, update and delete statements using syntax similar to the SELECT statement, and an insert statement. SQL also supports user views which are discussed later in this chapter. In addition, in the implementations of SQL mentioned previously — DB2 and Oracle — SQL can be embedded in a host language for application programming.

Finally an interesting feature of SQL is its ability to handle null values to cater for the 'not known' situation discussed in section 2.7. For this to be possible, 3-valued logic (true, false, unknown) is used, with appropriate truth tables which include the following:

Truth Table for 3-valued Logic	
A	T T T F F F ? ? ?
B	T F ? T F ? T F ?
A AND B	T F ? F F F ? F ?
A OR B	T T T T F ? T ? ?

4.5.3 QRS (The MDBS III Query Language)

The two formal query languages discussed so far have been designed for relational database systems. In this subsection, a query language for a network system based on the Codasyl proposals will be discussed. QRS is the query language of MDBS III, designed and developed primarily for micros by MDBS Inc. (MDBS 1981). MDBS III is based on the Codasyl proposals; it is only a subset of these proposals but it includes an additional feature — support for direct many-to-many relationships.

The syntax of the basic QRS retrieval command is:

LIST <target list> **FOR** <condition> **THRU** <pathlist>

The target list consists of a list of the required attributes, the condition consists of selection components and 'non-key' linkage components, while the pathlist provides 'key' linkage information by indicating the navigational route through the data model. The pathlist is a list of cosets which provide a continuous path in the data model starting with a system-owned (singular) coset. It is simpler than the linkage conditions in Quel and SQL; this is of course due to the fact that the relationships are explicit in a Codasyl data model and are hence implied by specifying the cosets involved in the query, while in a relational data model the relationships are implicit and have to be made explicit in the query.

Query nesting may be carried out by the following extension to the basic syntax:

LIST <target list> **FOR** <attribute> **IN**
  { **SELECT** <attribute> **FOR** <condition>
          THRU <pathlist> }
THRU <pathlist>

A grouping facility also exists but will not be considered here, and there are also facilities for ordering output and building query macros. Interactive updates may be performed by means of the IDML (Interactive Data Manipulation Language), which is an interactive version of the DML commands to be discussed later in the chapter.

Examples will illustrate the QRS query language. (Readers might like to refer back to the network version of the library data model in Figure 3.6.)

(1) Find the titles of all books by J. Austen.

  LIST Title
    FOR Author = "Austen J"
    THRU catalogue-list

(2) Print the title and author of all books due for return on 31.12.85.

  LIST Title, Author
    FOR Date-due-back = "851231"
    THRU catalogue-list, has-copy, lent-to

(Note: if attribute names are not unique they are prefixed by the relevant record name).

Since readers should by now be familiar with the target list and selection components in these two queries, only the pathlist will be explained. The pathlist in the second query replaces the two linkage conditions in the Quel and SQL queries, one linking Catalogued-Book and Book via Isbn, and the other linking Book and Loan via Book#. These are referred to as 'key' linkage components since in the relational model the attributes Isbn and Book# are keys (primary or foreign) in the relevant relations. The coset in the Codasyl model is used to indicate explicitly the relationships between records and hence it is not necessary to include foreign keys in records. (It was indicated in Chapter 3, though, that foreign keys could be included if required, but this is redundant data in a Codasyl model.)

A non-key linkage component is a condition which specifies a relationship between two record types which is not reflected in a declared coset type. For example, to find the names of persons who have currently borrowed their own books (i.e. their name matches the author's name, assuming these are unique), the query would be:

 LIST Name
   FOR Name = Author
   THRU person-list, has-loan-of, >lent-to, >has-copy

The component 'Name = Author' is a non-key linkage component since Author is not a key of Catalogued-Book, nor are Catalogued-Book and Person directly linked. The pathlist replaces three linkage conditions which would be necessary in Quel or SQL. The '>' symbol preceding a coset name is used to indicate movement up a coset from member to owner, rather than down a coset from owner to member which is the default direction. Thus to get from a Person record to a Catalogued-Book record via Loans, the entry is via the system-owned 'person-list' coset, and then the route is down through 'has-loan-of', up (from member to owner) through 'lent-to', and up through 'has-copy'.

As can be seen from the QRS examples, and by referring back to the network version of the Library data model in Figure 3.6, the pathlist provides access path information for navigating round the data model. The QRS query language therefore clearly separates logical access path (data model navigation) aspects from the rest of the query.

4.5.4 Prolog (A Logic Language)

As indicated in Chapter 3, Prolog is a logic language, based on predicate calculus, in which facts and rules are combined together in a program. A full description of the language, together with its relationship to predicate logic may be found in Clocksin (1981), while a more general discussion of logic as a database language is provided by Kowalski (1984). In section 3.5.3, *facts* and *rules* were introduced, although rules were not discussed in detail. Prolog notation was also introduced. Readers who are not well acquainted with Prolog should refer back to that section before continuing.

Both facts and rules correspond to predicates with one or more arguments. A query on a Prolog database resembles a fact or the head of a rule. In simple terms, a query causes Prolog to search the database of facts and rules to see if a match can be found; in the case of rules, each of the components in the body of the rule become goals which it attempts to satisfy, and the results of these attempts are combined as indicated by the connectives linking the goals. If the overall goal can be satisfied the rule evaluates to true and any variables in the head are instantiated. This is a very simplified explanation of the processing of a query; details of how it is done, and in particular the effect of 'backtracking' when goals fail, can be found in Clocksin (1981). A brief discussion and an example are also provided in the next chapter (section 5.4.2).

If a query contains only constants (actual data values) as the arguments of the predicate, Prolog answers 'yes' or 'no' as appropriate. For example, the question:

?- named (p002, 'Brown A.J.').

given the library database shown in Figure 3.13, would produce the answer 'yes'. A query may contain variables (indicated by an initial uppercase letter), in which case Prolog will instantiate the variables to actual values for which the predicate is true. For example, the question:

?- in-category (CB, 'QA264').

will produce the result:

CB = cb001

To obtain other values, if any, for which the predicate is true (i.e. to get Prolog to continue the search through the database), the continuation character ';' is required. If this is typed after each result the further results (instantiations)

CB = cb002
CB = cb004

will also be produced, followed by the word 'no' when no more matches can be found.

In some cases, in particular with n-ary predicates, not all the arguments will be of interest. In this case, the 'anonymous' variable '_' (underline) may be used. For example, if it is required to obtain the titles of all books, the catalogued-book identifier in the 'entitled' predicate is not of interest and this query may be represented as:

?- entitled (_, Title).

More complex queries can be specified in the form of the body of a rule, consisting of a number of linked predicates with connectives.

For example, the following would produce the catalogued-book identifier, author and title of all books:

>   written-by (CB, Author),   entitled (CB, Title).

The comma connecting the two predicates: 'written-by' and 'entitled' is the 'and' connective, and the variable CB ensures that author and title pairs are matched only if they have the same value in the CB argument position. Alternatively, for commonly required classes of queries rules can be built into the database. Suppose, for example, that it is commonly required to obtain catalogue details (excluding information regarding copies of books), or a subset of the catalogue entries, or selected catalogue attributes. For this purpose, the rule indicated in Figure 3.16 for deriving the catalogued-book predicate can be used to satisfy these three alternative requirements. For reference purposes, the rule was:

>   catalogued-book (Isbn, Author, Title, Publisher, Year, Classmark) :-
>   has-isbn (CB, Isbn),   written-by (CB, Author),
>   entitled (CB, Title),   published-by (CB, Publisher),
>   published-in (CB, Year), in-category (CB, Classmark).

In the first case (for full catalogue details), the query might be:

>   catalogued-book (Isbn, Author, Title, Publisher, Year, Classmark).

where each of the arguments are variables and could in fact be any character string so long as at least the first character is in uppercase. In the second case where a subset of the catalogue is required, a condition can be appended to the query or a constant can be used in place of a variable; for example, to obtain catalogue entries for books published in 1984 only, the query could be either: a)

>   catalogued-book (Isbn, Author, Title, Publisher, Year, Classmark),
>   Year=1984.

or: b)

>   catalogued-book (Isbn, Author, Title, Publisher, 1984, Classmark).

Note that in the case of conditions which are not simple equalities (e.g. 'Year >= 1982'), a constant cannot be used in place of a variable; the condition must always be appended to the query, as in the example a) above. In the third case where selected catalogue attributes only are required, the anonymous variable is used wherever necessary; for example,

>   catalogued-book (_, Author, Title, _, 1984, _).

would produce author and title only relating to catalogue entries for books published in 1984. All these classes of queries can be satisfied by a single rule.

Built-in navigation around the database can also be provided by rules. The 'book-loan' rule below, for example, will satisfy the class of queries which involve obtaining any or all of the author, title, name of borrower, and date due back of books on loan:

The 'book-loan' rule:
> book-loan (Author, Title, Name, Date) :-
> written-by (CB, Author),   entitled (CB, Title),
> has-copy (CB, B),   lent-to (B, L),
> has-loan-of (P, L),   named (P, Name),
> for-return-on (L, Date).

Note the use of linkage variables: CB, B, L and P, and the similarity with the link elements of QBE queries.

The two example queries of previous sections are now presented.

(1) Find the titles of all books by J. Austen.
> entitled (CB, Title),   written-by (CB, 'Austen J').

(2) Print the title and author of all books due for return on 31.12.85.
> entitled (CB, Title),   written-by (CB, Author),
> has-copy (CB, B),   lent-to (B, L),
> for-return-on (L, 851231).

(2a) or using the 'book-loan' rule:
> book-loan (Author, Title, _, 851231).

Note the anonymous variable in the book-loan query since the Name attribute is not of interest here.

Although Prolog is based on predicate calculus, when the predicates represent n-ary relations, as illustrated in Figure 3.15 in the previous chapter, the query language is more like domain-oriented relational calculus with the Prolog variables ranging over the domains underlying the relevant attributes. It is this aspect of Prolog which has given rise to research on Prolog interfaces to relational systems, and vice versa. One such interface from QBE to Prolog was mentioned in section 4.4.1 (Neves 1983); an interface from Prolog to SQL is described in Jarke (1984a), and one from an SQL-like language to Prolog is described in Johnson (1984).

4.6 High-level Procedural Languages

High-level procedural languages were included in the category of query languages in section 4.1, but it was indicated that such languages are suitable only for specialist end-users. Procedural languages are those in which the user has to specify in detail the steps to be taken to get the information he requires. They may be based on set-at-a-time logic or record-at-a-time logic (see section 4.1) but only the former are classified as high-level procedural.

The most widely available high-level procedural languages are those based on *relational algebra*. A formal definition of a relational algebra was presented by Codd, together with a definition of relational calculus and a discussion of the relational completeness of both languages, in Codd (1972b). Following this, a number of relational algebra systems were developed. PRTV (Peterlee Relational Test Vehicle) developed by IBM Peterlee is one system which was designed with a relational algebra interface (Todd 1976). As its name suggests, it was a research prototype and its user interface made use of a symbolic language (ISBL), rather than an English-like language, with the intention that a more user-friendly front-end would be developed for end-users. Another system which does provide a user-friendly relational algebra interface is Astrid (Gray 1984, ch.8). Amongst commercially available systems are micro DBMSs such as the well-known dBase II system (Ashton-Tate 1981). This has some relational algebra like facilities, as does Condor, another micro DBMS, but neither are full relational algebra implementations. Relational algebra will be used in this section to illustrate the nature of high procedural languages and to highlight the differences between procedural and non-procedural languages.

Both relational algebra and relational calculus based languages operate on the basis of 'set-at-a-time' logic, i.e. operations are performed on complete relations and produce relations as results. However, with relational calculus a query is expressed in a single retrieval statement (excluding declarative statements such as Quel's RANGE statement), while with relational algebra a query will in general consist of a sequence of relational algebra operations — the user must specify the 'procedure' necessary to obtain the result he requires. Hence relational algebra is at a lower level than relational calculus. However, any relational calculus query can be mapped (decomposed) into an equivalent set of relational algebra operations.

The query components: target list, selection condition, and linkage condition, are specified by means of *project*, *select (restrict)*, and *join* operations respectively, and in general each individual clause in the condition of a query corresponds to a separate select or join operation as relevant. As might be expected, the join operation is a binary operation (operating on two relations), while the select and project operations are unary operations. Relational algebra also contains relational division and cartesian product operations, and the traditional set operations of union, difference and intersection. The main query operations — project, select, join — will be discussed in detail, but the other operations will only be considered briefly. Since Codd (1972b) uses a mathematical notation for his description of relational algebra, a more user-friendly syntax will be used here with conventions similar to those used previously; relational algebra operations are in bold uppercase, relation names are in uppercase (separated by a comma in the case of binary operations), and attributes and expressions are enclosed in parentheses.

Relational project and select operations

Relational project and select are operations on single relations. Both produce a subset of the data in a relation, the project operation producing a vertical subset and the select operation a horizontal subset. A project operation has a relation name and a list of attributes as arguments; it extracts all values of the specified attributes from the named relation, producing a relation as a result which contains tuples formed from the attributes extracted, with duplicate tuples removed. For example:

PROJECT CATALOGUED-BOOK (Title, Publisher)

performed on a relation containing the data in Figure 3.1, would produce the result relation below.

Title	Publisher
Data Models	Ackson-Bull
Relational Systems	Wilkinson
Intro to DBMS	Porter
Query Languages	Clarkson
Database Systems	Clarkson

Note that duplicates have been removed; although the Title, Publisher pair: Data Models, Ackson-Bull, appear twice in Figure 3.1, only one pair appears in the result of the project operation; if both appeared it would not be possible to uniquely identify the tuples in the result and the result would not be a relation.

A select operation has a relation name and a condition as arguments; it selects tuples from the relation which satisfy the condition, producing a relation as a result which contains only the selected tuples. Each result tuple contains the same attributes as the original relation. The condition ranges over attributes in the specified relation and may be complex. For example, the following operation would select catalogued books with a classmark of QA264 and published after 1980:

SELECT CATALOGUED-BOOK (Year > 1980
$\wedge$ Classmark = 'QA264')

The result would contain just the second and fourth tuples from Figure 3.1.

Relational join

A join operation involves two relations and a join expression of the form:

Attribute1 = Attribute2

Every pair of tuples from the two relations, for which the values of the attributes in the join expression are equal, are joined together. The result is a relation containing the joined tuples; i.e. a result tuple consists of all the attributes from both relations, but with one of the join attributes omitted since the two join attribute values are identical. The primary key of the result is formed from the primary keys of the two joined relations. For example:

JOIN CATALOGUED-BOOK, BOOK (Isbn = Isbn)

produces a result relation with the following description:

RESULT (<u>Isbn</u> , Author, Title, Publisher, Year, Classmark, <u>Book#</u> , Shelf)

The join operation above produces catalogue information together with details of all copies of the catalogued books. The two relations are linked by means of the Isbn attribute. The fact that the join attributes in the two relations have the same name is immaterial; what is important is that they come from the same underlying domain.

Queries in relational algebra

In general, a query will require a combination of relational algebra operations. Operations can be combined in sequence ending with a project operation which represents the target list of the query. The result of one operation generally needs to be used in the next operation, and for this purpose there are two possibilities. One is to use a special character, e.g. '*', to indicate the result relation of the previous operation, while another is to assign each operation to a temporary named relation. The former is more concise if intermediate results do not need to be retained for later use. The two example queries used previously will illustrate how relational algebra operations are combined to form a single query.

(1) Find the titles of all books by J. Austen.

SELECT CATALOGUED-BOOK (Author = "Austen J")
PROJECT * (Title)

(2) Print the title and author of all books due for return on 31.12.85.

SELECT LOAN (Date-due-back = "851231")
JOIN BOOK, * (Book# = Book#)
JOIN CATALOGUED-BOOK, * (Isbn = Isbn)
PROJECT * (Title, Author)

Some relational algebra implementations enable the operations to be nested to form a single statement. The operations are kept separate here, however, so that they can be clearly recognised.

The above queries can be considered in terms of the basic query components mentioned in section 4.2.1. The final project operation is equivalent to the target list, the select operations are equivalent to the selection conditions, and the join operations represent the linkage conditions.

With a procedural language, it is possible to specify a sequence of operations which, although it produces the required answer to a query, is not very efficient. It is up to the user of such languages to understand what he is doing and specify an efficient sequence of operations. However, some implementations, e.g. PRTV (Todd 1976, Hall 1976) and Squiral (Smith 1975), contain optimisers to remove this responsibility from the user. The efficiency problem concerns the join operation which produces a result relation which contains all the attributes of both the joined relations, apart from one copy of the join attribute. A sequence of joins can therefore produce a result with a very large number of attributes. The join operation can be expensive in both processing time and storage space if used on large relations; hence it is important to minimise the size of the relations. By carrying out select operations as early in the sequence as possible, the number of tuples to be processed may be reduced. Also, by carrying out intermediate project operations to eliminate all attributes which are not relevant to the query, the number of attributes may be reduced. The join operations then not only operate on much smaller relations but also produce smaller results. An optimised form of query 2 is given below:

(2a)
```
    SELECT  LOAN  (Date-due-back = "851231")
    PROJECT  *  (Book#)
    JOIN  BOOK, *  (Book# = Book#)
    PROJECT  *  (Isbn)
    JOIN  CATALOGUED-BOOK, *  (Isbn = Isbn)
    PROJECT  *  (Title, Author)
```
Note the extra project operations, which reduce the size of the relations processed by the join operations which follow them.

In the section on SQL (section 4.5.2), it was mentioned that nested SQL queries contain relational algebra like features, including implicit join operations. Query (2a) above should be compared with the SQL nested query (2a). It will be seen that one is similar to the reverse of the other, SQL nested queries being processed bottom-up, while relational algebra queries are processed top-down. Readers should ensure that they recognise the similarities by associating each of the above relational algebra operations with a part of the corresponding SQL query.

It should be noted that all the non-procedural languages (QBE, Quel, SQL, etc.) have implicit joins wherever a linkage condition exists and hence implementations of these languages generally have built in optimisers at the query decomposition stage (i.e. the stage at which a query is broken down into its component parts for processing).

Other relational algebra operations

Before leaving relational algebra, the other operations will be mentioned briefly. Firstly, a return to the join operation. Codd defined a *generalised join* (or *theta-join*) enabling relations to be joined on any condition, not necessarily the equality condition. For example,

GENERALISED JOIN R1, R2 (A1 < A2)

would produce a result containing all the attributes of R1 and R2, including both of the join attributes, for all pairs of R1 and R2 tuples which satisfy the condition: A1 < A2. The join operation used in the examples above is referred to more explicitly as the *natural join* (or *equi-join*) in which the condition is always an equality condition and one copy of the join attributes is omitted in the result. It is called the natural join since it is the most commonly required form for queries, as can be seen from the above examples.

Other operations include cartesian product, division, and the traditional set operations: union, intersection and difference. The cartesian product is a relation multiplication operation which operates on two relations and joins together every possible pair of tuples from the two relations. Division is the means by which queries involving the universal quantifier ∀ can be implemented in relational algebra. For example if a relation CL contains the Isbn's of all the books on a particular course list, and a relation R contains just the attributes Isbn and Person# from the Reservation relation, then the division of R by CL will produce a relation containing the Person#'s of those persons who have reserved all the books on the course list.

Union, difference and intersection all operate on two relations, which must be union-compatible (i.e. they must have the same number of attributes, which must be drawn from the same domains and in the same order). Union and difference are useful operations for updating relations. Union may be used to add new tuples to a relation, while difference may be used to delete tuples from a relation (it should be noted that set difference can also be used instead of relational division and is actually more general). Intersection produces a set of tuples which exist in both the relations specified in the intersection operation.

A number of extensions to the relational algebra operations have been suggested, including enhancements to support additional semantics (Codd 1979), and some variations to the join operation to provide for more efficient processing of queries. Also, Gray (1984) has defined 'extend' and 'group-by' operations, which enable computation of derived fields in the Astrid system, corresponding to similar features in SQL.

Normal forms and relational algebra

In Chapter 2 (section 2.6), the normalisation approach to data modelling was discussed and the desirability of maintaining a database in a high normal form (3NF and above) was discussed. Before leaving this section on relational algebra, two points regarding normal forms should be mentioned. Firstly, it should be noted that the binary operations on relations, such as the join operation, produce results which are not generally in 3NF and above. For example, joining the Catalogued-Book and Book relations on Isbn produces a 1NF result relation. This is also true of result relations produced using other relational query languages, of course.

Secondly, it was mentioned in section 2.6 that the translation of relations from one normal form to another may be expressed in terms of relational albegra operations. The reader should now return to that section to transform the 1NF Employee relation and the 1NF Book-Loan-Data and Book-Reserved-Data relations of the library example to 3NF relations, by means of relational algebra operations.

4.7 Database Manipulation Languages

Only the lowest level of database language now remains to be discussed — the database manipulation language or low procedural level. Although referred to as 'low' level, it should be remembered that it is high level in relation to general purpose programming languages such as Cobol, Pascal, etc. It is only low level as far as database languages are concerned.

A database manipulation language (DML) is both procedural and based on record-at-a-time logic. Such languages are designed for application programming where manipulation of data prior to storage, or after retrieval, is required; they are **not** intended for the specification of ad-hoc queries by a user who is happy to have the answer presented in any understandable form so long as he can express his query easily and gets the answer quickly. A means of processing a record at a time is important in application programming. For example, a report may be required in a special format, with some entries in the report derived from data in the database by performing some arithmetic calculations. Before databases were around, such programming was done in a general purpose programming language, with data storage/retrieval carried out at the physical/internal level; the programmer navigated round the data in files and managed the relationships between files by himself, without any software tools to help him apart from indexed sequential, direct access, and sort file utilities.

With the advent of databases came the higher level database manipulation facilities. These are available in two main forms: hosted and self-contained.

Host language systems

In *host language* systems, the DML facilities come as a set of procedures/functions to be used with a general purpose language, thus enabling the programmer merely to call system procedures/functions for database access; this has the advantage that the programmer can use a host language with which he is familiar for the main data processing in the application. Hosted systems sometimes provide a preprocessor for the DML, which converts database access statements embedded in a host language program into appropriate host language procedure/function calls, rather than requiring the programmer to use the procedure/function calls directly. An example will illustrate the difference between these two approaches. In the preprocessor approach, the programmer might use a statement such as:

FIND NEXT MEMBER WITHIN has-copy

to find the logically next member record in the 'has-copy' coset of a Codasyl database. In the direct procedure call approach the same request might be specified as a Pascal function call like this:

status := **FNM** ('has-copy');

where FNM is the DBMS function call to find the next member in the coset specified by the parameter. This example is taken from MDBS III, the micro DBMS referred to in the section on QRS (section 4.5.3). The function returns a status value indicating the success or failure of the database access request.

Self-contained language systems

The second main form of database manipulation facility — the alternative to hosted systems — is the *self-contained language* system. In this case a complete high level language is provided for database access and standard data manipulation. The language is generally structured and often Pascal-like, providing assignment, conditional, and repetition statements, flexible input/output facilities, built-in functions, etc. Procedures and macros are also sometimes provided. Self-contained languages are frequently found in micro DBMS which are designed for end-users who are probably not conversant with a high-level language. Such systems frequently also provide form-based (full-screen) facilities for record definition, data input, editing, and reporting. Database retrieval usually consists of embedding query language commands or special high level commands for 'record-at-a-time' retrieval in the self-contained program where relevant. For other database access (storage, updates, etc.) appropriate high level commands will be available. Taking an example from Knowledgeman, which is a relational DBMS for a micro, the following two commands may be used either interactively or embedded in a program written in the self-contained language provided by the system. The first is an SQL-like SELECT command, and the second is a special command for record-at-a-time retrieval which is based on the syntax of the SELECT command. (Although the first command is identical to the equivalent SQL command, it is referred to only as 'SQL-like' since the syntax differs for retrievals involving multiple relations.)

(a) **SELECT** Title **FROM** CATALOGUED-BOOK
    WHERE Author = "Austen J"

(b) **OBTAIN RECORD FROM** CATALOGUED-BOOK
    WHERE Author = "Austen J"

The SELECT command will retrieve the titles of all the books by J. Austen, and display the result in a table in standard format. The OBTAIN command will retrieve only the first book which satisfies the condition; the complete record will be displayed in a standard format (unless display is suppressed) and all the attributes of the obtained record will be available for further use, if the command is used within an application program. To obtain the next and subsequent records for processing, a command such as:

    OBTAIN NEXT RECORD FROM CATALOGUED-BOOK
    WHERE Author = "Austen J"

is used in a 'while' loop. This record-at-a-time alternative allows a programmer to manipulate the data retrieved or format it as required for output.

4.7.1 An Example using a Self-contained Relational Database Manipulation Language

A complete example is given below to illustrate application programming using a self-contained DML. The DML is that of the Knowledgeman system, a micro-based DBMS (MDBS 1984). (Note: /* and */ are used to enclose comments; also, the example is in lowercase throughout except for relation and attribute names, which follow previous conventions.)

```
let e.supd = true        /* suppress display of an OBTAINed record */
clear       /* clears the screen */
at 3,30 output "BOOKS BY J. AUSTEN"
at 6,20 output "Title"
at 6,55 output "Number"
at 6,70 output "Classmark"
let line = 8      /* initialise a variable: line, to control the */
                  /* line no. for output of required data */
obtain record from CATALOGUED-BOOK where Author = "Austen J"
/* loop for each selected Catalogued-Book record */
while eot (CATALOGUED-BOOK) = false do
    at line,10 output CATALOGUED-BOOK.Title
    at line,55 output CATALOGUED-BOOK.Isbn
    at line,70 output CATALOGUED-BOOK.Classmark
    let line = line + 1
    obtain next record from CATALOGUED-BOOK where Author = "Austen J"
endwhile
```

The first line of the program suppresses the display of OBTAINed records, so that they can be formatted as required by the application; 'supd' is a built-in 'environment variable' recognised as such by the 'e.' prefix. The next 5 lines clear the screen, output a report title starting at line 3 column 30, and output the required column headings at line 6 columns 20, 55 and 70 respectively. A variable 'line' is then set to 8 ready for the output of the first set of catalogued book information on line 8. The first record is obtained from the Knowledgeman table (relation) called Catalogued-Book, then a 'while' loop is set up which is repeated while the end of the table has not yet been reached. In this loop, the required attributes from the retrieved Catalogued-Book record are output at the specified column positions in the line indicated by the variable 'line', which is then incremented, and the next record obtained. When the 'eot' (end of table) function returns the value true, the program terminates.

If it were required also to obtain information about copies of each book, an inner loop would be required using the following OBTAIN command:

OBTAIN RECORD FROM BOOK
   WHERE BOOK.Isbn = CATALOGUED-BOOK.Isbn

together with the OBTAIN NEXT RECORD command inside the inner loop. The WHERE clause in this OBTAIN command contains the linkage condition enabling the relationship between Catalogued-Book and Book to be made explicit. 'CATALOGUED-BOOK.Isbn' relates to the Isbn from the most recently obtained Catalogued-Book record.

4.7.2 An Example using a Hosted Network Database Manipulation Language

The DML of MDBS III (MDBS 1981) will be used to illustrate a DML for a hosted network system. Although it is only based on the Codasyl DML and does not use Codasyl syntax, it can be used to illustrate all the navigational features of a Codasyl DML. It is also available in an interactive version — IDML — which is very useful for quick, low volume updates to the database, and is also an important aid in building and testing DML logic. In this latter case, the application programmer can build up the database access logic for an application or part of an application by means of the IDML, and when he is satisfied that it is correct he can embed it into a host language application program as required.

In a DML for a Codasyl or network system, the concept of *currency* is very important. At any particular point in the running of a program (sometimes referred to as a run unit), there will be system variables with values identifying, amongst other things, the current record (i.e. the last one referred to), and the current record of each record type and set type. These values may of course be null in cases where no current record of a particular type has so far been identified in the run unit. These currency indicators are used by the system to determine the relevant record occurrence or coset occurrence upon which to carry out the specified operation.

In the MS-Pascal hosted version of MDBS (which will be used in the example), Pascal records are used as data blocks for the transfer of data between the database and the program. These data blocks are referenced in DML function calls by their address, which is obtained by means of a special 'ads' (address) keyword (other MDBS hosts use other mechanisms for addressing data blocks). A wide range of function calls are available, but only a small subset will be introduced here for the purposes of the example. The functions return a status value indicating the success/failure/status of the DML operation which has been carried out. It should be noted that virtually all the function calls are available in the IDML.

Summary of MDBS DML command types

Before the example is given the different types of MDBS DML command are summarised. Each type of command in general has a range of different formats to cater for different requirements.

Data retrieval:
Two separate types of command are provided for data retrieval. A record may need to be found (located) in the database for one of two reasons:
(i) retrieving attribute values from the record, and
(ii) navigating round the data model.
If attribute values from a record are required by the user's program, the 'Find' command is first used to locate the required record and the 'Get' command is then used to retrieve the required data values, while the 'Find' command is used on its own for data model navigation.

Database update:
The 'Put' command enables updates to be carried out on existing records, while the 'Create' and 'Delete' commands add new records to the database and delete complete records, respectively.
The Create command, as well as storing new records in the database, also inserts them automatically into cosets in which they are declared as automatic members.
Records which are optional members in a coset have to be manually inserted into that coset. This is done via the 'Insert' (connect) command. Optional members can also be removed from a coset without being deleted from the database; the 'Remove' (disconnect) command is used for this purpose.

Establishing currency:
For navigational purposes it is sometimes necessary to establish a record, which has been located as an owner or member of one coset, as the current owner or member of some other coset. The 'Set' command is provided for this purpose. It is used in conjunction with the Find command to enable the programmer to move from coset to coset, navigating round the data model.
(It should be noted that a different mechanism is used in the Codasyl proposals for establishing currency. The Codasyl 'Find' command establishes currency as a side-effect, and a 'retaining' clause can be used to suppress currency updates. However, the MDBS approach is useful in illustrating explicitly the data model navigation aspects of an application.)

Other commands include:
Commands to open and close the database, save database changes immediately (rather than at database closing time), and transaction logging.

Some commands used in the example

The DML commands which are used in the example below are described in detail first. The parameters in quotes ' ' contain database names such as coset, record, or item (attribute) names, which must have been declared previously in the relevant database schema. The following

Pascal declarations are assumed:
>   name: a character array of the same size as the Author attribute
>   catbook: a Pascal record containing the same attributes as those of the Catalogued-Book record type in the schema
>   book: a Pascal record containing the same attributes as those of the Book record type in the schema
>   status: an integer.

(a): FMI (Find Member based on Item)
> Example: FMI ('Author, catalogue-list', ads name);

This will find (locate) the member of the catalogue-list coset based on an Author value equal to the value in the variable: name.

FNMI (Find Next Member based on Item) is used to find the next member in the specified coset which has the relevant attribute value.

(b) FFM (Find First Member of coset):
> Example: FFM ('has-copy');

This will find the first member of the current has-copy coset occurrence.

FNM (Find Next Member of coset) is used to find the next member.

(c) GETM (GET data from Member):
> Example: GETM ('catalogue-list', ads catbook);

This will get data from the current member record of the catalogue-list coset and place it in the record variable: catbook.

GETO (GET data from Owner) is used to get data from the owner of a coset.

(d) GFM (Get Field from Member):
> Example: GFM ('Name, person-list', ads name);

This will get the value of the Name attribute in the current member record of the person-list coset, and place it in the variable: name. This is used instead of GETM when only one or two attributes from a record are required.

GFO (Get Field from Owner) is used to get the value of an attribute from the owner record of a coset.

(e) SOM (Set Owner based on Member):
> Example: SOM ('has-copy, catalogue-list');

This will establish the record which is currently the member of the catalogue-list coset as the current owner of the has-copy coset; it locates the relevant occurrence of the has-copy coset and hence provides access to its members.

Other functions for setting currency indicators and establishing coset occurrences include: SMM, SMO, SOO functions, where O and M indicate owner and member respectively.

The example

The objective in the example below is to find details of all copies of books by J. Austen. The part of the data model relevant to this procedure is illustrated below.

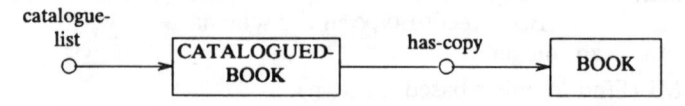

```
       catalogue-
          list        ┌──────────────┐   has-copy   ┌──────┐
          ○──────────▶│ CATALOGUED-  │──────○──────▶│ BOOK │
                      │    BOOK      │              └──────┘
                      └──────────────┘
```

To obtain the required data the member record of the catalogue-list coset with the required Author value must first be located (FMI) and data retrieved (GETM); this catalogued book record must then be established as the owner of the has-copy coset (SOM) in order for the system to locate the relevant coset occurrence. Once this has been done, data relating to all copies of the book member record can be obtained (FFM, GETM, FNM, GETM, FNM, GETM, ..., until the end of the current has-copy coset occurrence). The next member record of the catalogue-list coset with the required Author value is then located (FNMI) and the procedure is repeated until the end of the catalogue-list coset is reached.

The skeleton procedure in the MDBS DML embedded in MS-Pascal:
(comments are enclosed in { })

```
name := 'Austen J';
status := FMI ('Author, catalogue-list',  ads name);
        { find member in catalogue-list coset having the required author name }
while status = 0 do    { if status = 0, a record has been found }
  begin status := GETM ('catalogue-list',  ads catbook);
            { get data from the current member of the catalogue-list coset
              and put it into catbook for later use }
        status := SOM ('has-copy, catalogue-list');
            { find the has-copy coset occurrence which is owned
              by the current member of catalogue-list, so that
              the relevant book copy details may be obtained }
        status := FFM ('has-copy');
            { find the first member of the has-copy coset }
  while status = 0 do    { a member record has been found }
    begin status := GETM ('has-copy',  ads book);
            { get data from the current member of the has-copy
              coset and put it into the variable book }
        - - - - - - - -
            { produce required output using data which has been
              retrieved into the Pascal records: catbook and book }
        - - - - - - - -
        status := FNM ('has-copy');
            { find the next member of the has-copy coset }
    end;
  FNMI ('Author, catalogue-list',  ads name);
            { find the next member in the catalogue-list coset with the
              required author name }
end;
```

4.8 Views and the External Schema Revisited

In Chapter 3, the subject of user views / external schema was discussed. Two main approaches for defining user views were mentioned: the external schema DDL (generally applicable to hierarchical and network systems), and the view facility in query/manipulation languages (generally applicable to relational systems and Prolog). The former approach was discussed in Chapter 3, but the latter was left until this chapter in order that query and manipulation languages could be discussed first. In this section, then, examples of relational and Prolog user view specifications will be provided.

SQL provides a user view facility by means of the SELECT statement used within a DEFINE VIEW declaration. For example:

DEFINE VIEW DUEBOOK (Title, Author, Date) **AS**
   SELECT Title, Author, Date-due-back
     FROM CATALOGUED-BOOK, BOOK, LOAN
     WHERE CATALOGUED-BOOK.Isbn = BOOK.Isbn
     AND BOOK.Book# = LOAN.Book#

This defines a subset of the database, consisting only of the Title, Author and Date-due-back attributes of books on loan. The SQL view mechanism is basically a macro. The view is not instantiated until such time as it is used in a query. In a query, the name of the view, e.g. DUEBOOK, is used just like any other relation name although it only exists in intensional form (not in extensional form). Books due on 31.12.85 can be found, for example, by means of this view as follows:

   SELECT Title, Author
    FROM DUEBOOK
    WHERE Date = "851231"

Note that Date-due-back was renamed to Date in the DUEBOOK view.

Titles of books on loan can be found simply by:

   SELECT Title **FROM** DUEBOOK

And there are many other queries too which can be satisfied by means of this view.

SQL views can also be used to provide categorization as defined in Chapter 2 section 2.7. For example:

```
DEFINE VIEW   RECENT-BOOK  AS
    SELECT *
        FROM  CATALOGUED-BOOK
        WHERE  Year >= 1982
DEFINE VIEW   OLDER-BOOK  AS
    SELECT *
        FROM  CATALOGUED-BOOK
        WHERE  Year < 1982
```
Note: * is a shorthand notation for all attributes.

A *snapshot* is an alternative way of providing user views. (Note: this is not the same as the history snapshots mentioned in subsection 2.7.3 in relation to the time dimension in databases.) The macro-type view provided by SQL is only instantiated when the view is referred to in a query. A snapshot is an *instantiated view* which is stored in the database. The user will generally not be aware of whether the view he uses is implemented as a macro or as a snapshot. However, from the system viewpoint, a snapshot contains duplicated data which must be maintained to keep it up-to-date, while the macro-type view is always instantiated to the current database values automatically. It should be noted that view facilities are not provided by all relational systems.

The Prolog view mechanism has, in fact, already been introduced. A Prolog rule, such as the 'book-loan' rule in section 4.5.4, defines a view which is instantiated when the head of the rule is specified in a query. This was illustrated in section 4.5.4 in the alternative answer (2a) to the second example query.

4.9 Summary

In this chapter, various types of database query and manipulation language have been discussed and compared. The nature of queries was first discussed, including an introduction to predicate and relational calculus, in order to provide a basis for discussing the languages. Concepts and features of the different user interfaces were introduced in such a way as to highlight the similarities and differences between them.

The languages were classified into five groups, from the highest level: natural language, through graphics-oriented, formal query, and high-level procedural languages, to the relatively low level database manipulation languages designed for application programming.

Finally, user views, which were discussed in Chapter 3, were briefly reconsidered in relation to relational and Prolog systems. In these systems, view definition is closely associated with query language facilities, and therefore had to be left until this chapter.

It should be stressed that no attempt has been made to provide complete discussions of the various languages. It is beyond the scope of this book to do so, since it is aimed at broad coverage of a wide range of different concepts, approaches, and facilities, rather than detailed coverage of only the main approaches to DBMS. More comprehensive descriptions of the various systems and languages referred to in this chapter may be found in the various references provided.

CHAPTER FIVE

Database Management Systems: Facilities and Implementation Aspects

5.1. Introduction

It should be clear by now what a database is, how it is designed, and how it can be accessed by the end-user. But not much has yet been said about the database systems which support the database. It is time to consider what a database system really is, what facilities it should provide, and how it might be implemented.

In the section which follows, an attempt will be made to answer the question: 'What is a DBMS?', and the differences between file management and database management systems will be considered. The main facilities which are generally provided by currently available database systems will be summarised, and some products on the market will be reviewed briefly.

Following this, some important implementation aspects will be considered. Firstly, the organisation and storage of data in a database. The primary objective is to find a method of organising the data which enables the system to provide not only fast response to database requests from interactive users, but also efficient processing of large volumes of data by application programs. The methods available for data organisation and storage are dependent to a large extent on the conceptual basis of the database, and hence they will be considered in separate subsections. The first will cover relational databases, the second binary relationship databases, and the third network and hierarchical databases. The latter two are considered together since they rely on explicit logical pointers. The organisation of binary relationship data is considered after relational databases as there are some similarities (as well as significant differences).

The second implementation aspect to be considered is query processing. This aspect will also be covered in separate subsections — the first concerning relational database queries, the second concerning binary relationship queries, and the third, Codasyl-based database queries. The problem of processing a query expressed in a high level non-procedural language is primarily one of working out the most efficient sequence of lower level operations which are necessary to obtain the answer to the query. There may be many ways of obtaining the answer, and it is important to select a fast and efficient method. Generalised techniques are available for query decomposition, optimisation, and execution, and some of these will be discussed in the section on query processing.

The third implementation aspect, database protection, has three facets — reliability, security, and integrity, and each of these will be considered in the last main section of this chapter.

The implementation aspects mentioned above are sufficiently important to be given special attention in this book. It should be pointed out that for each of the implementation aspects to be considered, there are a great many alternative techniques available and it is only possible to discuss a few of these in this chapter. However, this should be sufficient to give readers an impression of the nature and complexity of DBMS implementation. There are, of course, other DBMS implementation aspects, but they do not involve such major design issues.

5.2 Database Management Systems

The micro revolution has given rise to the popularisation of the term 'database' and a wide range of different systems are now called 'database systems' or claim to have 'database management' facilities. The newcomer to databases must be wary, as many a file management system has been 'dressed up' in sales literature to look like a database system. Since the term 'database' is popularly used to refer to any collection of data, a full understanding of the difference between a file management system and a database system would not be possible without first understanding what a database is, in the specialist sense of the term. It is for this reason that a discussion of database systems has been left until now. The previous chapters in this book should have provided sufficient groundwork for this understanding.

Both a database system and a file system should contain standard file management capabilities, but a database system should contain additional facilities for handling highly structured data, normally stored in multiple files. The important difference therefore between a file management system (FMS) and a database management system (DBMS) is the ability of the DBMS to handle highly structured data. The main mechanisms for doing this should by now be obvious. Firstly, relationships amongst different data elements are reflected in the conceptual schema; in network and hierarchical systems this is done explicitly (for example, by linking different record types by means of the coset construct in Codasyl systems), while in relational systems the relationships are implicit (attributes drawn from a common domain in different relations). Secondly, very high level language facilities are provided for retrieving and manipulating the structured data. Such mechanisms do not exist in file management systems. Inevitably, there is no clear dividing line between a FMS and a DBMS. There is a 'grey' area in which lie systems with primitive and somewhat low level facilities for handling structured data.

Before listing some of the available DBMSs, an attempt will be made to answer the question: 'What range of facilities should be provided by a DBMS?'. The answer to this question depends partly on the type of machine for which the system is designed. If it is a single-user DBMS one cannot expect, and generally would not need, the same range and sophistication of facilities as in the case of a main-frame DBMS. Table 5.1 summarises the main facilities which are generally provided by currently available systems.

A few of the more well known DBMSs have been selected and listed in Table 5.2. It is not intended that this list should be comprehensive, but an attempt has been made to list DBMSs which are representative of the range available. For a somewhat more complete list, including file management systems, reference should be made to Wiederhold (1983, Appendix B).

Looking at Table 5.2, a number of comments can be made. Firstly, network and hierarchical systems are most likely to be found on mainframe or mini computers. This is due to the fact that such systems generally provide very good facilities for the management of large mainframe databases, but the initial setting up of the database can be complex and not worthwhile in a micro database environment. One or two network and hierarchical systems are however available on micros, but with limited facilities.

Secondly, it can be seen that most micro DBMSs are based on the relational model, but they vary in sophistication and in user-friendliness. The dBaseII relational facilities (i.e. facilities for linking files) are based on relational algebra and are hence not very user-friendly, but the enhanced version: dBaseIII, although very similar to dBaseII in most respects, provides improved facilities for specifying relationships between tables (files) of data and provides an "Assistant" facility, both of which

Facility	Comments
1. Data Description	
Record / relation / etc. description	
Structured data description	Not relational systems
View (subschema) description	Not always provided
2. Data Input/Edit/Update	
File-based	Important for large databases
Interactive / form-based	Important for micro DBMS users
3. Data Retrieval	
Interactive query language	Generally non-procedural and at various levels
Other data retrieval / manipulation language	May be record-at-a-time / may be extension of non-procedural query language
4. General Purpose Data Manipulation	
Application programming facilities via host language or self-contained language	
5. Data Presentation	
Tabular display of results	
Report facilities	Generally quite sophisticated in mainframe DBMSs
Graphical display	Not widely available yet
6. Database Protection	
Passwords / authorization rules	For access authorization
Backup copy / transaction logs	For recovery after a failure of some sort
Validation rules & Concurrent access locks and rules	For database integrity assurance
7. Data Administration	
Integrated data dictionary	Not always provided
Usage monitoring	
Physical organisation facilities (indexing / hashing / sorting / file characteristics / etc.)	For database tuning (micro DBMSs generally only provide sorting and indexing)

Table 5.1 Summary of Main DBMS Facilities

have improved the user interface. Knowledgeman on the other hand, provides an SQL-like query facility and has better multi-relation data retrieval facilities than the dBase systems; its general purpose programming capabilities are much the same as those in the dBase systems, but it also provides some non-database facilities such as spreadsheet operations.

DBMS	Developer	Structure	M/Mi/Mf (see key)	H/S (see key)	Comments
ADABAS	Software AG	see comments	Mf	H	Some relational features. Uses inverted file mechanism
CONDOR	Condor Corp.	limited relational	M	S	Files linked via 'join'
DATABASE 2	IBM	relational	Mf	H	SQL & QBE query languages
dBASEII	Ashton-Tate	limited relational	M	S	Files linked by 'join'
dBASEIII	Ashton-Tate	limited relational	M	S	Similar to DBaseII but with enhanced and more user-friendly facilities
DELTA	Compsoft	limited hierarchical	M	S	In the 'grey' area between DBMS & FMS
DMS1100	Univac	network	Mf	H	Codasyl-based
IDMS	Cullinane	network	Mf	H	Codasyl-based Nat.lang.query facility
IDSII	Honeywell	network	Mf	H	Codasyl-based
IMAGE	Hewlett-Packard	network	Mi	H	
IMS	IBM	hierarchical (linked)	Mf	H	Limited network via linked hierarchies
INGRES	UCal.Berkeley & Relational Technology	relational	Mi/Mf	H	Quel(rel.calc.based) query language
KNOWLEDGEMAN	MDBS Inc.	limited relational	M	S	SQL-like retrieval facility
MDBSIII	MDBS Inc.	network	M/Mi	H	Codasyl features
MRDS	Honeywell	relational	Mf	H	
ORACLE	Oracle Corp.	relational	M/Mi/Mf	H	SQL query language
PROLOG		bin.reln./logic	M/Mi/Mf	S	Pred.calc. based language
RAPPORT	Logica	relational	M/Mi/Mf	H	RaSQL query language (SQL-based)
SYSTEM 2000	MRI	hierarchical	Mf	H	
TOTAL	Cincom Inc.	limited network	Mi/Mf	H	

Key: M micro   H hosted
     Mi mini   S self-contained
     Mf mainframe

Table 5.2 A Selection of Available Database Management Systems

A third point to note is the tendency towards SQL as the high level query language. This tendency probably owes much to the fact that it is an integrated and comprehensive language, providing data description, input, update and other data manipulation facilities, as well as query facilities.

It can be seen that mainframe systems tend to be hosted by a conventional general purpose programming language (Cobol, Pascal, etc.), while micro systems tend to provide their own self-contained language for general data manipulation. This can be explained by the greater significance of application programming in the mainframe environment, with greater dependence upon experienced programmers; hence, a familiar host language for application programming is an important advantage. Micro database applications are usually relatively small and often written by non-specialists who are not experienced in any programming language. For such people, an integrated and user-friendly environment is very essential.

Two of the relational systems listed: Oracle and Rapport, and also Prolog, have micro as well as mainframe versions. Also, MDBS III, although basically a micro system, is available on minis. Mainframe / mini / micro versions of the same package will become increasingly important in the future as more companies move towards providing distributed computing facilities and require DBMSs on both departmental micros and centralised mainframes which can 'talk' to each other.

It is worth pointing out two further tendencies in micro-based facilities which are having an impact on DBMSs in general. Firstly, micro DBMSs have tended to lead the way as far as end-user interfaces are concerned, and have provided the impetus for the development of better facilities for non-specialist, casual users. The micro has very much changed the ratio of non-specialist to specialist computer users, and demand for more user-friendly systems of all types (including operating systems!) on mainframes as well as micros has resulted. Secondly, a number of integrated packages have become available on micros. The types of facility which have been integrated are spreadsheet, word processing, file management, and graphics. In general, though, such packages provide comprehensive facilities in one area and more limited facilities in the other areas. Examples are Lotus 1-2-3 and Symphony (from Lotus Corp.) which are basically spreadsheet packages but also include file management and business graphics (and also word processing in Symphony), and Knowledgeman which is basically a database system (see Table 5.2) but also includes spreadsheet facilities in the basic system, and 'add-on' business graphics and word processing facilities. The idea of integrating packages is gathering pace, and mainframe DBMSs are beginning to move in the same direction. Integrated systems pose additional problems though, and conventional database techniques are not always adequate.

5.3 Database Organisation and Storage

The first DBMS implementation aspect to be considered is that of how to organise and store the data in a database to permit fast and efficient retrieval of single or multiple units of data. Database organisation and storage relate to the physical database, and hence are associated with the *internal model*. At this level, one is not concerned with real world aspects of the data, but with computer-oriented aspects instead. Physical units of data (e.g. blocks of bytes) are of interest here, but entities, attributes and relationships are not directly of interest; only their relationship to the physical units is important (e.g. a particular entity may be represented by a physical record in the database, with its identifier used as the key for storage and retrieval purposes).

In this chapter, the term 'record' will be used to refer to a physical record (i.e. block of bytes forming a single unit); this is consistent with conventional data processing terminology. A physical record may actually be identical to a logical record, but it will more likely be a compact representation of the version of the record which is seen by the user.

It is assumed that readers are already acquainted with methods of file organisation. However, some techniques are briefly outlined as an 'aide memoire' and references are given to full descriptions and discussions of the different techniques. It should be noted, in particular, that the techniques which are introduced in the subsection on relational database organisation are standard file organisation techniques and can therefore be applied to other types of database organisation as appropriate. Mention will be made of this where relevant.

5.3.1 Relational Database Organisation

The internal model of a relational database is generally a set of physical files, one per relation, and with one physical record per tuple in each relation. It is also quite common for the schema and other metadata (data dictionary information) in a relational database to be modelled as relations and hence stored in the same way as the basic relations. This has the advantage that DBMS facilities can be used for metadata access as well as for data access.

The three main options for physically organising data in relations are: *heap, hash table,* and *index,* and these will be considered in turn.

Heap or pile

The *heap* or *pile* is a type of organisation in which new records are simply added at the end of a file and hence they are in purely random order — just a heap of records. To find a particular record, a sequential search must always be carried out, starting from the beginning of the file. To delete a record, the record can be found and marked for deletion with a special marker (and the files can later be 'tidied' by physically removing (or archiving) marked records, at some slack period in the use of the database (e.g. overnight)).

While this is the simplest method of organisation, it is the slowest for anything but simple retrievals on small files. In particular, for multi-relation retrieval requiring join operations, either both relations in a join must be sorted prior to processing, or, for each tuple in the first relation of a join the complete second relation must be scanned.

The Ingres database system provides heap organisation by default, but also provides hashing and index mechanisms which the user can specify when creating his database. The heap is a good method for storing metadata if the metadata for each relation is itself kept in a separate relation. Such relations are likely to be quite small as the number of tuples will be a function of the number of attributes in a relation. However, such metadata structure is rather primitive and inflexible, and is not likely to be suitable for the knowledge bases of the future (see Chapter 7).

To summarise the characteristics of a heap:
- additions are very fast;
- single relation retrievals require searching the complete file;
- multi-relation retrievals can be very slow for large files;
- single alterations require searching the complete file until the relevant record is found; then that record can be changed and the old one overwritten;
- single deletions require searching the complete file until the relevant record is found; then it can be marked for deletion and the file tidied at a later stage;
- large volume multi-relation retrievals and updates would require the relevant files to be sorted before processing.

Hash table

For fast access to individual records the ideal situation is to be able to locate the required data directly in one database access, instead of the many accesses which may be required with heap organisation. With compact and complete primary key values (e.g. 100 records with key values from 1 to 100 inclusive), records can be stored in the file in the physical record position which corresponds to their logical key value. However, such a situation is very rare; identifiers are generally not so compact and definitely not complete. Codes used as identifiers often have some intrinsic meaning (e.g. SSCS1008 may be a code to identify a Stainless Steel Counter Sunk 1.0" 8 screw) and not all possible combinations of letters and digits in the code will be used. Also, codes which are consecutive numbers may soon become incomplete due to the dynamic environment of a database; for example, employees come and go, and the set of employee numbers in the database at any one time will be very randomly distributed. For these reasons, the direct method suggested above is generally out of the question as it would result in large amounts of empty space in files.

An alternative is *hash* organisation. It is, for example, available in both the Ingres and Rapport relational DBMSs, and has been widely used in conventional file environments. Hash organisation requires the setting up of a hash table (or file), with sufficient space to store a fixed number of records. Hashing involves taking the primary key value of a record (converting it to a numeric value if necessary), and passing it through an algorithm which returns a value — the *hash key* — which represents the physical record position. The objective of the hashing algorithm is to map primary key values into unique hash keys with a restricted range corresponding to the number of records which can be stored in the allocated table space. However, the uniqueness of the derived hash key cannot be guaranteed, and clashes may arise such that for some different pair of primary key values Pk1 and Pk2

$h(Pk1) \rightarrow Hk$
and $h(Pk2) \rightarrow Hk$

where h is the hashing algorithm and Hk is the resulting hash key value, which is identical in the two cases. Hashing algorithms therefore also have *clash* or *collision mechanisms* associated with them.

A number of hashing algorithms have been devised over the years and many papers on the subject may be found in the literature. *Prime division* is one technique which has been found to perform well in most circumstances, and this will be described briefly. The approximate capacity of the file (in terms of records or addressable units such as pages or buckets) is first determined by reference to required load factors. (The load factor is the proportion of the file which is filled by records, i.e. not empty. A high load factor, say 90%, minimises wasted space at the expense of increased retrieval time, and vice versa for low load factors.) The actual capacity (C) is then chosen as a prime number (or a number with at least no prime factors < 20) which is close to the approximate capacity. The hashing algorithm is:

Hk:= rem (Pk div C)

i.e. the hash key is the remainder after dividing the primary key by C. For example, suppose the approximate capacity is to be 700, the value of C can be 701 (since this number has no prime factors < 20). A key value of 654321 when divided by 701 gives a remainder of 288 which will be the hash key for locating the position of the relevant record.

As mentioned earlier, there can be no guarantee that the hashing algorithm used will generate unique hash keys. In fact, the above algorithm will produce a result of 288 for many other primary keys; one example is 329758, but it is possible that this particular primary key value may never actually occur, thus avoiding a clash. However, clashes will sometimes occur, in particular if the load factor is high, and in practice, load factors between 50% and 80% are advisable, the actual factor chosen depending on how fast, and by how much, the number of stored records is likely to increase.

As with hashing algorithms, there are a number of *clash* or *collision* techniques, including open addressing, rehashing, and overflow table. With *open addressing* a record whose hash key clashes with one already stored, is placed in the next available free slot in the file; the disadvantage is that clustering of records can occur, leading to lengthy searches for records not found at their hash key address. With *rehashing* a secondary hashing algorithm is applied to the key of a record which clashes, to obtain a new hash key; the new hash key could, of course, also clash with some other record but rehashing should produce a more even distribution of records and faster access time than open addressing. The *overflow table* technique requires a separate table to be used to store those records whose hash keys clash with an already stored record. This table may be stored as a separate file or as a separate part (an extension) of the main file. Records may be stored serially in the overflow table, or alternatively, records with the same hash key value may be chained together to provide faster access (*overflow with chaining*).

Detailed discussions of hashing techniques may be found in Cunningham (1985), Wiederhold (1983), Knuth (1973), and others.

The main advantage of hashing is fast access to data when a file is relatively stable (a hashing algorithm can be carefully selected to suit the specific data in the file). There are two main disadvantages; the first is the inability to access the data in sequential order of key value without prior sorting, and the second is the degradation in performance which can occur if the file is dynamic and the load factor increases to a high level. To overcome the second problem *dynamic hashing*, and related techniques: *extendible hashing* and *virtual hashing*, have been designed (Larson 1978, Fagin 1979, Litwin 1978). These are briefly summarised in Scholl (1981), together with two variations designed to increase the load factor with only a slight cost as far as performance is concerned. Dynamic and extendible hashing both employ an index mechanism (to be discussed later), together with a 'dynamic' hashing algorithm. The index expands and contracts as records are added and deleted.

In extendible hashing, for example, if the index has 2^n entries, then to access the index, the leftmost n bits of the hash key (derived using a hashing algorithm such as prime division described above) will be used. Each index entry will contain a pointer to a bucket or page of the file. Due to the design of the index (i.e. two or more entries may point to the same bucket), overflow of a bucket may merely require a new bucket to be created, an index pointer to be changed, and some records to be split between the old and new buckets. It is possible though that overflow may cause the index to be increased (doubled in size), with corresponding alterations to index entries. When this occurs the algorithm for accessing the index now requires the leftmost n+1 bits of the hash key to be used, since the index will have expanded to 2^{n+1} entries. Full details of this technique may be found in Fagin (1979). It provides fast access to dynamic files but with a load factor of approximately 69% (ln 2) only.

To summarise the characteristics of hash organisation:
- access (retrieval and updates) via the primary key may be very fast especially for relatively stable files;
- there is a trade-off between fast access and high storage utilization; improving the former generally means reducing the latter and vice versa;
- sequential access in key order is not possible without prior sorting.

Index

An alternative to hash organisation, which not only provides direct access to individual records but also provides sequential access to sets of records, is to use some form of *index* mechanism. An objective of indexing is to hold as much of the index as possible in main memory to provide fast access to the index with (if possible) only one disc access to obtain the required record.

There are various different types of index; the basic types are partial indexes and full indexes, both of which may be single-level or multi-level. These will be discussed briefly, and then a particular form of full index — the B-tree, which is becoming widely used in relational database systems, will be discussed.

Partial indexing requires the file of records to be sorted in key order. A *partial index* provides an index to individual buckets or pages in the file, each of which contains a group of records. A particular record is found by first searching the index to locate the relevant bucket, and then searching serially through the bucket for the actual record required. This is the basis of the *indexed sequential* access mechanism.

An example of a single-level partial index is illustrated in Figure 5.1.

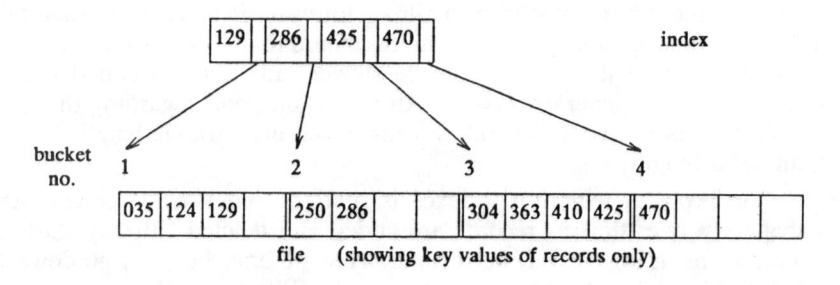

```
                    | 129 | 286 | 425 | 470 |                    index


 bucket        1              2                 3               4
  no.
           | 035 | 124 | 129 |    | 250 | 286 |    | 304 | 363 | 410 | 425 | 470 |    |    |
                    file     (showing key values of records only)
```

Figure 5.1 A Single-level Partial Index

The index entry contains the key of the last record in a particular bucket and a pointer to that bucket. To find the record with key 410, for example, the index is searched for the first key which is greater than 410, then the bucket pointed to (i.e. bucket 3) is searched serially until record 410 is found. The records are maintained in the file in sequential order and hence records may easily be accessed either sequentially or at random.

A *full index* provides an index entry for each record. Except for the smallest of files, a full index will be multi-level, representing an inverted tree structure. An example is illustrated in Figure 5.2.

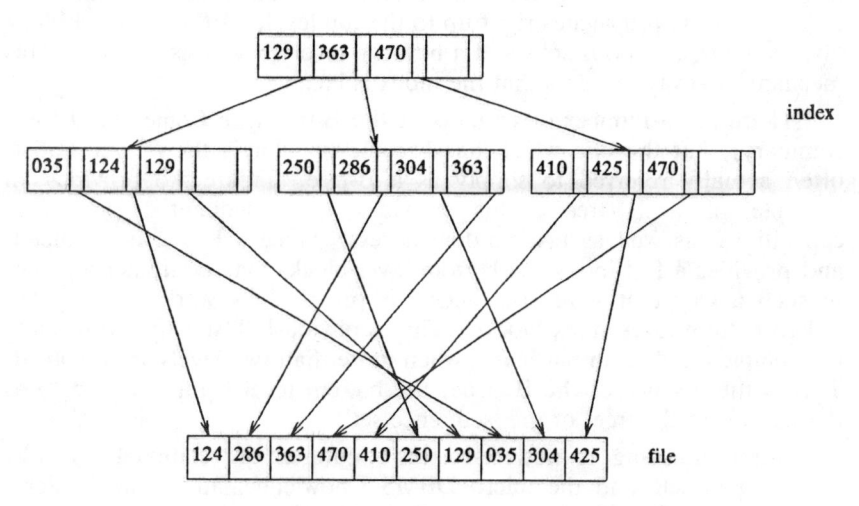

```
                    | 129 | 363 | 470 |    |    |

                                                                       index

| 035 | 124 | 129 |    |    |   | 250 | 286 | 304 | 363 |    |   | 410 | 425 | 470 |    |    |



             | 124 | 286 | 363 | 470 | 410 | 250 | 129 | 035 | 304 | 425 |     file
```

Figure 5.2 A Multi-level Full Index

Note that the records can be stored in any order in the file, since the index is maintained in sequential order, although this means that the index must be traversed for sequential retrieval, which is not as fast as retrieving records serially from a file. However, it is easier to maintain an index in sequential order than to maintain a file of records, and although sequential retrieval may be slower, additions to and deletions from the file are generally faster. An important point regarding this type of index is its ability to support records which are variable-length (rather than fixed-length).

One problem with full indexes is that the index may become very unbalanced over time as records are added and deleted. It may start off balanced, as in Figure 5.2, but eventually some branches may go down to many levels while others are only one level. With large files, only part of the index (possibly only the top level) will be able to be maintained in main memory. Hence with an unbalanced tree a number of disc accesses may be required in order to access a specific record. A particular technique for organising a full index which remains balanced over time is the B-tree.

A *B-tree* (Comer 1979, Wiederhold 1983) is a multi-level balanced index, each index block containing space for a fixed number of pointers. Index blocks are initially created only half full to allow for easy updating; rearrangement of the index blocks is only necessary when one overflows. When this happens, it is split in two with a new entry being made in the parent index block (i.e. the block at the next higher level which currently points to the overflowed block). If the parent block overflows, it is split in the same way. In the worst case situation in which each parent block is full, splitting propagates right up to the top level. If the top level block also overflows, it too is split and a new top level above it is created. This mechanism always ensures that the index is balanced.

There are a number of variants of the B-tree (see Comer 1979 for a summary), but the one which has become popular is the B^+-*tree* and is often actually referred to simply as a B-tree. Figure 5.3 provides an example of a B^+-tree. This provides good sequential processing capabilities, as well as fast random access. Since a B-tree is balanced, and provides a full index, its bottom level blocks may be linked together in such a way that sequential access is provided by working along the linked bottom level index blocks. This is obviously faster than traversing the complete index, in particular when more than two levels are involved. This is the essence of the B^+-tree, the bottom level being referred to as the 'leaves' of the tree, or the 'sequence set'.

B-tree indexing is now used in a number of relational DBMSs, including Oracle and the micro DBMS Knowledgeman. Other systems (e.g. Ingres, dBaseII) provide some form of indexing.

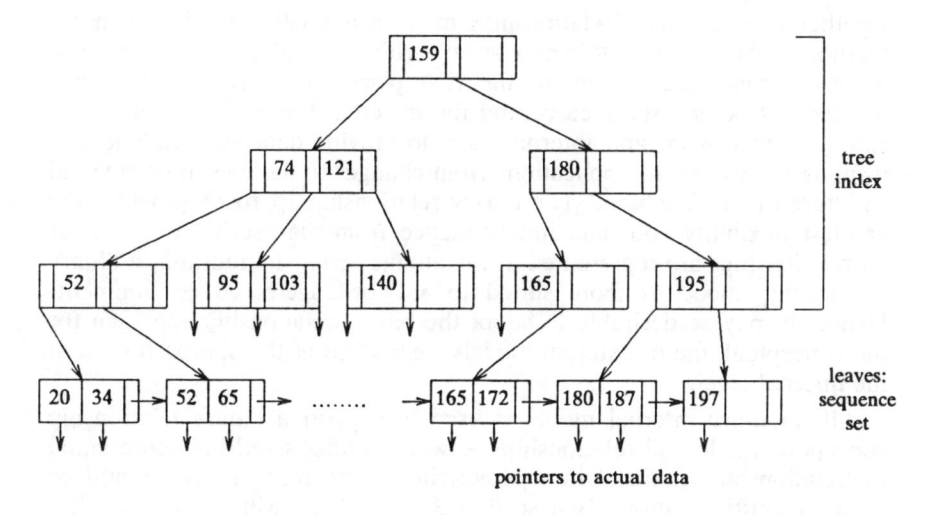

Figure 5.3 An Example of a B^+-tree Index

In summary, the characteristics of B-tree index organisation are:
. fast access via primary key to records at random, with predictable efficiency because index is balanced;
. good support for sequential retrieval;
. index may be quite large though.

Comments on relational database organisation techniques

The B^+-tree index is flexible and performs well for both random and sequential access; however, it will be seen in a later section that hashing techniques may also be used effectively in the processing of relational queries. It will also be seen that hashing and indexing techniques in general are applicable to other types of database.

5.3.2 Binary Relationship Databases

There are a number of possible alternative ways in which binary relationship databases may be physically stored.

N-ary relation organisation

The first alternative to be considered is to store the data as an n-ary relational internal model (see previous subsection) and map between the binary conceptual and n-ary internal views. This will entail collecting together related binary relationships to form a smaller number of n-ary relations. At first sight this may seem a ridiculous idea — why not have an n-ary conceptual model in the first place! However, as has been pointed out before, the idea behind the different levels of data model — external, conceptual and internal — is to provide data independence, to insulate the users and applications from changes to the logical or physical structure of the database. The binary relationship approach provides the greatest flexibility and data independence from the user's viewpoint, as all relationships are represented at the atomic level. In addition, a binary relationship model is more suited to a knowledge-based environment. Hence, it may be desirable to adopt the binary relationship approach for the conceptual and/or external models, regardless of the approach used at the internal level.

If an n-ary internal model is used to support a binary relationship conceptual model, all relationships between entities should be represented as 'relationship relations' in separate files — no foreign keys should be used in entity relations (see section 3.2.2). This will greatly simplify mappings between the conceptual and internal models, although there will be more relations to be stored.

Binary relation organisation

The second alternative is to store the binary relationships as actual binary relations, with each relationship type stored in a separate file. The relational database organisation techniques discussed in the previous section may be applied in this case. The advantages of this approach are firstly that the system is required to handle somewhat smaller files than in the n-ary approach, and secondly that all relations are of the same binary structure and hence simpler to manage (although the objects (attributes) will be of different types). Indexes can be set up to provide fast access to each relation in both the primary and the inverse direction.

One disadvantage, though, is the amount of storage space required by the relations and indexes, but this may be reduced by not providing indexes for all objects. Indexes may be created for selected objects only, with a possibility of hashed organisation being used for certain primary relationships, and heap for small relations. Some inverse relationships may be used so infrequently that indexes are not cost effective. For example, consider the 'located-at' relation:

located-at (Person, Address)

It is likely that this will only be used in the primary direction to find the address of a person, and not in the inverse direction to find the person with a particular address.

A second disadvantage is that the problem of multi-relation retrievals is many times greater than with n-ary relations due to the multiplicity of relations. The equivalent of a single record in an n-ary relation model is a set of binary relations, and to obtain related data about an entity therefore requires access to many relations, instead of just one in the n-ary approach. Techniques may be devised to minimise this problem though. For example, if, by means of appropriate rules/integrity constraints, the system can deduce that if a person entity has an entry in the 'is-named' relation, it must also have an entry in the 'located-at' and 'has-status' relations, then it can arrange to store the related information about a person by position so that a positional retrieval mechanism can be used. In this way, if a person's name is stored in the 'is-named' relation at record position n, then that person's address and status will also be stored at position n in the relevant relations. Thus, after having located one of these items by some mechanism (e.g. serial scan, hash table or index), the others may be directly located. However, this technique may give rise to a consequent reduction in flexibility.

Triple organisation and extensions

A third alternative for the binary relationship internal model is to store the facts in a single ternary relation — known as a *triple*. The triple consists of three elements: the two related objects and the name of the relationship between them; for example,

(p002, has-status, staff)

where 'has-status' is the relationship, and 'p002' and 'staff' are the two related objects (object1 and object2). Multiple indexes or hash tables can be used for accessing the triples. This solution is the simplest but most costly in terms of storage space and access time, given the current state of the art. A system which has been developed using the triple method is Asdas (Frost 1980), an experimental system for research into new storage organisations. The problem of access time has been overcome in this system by means of replicated data and dynamic hashing, but at the expense of storage space and additional overheads when updating data. The triples are held as a single set of data, replicated in six dynamic hash tables, one for each element and pair of elements in the triples; that is, there will be one table hashed on object1, one on object2, one on the relationship, and also tables hashed on the combinations: object1 + relationship, object1 + object2, and relationship + object2. Thus, if it is required to find out who has a status = 'staff', the query template would be:

(?, has-status, staff)

and the last hash table mentioned above will be accessed with the relationship value equal to 'has-status' and the object2 value equal to 'staff'. Some other implementations of binary relationship databases are summarised in Frost (1982).

Prolog binary facts could of course be stored as triples, since the predicate and the two arguments of a binary fact correspond to the relationship name and the two related objects of the triple. The Asdas mechanism cannot be used for Prolog rules which are in general n-ary. However, a Prolog binary database could be divided into a 'binary fact base' stored as triples and an 'n-ary rule base' stored in a different way. A rule could, for example, be identified in the triple fact base as follows:

(< rule name >, ref-rule, < identifier in rule base >)

e.g. (book-loan, ref-rule, r001)

where the relationship name 'ref-rule' identifies this fact as a reference to a rule called 'book-loan' with identifier 'r001'. The rules could be stored in the most convenient way (e.g. as strings or linked lists, identified internally by the identifiers in the fact base).

The triple (or 'heap of facts') approach is well suited to natural language query systems and artificial intelligence problems, since it has the simplest structure and facts can simply be added or removed as required. One major advantage of this approach is the ability to incorporate more meaning into the database by automatic, extensive and hierarchical indexing, thus providing categorization, generalization and inferencing mechanisms. Rules can of course be used for these purposes, as indicated in section 3.5.3, but extensive indexing provides greater flexibility and faster response, though at a cost in terms of index storage space and additional updating complexity. Indexing in relation to natural language fact retrieval is further discussed in Kolodner (1983). Kolodner points out that automatic indexing can get out of hand if unconstrained, but types of features relevant to certain categories may be defined in advance so that similar features do not get indexed separately.

Quadruples (McGregor 1984) and *quintuples* (Jiang 1985) are extensions of triples, designed to provide a more efficient and flexible basis for the storage and retrieval of binary relationship data. The quadruples are triples with a 'fact number' added as the fourth element; this enables facts to be combined so as to represent information of arbitrary complexity. McGregor & Malone have designed and developed hardware — the Fact machine — to provide high performance support for the quadruple storage structure. The quintuples have a fifth element — a 'truth' value (true, false, probable, etc.) — which is useful in an expert system environment.

Comments on binary relationship database organisation

In this discussion of the organisation and storage of binary relationship data, it may have been noticed that no mention has been made so far of the suitability of the different storage structures for the large volume data retrieval requirements of data processing applications. It is true to say that such requirements have been inadequately addressed (if at all) by those developing binary relationship systems. The first two storage approaches — n-ary relation, and binary file with positional retrieval facilities — can be adapted for large volume retrieval with sequential access capabilities by means of indexes, but more research needs to be carried out on the triple and other similar storage approaches.

5.3.3 Networks, Hierarchies and Database Organisation

In network and hierarchical data models, relationships between entities are explicit. In the associated internal models for such systems these relationships are commonly implemented by means of pointers, using such structures as linked lists, rings, and pointer arrays. These systems also use hashing or index mechanisms to provide initial entry points to the databases.

Network databases

Codasyl storage structures will be used to illustrate network database organisation. Cosets may be implemented by means of rings or pointer arrays. A *ring* is a linked list with the last object in the list pointing back to the first object. A coset implemented as a simple ring structure is illustrated in Figure 5.4.

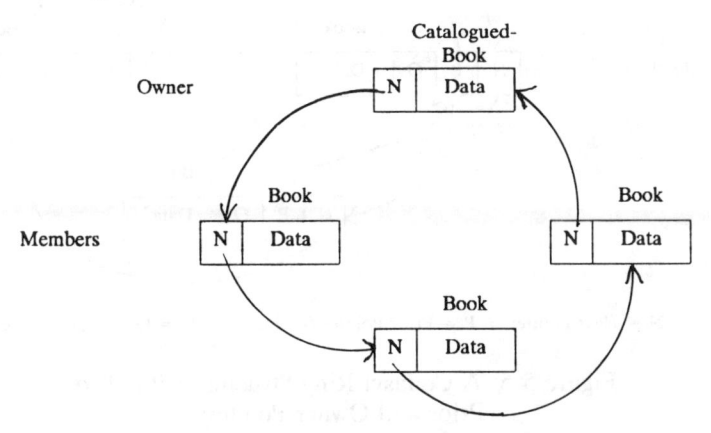

N = Next Pointer

Figure 5.4 A Simple Codasyl Ring Structure

This shows an occurrence of the 'has-copy' coset, with a Catalogued-Book record as owner and three Book records as members. The 'Data' indicates the data which the user sees in the relevant records. The pointer labelled N ('next' pointer) is transparent to the user and is used purely by the system for data retrieval purposes. The 'next' pointer points to the record which is physically next in sequence in a particular coset, with the owner of the coset pointing to the first member and the last member pointing back to the owner. In a Codasyl database, 'next' pointers are automatically provided by the system, but 'prior' and/or 'owner' pointers may optionally also be provided. This was briefly mentioned in section 3.3.3. The two relevant optional clauses provided by the Codasyl Schema DDL are 'SET IS PRIOR' indicating that prior pointers are to be set up to enable the coset to be accessed in a backwards direction, and 'LINKED TO OWNER' to indicate that pointers from each member record to the owner are to be set up. Figure 5.5 illustrates the previous coset with next (N), prior (P) and owner (O) pointers, all of which are transparent to the user.

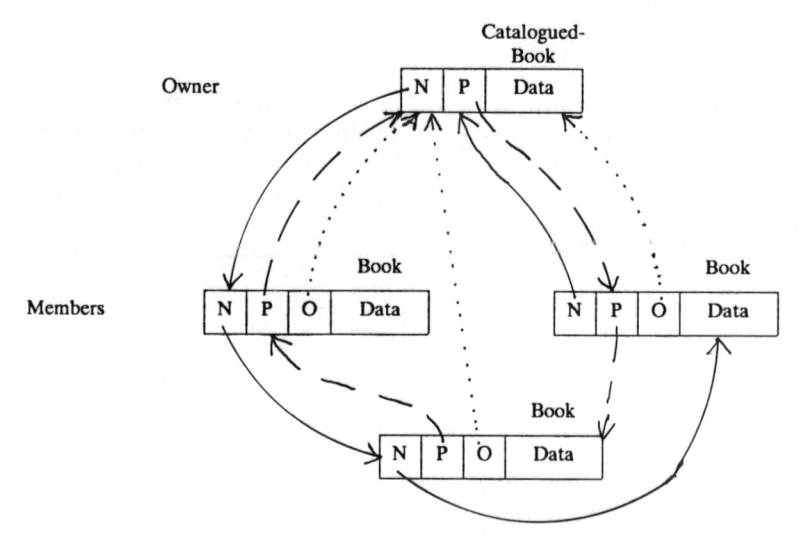

N = Next Pointer   P = Prior Pointer (optional)   O = Owner Pointer (optional)

Figure 5.5 A Codasyl Ring Structure with Next,
Prior and Owner Pointers

Note that the owner record does not, of course, need an owner pointer; it only has next and prior pointers. For each coset in which a particular record participates as a member, there will be a next pointer, and optionally, prior and owner pointers, while for each coset in which that record is an owner, there will be a next pointer, and optionally, a prior pointer. Thus a record which is an owner or member in n cosets will have n sets of coset pointers.

At first sight it might appear that the optional prior and owner pointers merely increase the storage requirement of the database. However, they are important for reducing access time for certain types of access. Hence, as usual, there is a trade-off between storage space and access time, and the database designer must refer to functional requirements and other usage information obtained during data investigation in order to determine the best combination of pointers for each coset type.

How can prior and owner pointers speed up database access? With next pointers only, efficient processing is possible from the owner record to all related member records in the coset. If one wishes to find the owner record for a given member record, however, the system must follow all the pointers from that member record round the ring to the owner record, which may be time-consuming if the coset has a large number of members. If owner pointers exist as well, finding an owner record is accomplished directly by following one pointer.

Prior pointers are particularly useful for updates. Adding or deleting member records in a coset requires the alteration of pointers. The pointers of records either side of a record to be deleted need to be altered and this is accomplished very simply with both next and prior pointers, but is more time-consuming with next pointers only, since the only way of accessing the record preceding the current one is to follow next pointers all the way round the coset.

Pointer arrays are an alternative to rings for implementing cosets. Such arrays would be associated with the owner record of a coset and would contain all the next pointers. The actual records would then contain only the user-defined data, plus owner pointers in member records if required.

Codasyl systems generally provide an optional hashing mechanism for accessing particular records directly rather than via coset membership. In addition, singular (system-owned) cosets provide fast access to the complete set of records of a particular type (a singular coset is similar to a relation). For a comprehensive discussion of storage and retrieval mechanisms in Codasyl databases, reference may be made to Olle (1978).

Hierarchical databases

IMS storage structures will now be considered briefly, as examples of a hierarchical internal model. IMS, developed by IBM, provides four storage structures: HSAM and HISAM (Hierarchical Sequential and Indexed Sequential Access Methods), and HDAM and HIDAM (Hierarchical Direct and Indexed Direct Access Methods). In IMS terminology, a complete hierarchical occurrence is referred to as a 'record', while the individual objects making up the hierarchy are referred to as 'segments'. Hence, looking back at Figure 3.9, the complete diagram would be referred to as an IMS record, while the individual objects: the Catalogued-Book object, together with related Book, Loan and Person objects, would be referred to individually as IMS segments, Catalogued-Book being the root segment. To avoid confusion with the conventional use of the term 'record', the term 'IMS record' will be used where relevant.

In a HSAM database the IMS records are stored serially, with the hierarchical sequence for the segments within an IMS record represented by physical contiguity. Thus the Catalogued-Book hierarchical occurrence illustrated in Figure 3.9 would be stored as follows:

...	CAT-BOOK 0-999-99999-0	BOOK 00023	BOOK 00060	LOAN 851231	PERSON Bloggs	BOOK 12345	LOAN 860115	PERSON Smith	...

To find specific hierarchical occurrences the database must be searched serially (cf. Cobol hierarchical files). HISAM basically provides indexed access to the root segments (Catalogued-Book records in the library example) and serial access to the other segments, although this is a slight simplification of the actual situation.

HDAM provides a hashing mechanism for storage of, and access to, the root segments, with a chaining mechanism for collisions, while HIDAM provides indexed access to root segments. With both HDAM and HIDAM hierarchical or child/twin pointers may be used for access to the other segments. Hierarchical pointers provide an unbroken sequence from a root segment occurrence to all other related segment occurrences. The logical sequence of segments would be the same as in the above example, but the physical sequence would be maintained by pointers rather than physical contiguity. Child/twin pointers, on the other hand, provide access from a 'parent' segment occurrence directly to the first occurrence of each related 'child' segment, and from a child segment to all of its 'twins' (related segment occurrences of the same type). This type of structure resembles the Codasyl coset structure, and provides access more directly to related segment occurrences than hierarchical pointers. An example to illustrate this type of structure is given in Figure 5.6. In the example, the pointers are 'child' (owner-to-member) and 'twin' (member-to-member) pointers. Catalogued-Book may have both Book and Reservation segments as children and therefore has two child pointers, but for the entry for the catalogued book with Isbn 0-999-99999-0 there are currently no reservations so only the Book child pointer is in use. Book 00023 only has a twin pointer to the next book which relates to the same catalogue entry, while Book 00060 has both a twin pointer and a child pointer to the related Loan segment. Book 12345 is the last book for this catalogue entry so has no twin pointer but it does have a child pointer.

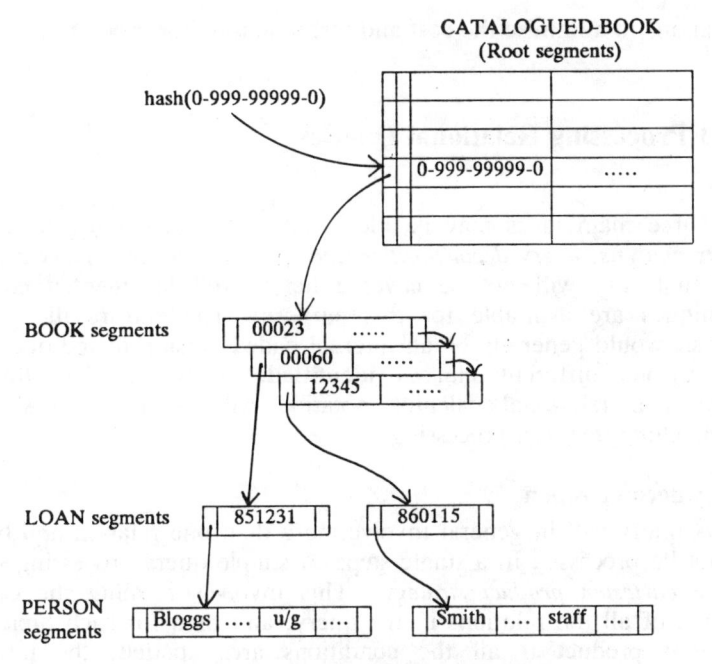

Figure 5.6 Example of IMS Hierarchical Direct Structure

This has been a very brief introduction to IMS storage mechanisms and readers are referred to Date (1981) for a fuller discussion, and to McGee (1977).

5.4 Query Processing

The second DBMS implementation aspect to be considered is that of query processing. It is particularly important in an interactive environment where fast response to ad-hoc queries is required, and hence efficient techniques must be employed. The execution of a query will generally involve a sequence of relatively low level database retrieval operations. When the query is expressed in a high level non-procedural language (e.g. QBE, Quel, QRS, and others discussed in Chapter 4), it must be decomposed into an appropriate sequence of these lower level operations. The fundamental problems of query processing relate to this decomposition task and also to the task of optimising the sequence of operations to minimise the cost and response time for processing.

5.4.1 Processing Relational Queries

Three main tasks may be identified in the processing of a query: *syntax analysis*, *query decomposition and optimisation*, and *query execution*. The first task will not be covered here; well-documented compiling techniques are available for this purpose. The end result of syntax analysis would generally be an internal coded version of the query, with the various different clauses identified. However, for illustrative purposes a relational calculus notation will be used to show the intermediate stages in processing.

Query decomposition

A query will in general involve more than one relation and hence it cannot be processed in a single step. A simple query processing strategy is the *cartesian product strategy*. This involves forming the cartesian product of all the relations in the query, and then for each tuple in the cartesian product if all the conditions are satisfied, the target list attributes for that tuple are placed in the result relation. The advantage of this strategy is its simplicity but the big disadvantage is the amount of storage space required for intermediate results and the time needed to form the cartesian product. A three-relation query, for example, with 5, 8 and 6 attributes respectively, and 20, 100, and 50 tuples respectively, would produce a cartesian product with 5 + 8 + 6 = 19 attributes and 20 x 100 x 50 = 100,000 tuples! A strategy such as this is obviously not economically feasible.

An alternative strategy is to break down a query into a sequence of subqueries, each of which can be processed in a single step, with the last subquery in the sequence producing the required results. This is referred to as the *decomposition strategy*.

To illustrate the decomposition process, consider the following query:

Find the title and book number of all books by J. Austen in the QA category due back after 31.12.85

The relational calculus version of the query is:

result (cb.Title, b.Book#) <—
  (∃ cb ∈ CATALOGUED-BOOK) (∃ b ∈ BOOK) (∃ l ∈ LOAN)
    cb.Isbn = b.Isbn ∧ b.Book# = l.Book#
    ∧ l.Date-due-back > "851231"
    ∧ cb.Author = "Austen J"
    ∧ cb.Classmark = "QA*"

("QA*" indicates all values which start with the characters "QA").

As can be seen, this query involves three relations: Catalogued-Book, Book and Loan. The query is first split into its individual components: the target list (labelled T), the linkage conditions (labelled L1 and L2), and the selection conditions (labelled C1, C2 and C3). The individual components of the query are listed in Figure 5.7.

    T: cb.Title, b.Book#
    L1: cb.Isbn = b.Isbn
    L2: b.Book# = l.Book#
    C1: l.Date-due-back > "851231"
    C2: cb.Author = "Austen J"
    C3: cb.Classmark = "QA*"

Figure 5.7 Query Components

An *incidence matrix* can now be formed with relations in the columns and the query components in the rows. A '1' is placed in a cell of the matrix if the relation represented by the column of the cell is involved in the query component represented by the row of the cell; the cell value is '0' otherwise. The incidence matrix for the above query is shown in Figure 5.8.

Query Component	Relation Name (tuple variable)		
	Catalogued Book (cb)	Book (b)	Loan (l)
T	1	1	0
L1	1	1	0
L2	0	1	1
C1	0	0	1
C2	1	0	0
C3	1	0	0

Figure 5.8 A Query Component Incidence Matrix

A *query tree* may be built up from the incidence matrix using the following rather simplified rules:
a) the selection conditions are used to create a set of subqueries which may be placed in any sequence at the top of the tree; all conditions relating to a particular relation are placed in the same subquery;
b) any linkage condition(s) involving the relation(s) in the target list form a subquery (or subqueries) which are last in sequence;
c) any remaining linkage conditions form subqueries in between those of a) and b).

From the above rules, according to a) C2 and C3 may be combined into one subquery and C1 will form another; according to b) T and L1 will form the last subquery in the sequence; this leaves L2 which according to c) will form a subquery in between. The query tree in Figure 5.9 is thus produced.

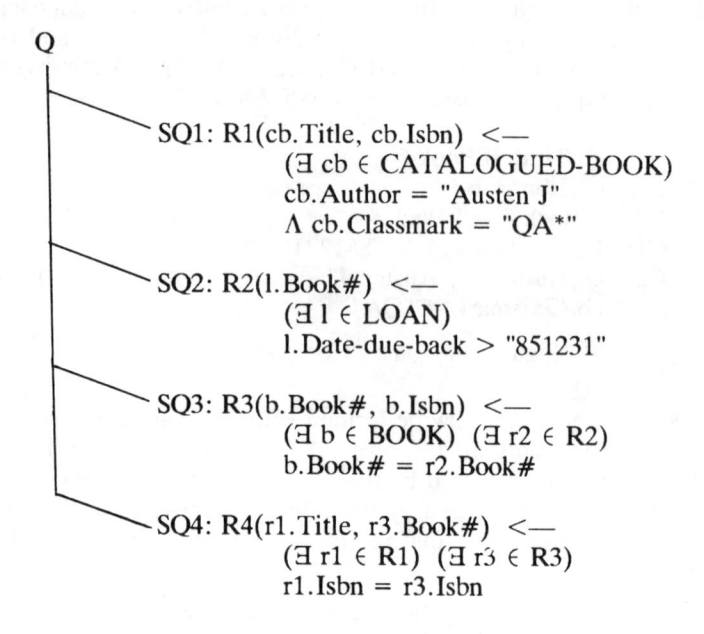

```
Q
├──▶ SQ1: R1(cb.Title, cb.Isbn) <—
│        (∃ cb ∈ CATALOGUED-BOOK)
│        cb.Author = "Austen J"
│        ∧ cb.Classmark = "QA*"
│
├──▶ SQ2: R2(l.Book#) <—
│        (∃ l ∈ LOAN)
│        l.Date-due-back > "851231"
│
├──▶ SQ3: R3(b.Book#, b.Isbn) <—
│        (∃ b ∈ BOOK) (∃ r2 ∈ R2)
│        b.Book# = r2.Book#
│
└──▶ SQ4: R4(r1.Title, r3.Book#) <—
         (∃ r1 ∈ R1) (∃ r3 ∈ R3)
         r1.Isbn = r3.Isbn
```

Figure 5.9 A Query Tree

The query tree represents the original query decomposed into a sequence of subqueries involving either a single relation or two relations. The target lists in each subquery consist of attributes which are used in other subqueries or which are referred to in the target list of the original query; e.g. Title and Isbn in R1 are used in R4. The set of single relation subqueries (SQ1 and SQ2 in the example) are in the top part of the tree and may be carried out in any sequence or in fact in parallel if parallel processing capabilities exist; the set of two-relation subqueries in the bottom part of the tree generally need to be carried out in sequence.

The query decomposition process described above is based on that presented in Wong (1976), but is a somewhat simplified version. The process of producing the query tree may also be referred to as *query detachment*.

The query tree can be mapped into an *object graph*, in which the objects (ellipses) represent either actual relations or single-relation subqueries which generate subrelations, and the edges (lines joining the ellipses) represent two-relation subqueries. An important property of object graphs is that they are based on a relational calculus version of the query (or similar representation), and although minor variations exist, all possess this property. An example of an object graph, representing the query tree in Figure 5.9, is given in Figure 5.10.

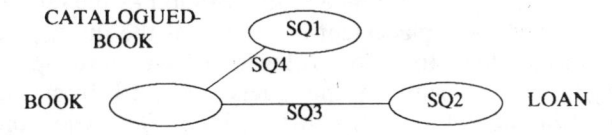

Figure 5.10 Object Graph Query Representation

An alternative graphical representation of a query is an *operator graph*, which is based on relational algebra. An example is given in Figure 5.11, derived from the subqueries in Figure 5.9.

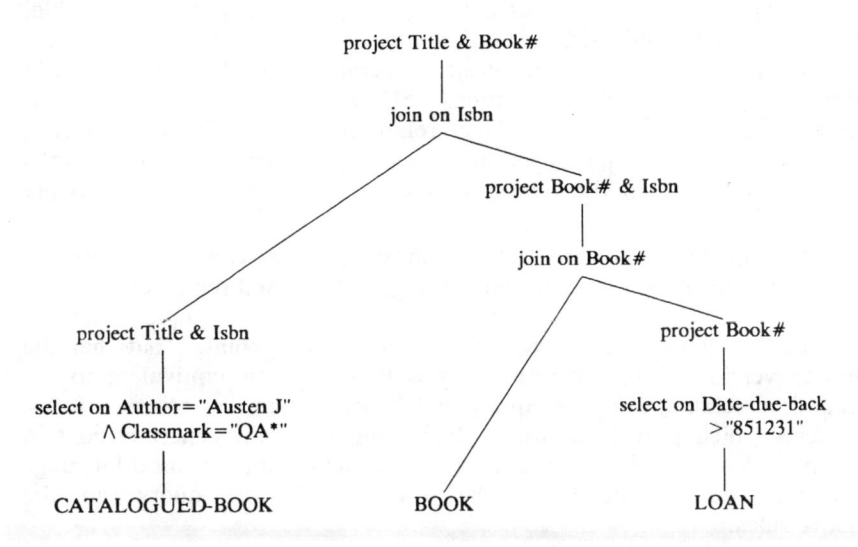

Figure 5.11 Operator Graph Query Representation

In this graph, the bottom level contains the relations in the query, while higher levels contain relational algebra operations to be performed on the relations or on the results of previous operations. At the top is a single operation which produces the final result.

Query optimisation

In the query decomposition process described above, the rules for building the query tree from the incidence matrix incorporate some elements of *query optimisation*. In the same way as one can write both efficient and inefficient computer programs to achieve the same result, one can express a query as an efficient or inefficient sequence of operations. The objective of optimisation is to transform an inefficient sequence into an efficient sequence.

In the decomposition process, the creation of the set of single-relation subqueries and their placement at the top of the query tree, ensures that relations which have to be joined together have those tuples and attributes which are not relevant to the query removed from them first, thus reducing the size of relations to be joined. The selection conditions in the single-relation subqueries reduce the number of tuples, while the target lists reduce the number of attributes. Thus, two basic rules for query optimisation are:

    (i) perform selections as early as possible in the processing;
    (ii) remove non-relevant attributes as soon as possible.

In relational algebra terms, this is equivalent to carrying out select and project operations on relations before join operations wherever possible. Note that SQ1 and SQ2 in the query tree of Figure 5.9 represent relational algebra select and project operations, while SQ3 and SQ4 represent join and project operations. SQ1 and SQ2 will produce subsets of the Catalogued-Book and Loan relations respectively, which means that the subsequent join operations will involve smaller relations than would be the case if the relations were joined before the selections are processed.

The application of the basic optimisation rules can also clearly be seen in the operator graph example of Figure 5.11, and readers may recall that these basic rules were applied to the second example relational algebra query in section 4.6; in addition, it was pointed out that the nested version of the corresponding SQL query was equivalent to the optimised relational algebra query and hence was in an optimised form. Systems which provide non-procedural languages will generally contain some form of optimiser, while those which provide a procedural language sometimes do not, and the user has to optimise his own query using the above rules.

Other optimisation rules can also be applied to queries, in addition to these basic rules. The optimisation of relational algebra queries is discussed in detail in a paper by Smith & Chang (Smith 1975); they adopt an operator graph form of query representation, with special symbols used to represent the relational algebra operations. A comprehensive discussion of query optimisation (including other aspects of query processing) is presented in Jarke (1984b). Query optimisation has a much larger role to play in the processing of a query in a distributed database environment and this will be discussed further in the next chapter.

Query execution

The decomposition and optimisation processes produce a sequence of subqueries which represents an optimised version of the original query. The next task in the processing of a relational query is *query execution*. The method of executing the subqueries which represent selections will depend on the organisation of the relevant relations. If at least one of the attributes in the selection condition of a subquery is indexed, then the index can be used for fast execution of the query, in particular in the case of an '=' condition. If one of the selection attributes is hashed, then the hashing algorithm can be applied but only if the conditional operator is '='. In all other cases a complete scan of the relation is necessary.

To execute the linkage subqueries a *join strategy* is required. Various strategies have been proposed over the years and a few of the alternatives are considered here.

In Ingres, for example, a tuple-substitution mechanism is used in conjunction with a 'one-variable query processor' (OVQP). The OVQP, as its name implies, processes subqueries involving one relation only. The selection subqueries are processed by the OVQP as well as the linkage subqueries, but in the latter case each linkage subquery is converted into a set of single-relation subqueries by means of tuple substitution. This is done by selecting the relation with the smallest number of tuples, and substituting relevant attribute values from each tuple of that relation into separate subqueries as constants (Stonebraker 1976).

Taking SQ3 as an example, the relations involved are Book and the Loan subset after selection (R2). It can be assumed that R2 will have fewer tuples than Book and hence R2 will be the tuple substitution relation. Using the Ingres strategy, SQ3 will be converted into the following set of single-relation subqueries, which will then be processed by the OVQP:

$R3_i$: (b.Book#, b.Isbn)
　　　($\exists$ b $\in$ BOOK)
　　　b.Book# = i^{th} Book# value from R2
for i = 1 to no. of tuples in R2

and R3 will then be formed from the union of all the $R3_i$ relations. Also, assuming R1 is selected for tuple substitution in SQ4, the following set of single-relation subqueries will be produced and processed:

$R4_i$: (i^{th} Title from R1, r3.Book#)
　　　($\exists$ r3 $\in$ R3)
　　　r3.Isbn = i^{th} Isbn from R1
for i = 1 to no. of tuples in R1

and R4 (i.e. the query result) is then the union of all the $R4_i$ relations. (Note the constant in the target list of $R4_i$, as well as in the selection condition.)

The execution of such a large number of subqueries might at first sight appear to be an inefficient strategy but two important points should be made. Firstly, Ingres hashes the relation which is not selected for tuple substitution on the linkage (join) attribute before executing the subqueries. This attribute becomes a selection attribute in the tuple-substitution subqueries, and since the conditional operator is '=', tuples which satisfy the condition may be found directly by hashing the constant in the condition. Hence, each subquery will involve a minimum of database accesses. A second point to note is that the Ingres strategy lends itself to application in a parallel processing environment. Not only can the original single-relation queries (e.g. SQ1 and SQ2) be carried out in parallel, but each set of tuple substitution subqueries can also be carried out in parallel. Thus, with parallel processing facilities available this strategy can produce very fast response times.

Some join strategies do not use Wong's query tree but instead use a set of join subqueries which can be derived from the individual query components (Figure 5.7) and the incidence matrix (Figure 5.8) during query decomposition. Each join required is identified by reference to the linkage components, and for each join the relevant selection components and target list elements are combined with the linkage component to form one of the subqueries. Referring to the example query, two join subqueries would be produced, one formed from C1 and L2 and based on the join of the Book and Loan relations, and the other formed from C2, C3, L1 and T and based on the join of the Catalogued-Book and Book relations. The two join subqueries are:

JSQ1: JR1 (b.Book#, b.Isbn)
($\exists$ b $\in$ BOOK) ($\exists$ l $\in$ LOAN)
b.Book# = l.Book#
$\wedge$ l.Date-due-back > "851231"

JSQ2: JR2 (cb.Title, jr1.Book#)
($\exists$ cb $\in$ CATALOGUED-BOOK) ($\exists$ jr1 $\in$ JR1)
cb.Isbn = jr1.Isbn
$\wedge$ cb.Author = "Austen J"
$\wedge$ cb.Classmark = "QA*"

Blasgen (1977) describes four join algorithms, whose performance depends on a number of factors, including the organisation of the relations (in particular, whether indexes exist for appropriate attributes), the number of tuples in the relations, the amount of main storage space available for intermediate results, the ratio of the number of tuples in each relation after applying the selection conditions to the original number of tuples, etc. Of Blasgen's four algorithms, the first one performs well under most conditions so long as indexes exist on the join attributes. It is applied to join subqueries as described above, and is given below in outline. R1 and R2 represent the two relations involved in a particular join subquery, and I1 and I2 represent the respective indexes on the join attributes.

The *index nested loop* algorithm:
    scan I1 and I2 to find a pair of tuples with a matching
        join value.
    if a match is found then
        if there is no selection condition for R1
            then retrieve the first tuple from R1 with
                the relevant join value
            else retrieve tuples from R1 with the relevant
                join value until one is found which
                satisfies the selection condition or there
                are no more tuples in R1 with that join value
    if a satisfactory R1 tuple has been found then
        retrieve all tuples from R2 which match the
            join value, apply the selection condition,
            and store the required attributes
            in temporary storage if the condition is
            satisfied.
        if any satisfactory R2 tuples have been found
            then join the required attributes from
                the R1 tuple with each of the
                tuples in temporary storage
            retrieve any other tuples from R1 with
                the same join value, and join
                those which satisfy any R1 selection
                condition with each of the tuples
                in temporary storage
    return to the beginning and continue the
        scan of I1 and I2 to find a
        pair of tuples with another matching join value.

An algorithm similar to this can be used if the relations are hashed on the join attributes, rather than indexed.

Blasgen's second algorithm is a *sort/merge* algorithm and works with subqueries in Wong's query tree form. The single-relation subqueries are processed first, and then the two-relation subqueries are processed by sorting the relations on the join attribute and scanning the two sorted files to find pairs of tuples with matching join attribute values. This algorithm does not depend on indexes but incurs the cost of two sort operations.

The third algorithm performs well if sufficient main memory is available to hold one of the relations after applying any selection conditions and removing attributes which are not required, while the fourth performs well if indexes exist on the selection attributes as well as the join attributes. These are not described here.

It is, of course, possible to implement more than one join algorithm in a system and select the algorithm for each join as appropriate to the relations involved. This approach has been adopted in System R (Chamberlin 1981).

The objective of this subsection has been to give some impression of the different approaches which have been used in the processing of relational queries. These are aimed at minimising the number of accesses required to external storage, in order to provide fast response to ad-hoc queries. It should be noted that most depend on the availability, or the creation, of appropriate indexes or hash tables to improve performance. Many other approaches also exist.

5.4.2 Processing Binary Relationship Queries

In this subsection, two strategies for processing queries on a logic database composed of facts and rules are discussed, together with some comments about binary relationship query processing in general. The first strategy is that adopted in Prolog (Clocksin 1981) and the second is a relational algebra approach (Ullman 1985). In both cases a query is assumed to consist of a conjunction of 'goals' (i.e. the components (goals) of the query are linked by the 'and' connective). As a reminder, a Prolog query is specified using a fact or the head of a rule as a template. If the query involves a rule, the body of the relevant rule contains the goals to be satisfied, and the goals are either fact templates or rule templates. The query represents a conjunction of goals if they are all linked by a ',' (the Prolog 'and' connective) (discussed in section 4.5.4). Both of the strategies which will be considered can be applied to a database of n-ary facts and rules, as well as binary fact databases.

The Prolog strategy

The strategy adopted by Prolog is to attempt to satisfy each goal involved in the query from left to right. Prolog starts its processing from the beginning of the database and whenever a particular goal is satisfied, a labelled place-marker is left in the database at the point of satisfaction. Relevant variables in the goal become instantiated at that point, and all occurrences of those variables in the query also become instantiated. Prolog then moves to the goal next on the right and attempts to satisfy it, again starting from the beginning of the database and again leaving a labelled place-marker if it can satisfy the goal. When a goal fails (e.g. no matching fact can be found), Prolog *backtracks* by returning to the goal on the left of the failed goal, which becomes the new current goal, uninstantiating all variables which were previously instantiated at that goal, and then attempting to resatisfy that goal by restarting the database search at its place-marker. If, by successive backtracking, Prolog eventually ends up back at the leftmost (first) goal and this goal fails, the query fails (i.e. it produces a null response).

An example will illustrate this process. Consider the rule:

recent-titles (T, A) :-
    entitled (CB, T),   written-by (CB, A),
    published-in (CB, Year),   Year > 1984.

The query:

recent-titles (Title, 'Austen J').

requests the titles of all books by J. Austen published since 1984. The expanded query, with actual variables and constants replacing the relevant arguments in the rule, is:

recent-titles (Title, 'Austen J') :-
    entitled (CB, Title),   written-by (CB, 'Austen J'),
    published-in (CB, Year),   Year > 1984.

Prolog first attempts to satisfy the goal: entitled (CB, Title); as soon as a fact is found which satisfies this, a marker with a label identifying this goal is placed at that point. The variables CB and Title are instantiated with the values in the fact which has been found (e.g. CB = cb001 and Title = 'Data Models') and CB is also instantiated to the value: cb001 in the other goals in the query. Prolog then moves on to the next goal, which is now: written-by (cb001, 'Austen J'), and starts searching the database again from the beginning. If a matching fact can be found, another marker is placed at that point and the 'published-in' goal is then considered. Assuming that can be satisfied, Year will be instantiated, and the final goal is the simple condition: Year > 1984. If that is satisfied, the complete query is satisfied, and one answer is produced, with the variable referred to in the query, i.e. Title, instantiated to the relevant value. Further answers are obtained by continuing the database search from the last place-marker which was left in the database, i.e. that relating to the 'published-in' goal in the example. When the search relating to that is exhausted, Prolog backtracks to the 'written-by' goal and continues its search for further answers to the query from that place-marker. If another matching 'written-by' fact is found, Prolog moves to the goal on the right again and a search through the database for satisfactory 'published-in' facts is again made. This procedure is continued, until eventually the place-marker for the leftmost goal, i.e. 'entitled' in the query, has reached the end of the database, and all possible answers to the query will have been located.

The Prolog query processing strategy is sometimes referred to as a *depth-first*, a *nested loop*, or a *tuple-at-a-time* strategy. Note that the use of place-markers in this strategy has some similarities with the currency indicators used when navigating round a Codasyl data model.

Logic-based relational algebra strategy

Ullman has commented that the Prolog strategy does not enable one to use efficient methods for linking (joining) goals, and suggests alternative strategies for logic query processing (Ullman 1985). The strategy to be discussed here is a *logic-based relational algebra strategy* and can be used as long as the rules involved are not recursive. A query is first represented as a rule/goal tree with each node representing a rule or a fact. Then, starting from the bottom of this tree, a relation is built for each node according to certain rules. A simplified version of the rules for building relations from the nodes are as follows:

1. If the node is a leaf node representing a fact:
    the value of that node is the relation representing that fact after any selections implied by the arguments associated with the fact have been applied (i.e. if there is a constant instead of a variable in a particular argument position, this implies a selection on the associated attribute).
2. If the node is a leaf node representing a condition:
    the value of that node is the unary relation representing the set of values satisfying the condition. (Note: an infinite set, such as Year > 1984, can be replaced by its finite complement, i.e. not (Year <= 1984), assuming positive years; alternatively, if there is a range constraint on Year in the database, a finite set can be produced e.g. [1985, 1986]).
3. If the node represents a rule for which
    all 'child' relations have been computed:
    the value of that node is the relation computed by the natural join of the 'child' relations using variables with the same names for joining, followed by the projection of attributes corresponding to the variables referred to in the rule head.
    (Note: join strategies were discussed in subsection 5.4.1.)

An example will illustrate this approach. Assume that the 'recent-titles' rule introduced earlier in this subsection has a modified head as follows (with the body of the rule as before):

recent-titles (CB, T, A) :-
    entitled (CB, T),   written-by (CB, A),
    published-in (CB, Year),   Year > 1984.

Assume also that two other rules exist:
    onloan (CB) :-
        has-copy (CB, B),   lent-to (B, L).

```
recent-titles-onloan (T, A) :-
    recent-titles (CB, T, A),    onloan (CB, Isbn).
```
Consider the query:
```
recent-titles-onloan (Title, Author).
```
This will produce the rule/goal tree in Figure 5.12.

```
                    1. recent-titles-onloan (Title, Author)
                                     |
                    2. recent-titles-onloan (T, A) :-
                           /                      \
          3. recent-titles (CB, T, A)          4. onloan (CB)
          /       /        \        \           /            \
5. entitled  6. written-by  7. published-in  8. Year > 1984  9. has-copy  10. lent-to
  (CB, T)    (CB, A)        (CB, Year)                        (CB, B)      (B, L)
```

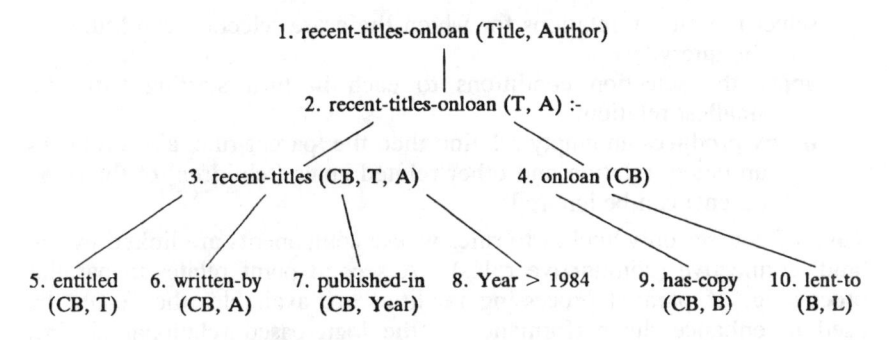

Figure 5.12 A Rule/Goal Tree

In the tree, node 1 is the original query as input by the user. Node 2 is the rule associated with that query; note that the variables specified by the user have been replaced by variables in the rule as stored in the database. The nodes at lower levels represent the rules expanded according to their bodies. The leaves of the tree are facts or conditional expressions.

Applying the rules which were given earlier for building relations for each node, rule 1 applies to nodes 5, 6, 7, 9 and 10, and the relations representing these facts will be generated. Rule 2 applies to node 8 and a unary relation corresponding to the set [1985, 1986] will be generated (assuming a range constraint on Year exists). Rule 3 then applies to node 3 and node 4. In the case of node 3, the relations generated at nodes 7 and 8 will be joined on the variable Year and the result will be joined with nodes 5 and 6 on the variable CB to produce a relation containing the variables CB, T, A and Year; CB, T and A will be projected from this to produce the relation representing the rule in node 3. In the case of node 4, the relations generated at nodes 9 and 10 will be joined on the variable B, and CB will be projected from the result to produce the relation representing the rule in node 4. Rule 3 applies to node 2, relations at nodes 3 and 4 being joined on CB, and T and A projected. Finally, the relation at node 2 becomes the result relation at node 1 by renaming the variables.

Comments on binary relationship query processing

Some general comments regarding binary relationship query processing will now be made. Firstly, if the logic-based relational algebra strategy discussed above is used with a binary relationship database in which each binary relation is stored in a separate file (as in the second approach discussed in subsection 5.3.2), an optimised version of rule 1 might be:

- select the binary relations for which there are selection conditions in the query;
- apply the selection conditions to each in turn starting with the smallest relation;
- if any produces an empty relation then the 'parent rule' also produces an empty relation and other related goals ('children' of the same parent) can be ignored.

This, of course, only applies to rules whose components are linked by the 'and' connective (conjunctive rules). A second point relates to parallel processing; if parallel processing facilities are available, they could be used to enhance the performance of the logic-based relational algebra strategy. This is an important point considering the comment made in subsection 5.3.2 regarding the multiplicity of joins in the binary relationship approach. Parallel processing of goals could make a significant difference to performance. A further comment: although Ullman has criticised the Prolog strategy as being one which does not permit the use of efficient methods for linking goals, it should be noted that if the database is organised using hash tables or indexes, efficient processing using the Prolog strategy is possible. The value of a variable which has been instantiated by the satisfaction of one goal can be used to access the appropriate hash table or index (if one exists) for the next goal.

5.4.3 Processing Codasyl Queries

In this subsection the processing of queries on a database with physical pointers will be illustrated by means of a Codasyl example. The important advantage of the Codasyl coset and associated storage organisations is that they provide fast access to data for predictable data retrieval requirements. Access to a complete set of records of a particular type can be obtained by means of a singular coset, assuming such a requirement is known at the database design stage. Access to related records of different types is achieved by following the relevant pointers from owner to member, or vice versa, and from coset to coset. Assuming the relevant relationships have been identified at the data modelling and database design stages, related records will be explicitly linked and no specific join mechanism is required.

However, additional techniques can still be used to improve retrieval efficiency even for predicted retrievals where access paths have been built into the data model. Two possibilities are considered here. One is to change the order of traversing the network model from that given in the query. The second is to defer retrieval of a record to avoid duplicating retrievals.

Changing order of traversal

To illustrate the first case — changing the order of traversal — an example query will be used. Suppose it is required to find the names of those people who have reserved books by J. Austen. Referring to the Codasyl network diagram in Figure 3.6, the QRS (MDBS III) query might be expressed by a user as:

LIST Name **FOR** Author = "Austen J"
    THRU person-list, has-reservation-of, > reserved-by

In outline, this might be processed as follows:

for each Person in the person-list coset
  for each Reservation in the associated has-reservation-of coset
    find the relevant Catalogued-Book record
      (i.e. the owner of the reservation
      in the reserved-by coset)
    and if the Author is "Austen J"
      print the current Person's Name

This particular query has a selection on Catalogued-Book, and it may be remembered that in the processing of relational queries, selections were, if possible, executed first to reduce the size of relations for subsequent joins. Similarly in the case of Codasyl queries, efficiency of processing can be improved if selections are processed as early as possible. Hence, an optimised form of the QRS query would be:

LIST Name **FOR** Author = "Austen J"
    THRU catalogue-list, reserved-by, > has-reservation-of

processed in outline as:

for each Catalogued-Book in the catalogue-list coset
    for which the Author = "Austen J"
  for each Reservation in the associated reserved-by coset
    find the relevant Person record
      (i.e. the owner of the reservation
      in the has-reservation-of coset)
    and print the Person's Name

In this case, instead of locating all the reservation records in the database as previously, only those related to catalogued books which satisfy the condition will be located. Also, if the member record type of the catalogue-list coset has been declared to be sorted by Author in the schema, searching through the catalogue-list coset can stop when a Catalogued-Book record with Author > "Austen J" is found.

In the MDBS system it is actually up to the user to specify his query efficiently, but an optimizer could be provided for this purpose to remove the responsibility for efficient query specification from the user.

Deferred retrieval

The second technique for improving efficiency of Codasyl query processing will now be considered; this is the deferred retrieval of records. The optimised query in the previous case will be used as an example. The general algorithm for processing a query, which was outlined above, may be referred to as a *record-at-a-time following links method*. H. Chen (1984) has suggested an alternative mechanism which may be referred to as the *sort owner key method*. It can only be applied when owner pointers exist in the relevant cosets or when owner keys are held as attributes in the member records. He provides three variants of the method: a one-relation, two-relation, or parallel variant; which one of these should be selected depends on the nature of the query in relation to the database. The one-relation strategy is considered here. It requires a single sort and merge for each retrieval which involves following a path from member to owner record type in a coset. For the previous query, the outline procedure following Chen's method would be as follows:

for each Catalogued-Book in the catalogue-list coset
    for which the Author = "Austen J"
  for each Reservation in the associated reserved-by coset
    save the pointer to, or key of, the owner of
      the reservation in the has-reservation-of coset

sort the saved owner pointers/keys and eliminate duplicates

for each pointer/key, retrieve the corresponding Person record
    and print the Name

If owner pointers are available, these are saved in preference to the owner keys. The cost involved is that of storing and sorting the owner keys or pointers; the saving is in not retrieving multiple copies of the same record, which can be very significant with some large databases.

Chen shows that this is a good strategy to use when there is a true many-to-one relationship between member and owner record types in a coset which is to be traversed from member to owner, and when no target list or selection attributes are involved in the coset. If the relationship is really one-to-one, the general algorithm is best — there is no possibility of duplicate owner records being retrieved; and when attributes from the records in the coset need to be saved for the target list or use in later selection operations, this increases the size of the information to be saved and sorted, and it may not be possible to process this information in main memory. The other two variants proposed by Chen — two-relation and parallel — involve two sorts in each case but may produce better results when target list and selection attributes are involved.

5.5 Database Protection — Reliability, Security and Integrity

The third DBMS implementation aspect to be considered is database protection. In Chapter 1 it was mentioned that one of the problems of the traditional file approach is the lack of centralised control over the reliability, security and integrity of the database. One of the important tasks of a DBMS is to ensure that the database is protected as far as possible against
(i) accidental loss or damage,
(ii) unauthorised access,
(iii) violation of integrity and consistency.

The first type of protection is referred to as *reliability*, the second as *security*, and the third as *integrity*. Different techniques are appropriate for the different types of protection and each of these are considered in turn. They are summarised in Table 5.3.

Type of protection	How to achieve it	Techniques available
Reliability	Ensure that the database can always be recreated, following corruption, loss or damage	Backup copies Transaction logging Before- and after-images Checkpoints
Security	Ensure that only those who are permitted access may gain access	Privacy locks and keys (passwords) Authorization rules
Integrity	Ensure that the database is internally consistent and valid	Validation rules Concurrent access locks and rules

Table 5.3 Database Protection

5.5.1 Database Reliability

A company whose operations revolve round the database cannot just stop working if the database is unavailable for some reason; it must always be available, or at least any down-time must be minimal. This means that facilities must be available for the fast recovery of the database to a usable state if it becomes corrupt or is accidentally damaged in some way. Facilities available for this purpose are *backing up* and *transaction logging / audit trails*, together with *before- and after-images*, and *checkpoints*. These facilities will first be discussed, followed by a discussion of the recovery methods used for the different types of failure.

Recovery facilities

It is important that *backup copies* of the database are held, with at least one copy in a separate location to guard against destruction in the event of fire, flood, etc. How frequently the backing up is done depends on the size and importance of the data, how frequently it is changed, etc. If some parts of the database are more volatile than others, and these parts are in separate physical files, full backups need not be done so frequently. Instead, partial backups of the volatile files can be done when considered necessary.

Transaction logging involves the creation of a special file which contains information about the start and end of each transaction and any updates which occur in the transaction. It is sometimes referred to as an *audit trail*. At any point in time it is likely that there will be many users or applications currently using the database. Each user or application will carry out a series of transactions on the database. A single command/statement may represent a separate transaction, or a sequence of commands/statements may be grouped together to represent a transaction. Each transaction will be identified according to the user or application program initiating it.

When a transaction requires an update to be carried out on the database, *before-images* and *after-images* will be placed in the transaction log. A before-image is a copy of an object (e.g. a record) as it exists in the database before it is updated. An after-image is a copy of an object taken immediately after it has been updated. The use of these 'images' will be illustrated later. They are sometimes referred to as before- and after-looks.

A *checkpoint* is a marker placed in the transaction log at a point in time when any outstanding updates which are in temporary buffers are written permanently to the database; this will occur periodically. It provides summary information regarding all active transactions at that point in time.

Recovery methods

Recovery from different types of failure will now be considered. Firstly, a *disc failure*. If a disc failure occurs and the contents of the disc are corrupted, the most recent backup copy will need to be brought into use. It will be brought up-to-date as far as possible by applying the after-images on the transaction log up to the latest checkpoint in the log. At this point, those transactions which were active will need to be 'undone' by means of the before-images in order to restore the database to a consistent state. This recovery mechanism is illustrated in Figure 5.13.

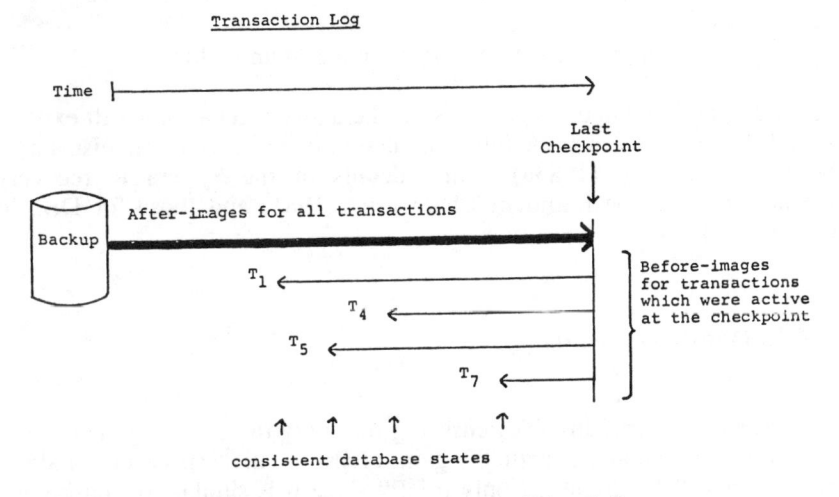

Figure 5.13 Recovery from a Disc Failure

A second type of failure is a *system failure*. In this case, the current version of the database may be usable but cannot be guaranteed to be consistent or valid. To restore it to a known valid state, before-images are applied from the transaction log back to a checkpoint, and then back further for those transactions which were active at the time the checkpoint was taken. This is illustrated in Figure 5.14.

Finally, a *transaction failure* only requires the before-images for the failed transaction to be applied to the current database. This type of recovery can take place online without affecting other active transactions. The other two types require that the database is taken out of use for a period, which should be quite short in the case of a system failure but may be longer in the case of a disc failure since a backup copy needs to

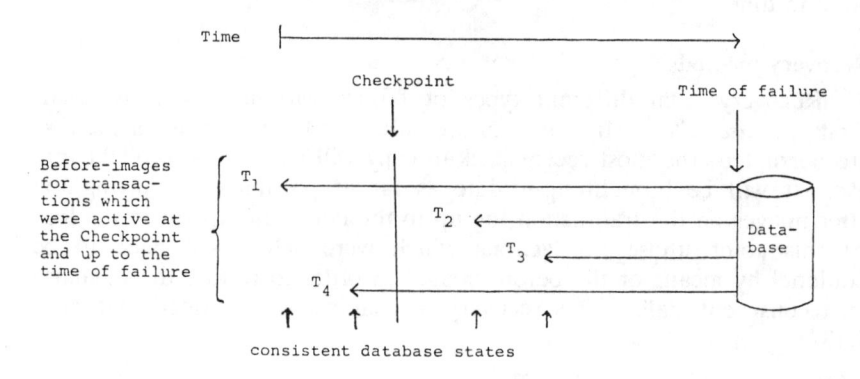

Figure 5.14 Recovery from a System Failure

be loaded and updated. Variations on the above mechanisms will exist in actual database systems. A fuller discussion of recovery mechanisms may be found in Date (1983a), while details of the System R recovery mechanisms may be found in Chamberlin (1981) and those for DB2 in Crus (1984).

5.5.2 Database Security

Database security involves ensuring that only those who are permitted access to the database actually gain access. This aspect of database protection will be discussed only briefly since it is similar to well-known file security and computer security mechanisms.

Database security involves providing *passwords* and *authorizations*. Users may need to provide passwords to access the database at different levels. Codasyl systems, for example, provide an optional privacy lock mechanism which can be set at database, coset, record, and data item levels for different types of operation such as read, modify, delete, etc. An alternative is to provide an authorization rule mechanism so that rules can be specified to authorize specific users to access certain parts of the database for certain operations. In System R, for example, a SQL GRANT statement is available for this purpose. Authorizations can be granted by the creator of a relation to other users for read only, update, and/or delete operations. The owner of the relation can also give other users grant privelege, and he can also revoke previously granted authorizations. Authorization rules can also be applied to views, providing control over access in smaller units than a complete relation, maybe to a single tuple only. This is discussed in Chamberlin (1981). Other aspects of database security are discussed in Date (1983).

5.5.3 Database Integrity

The primary reason why maintaining the integrity of the data is a problem in a database environment is that there may be many users accessing the database at the same time. Without careful control their transactions may interfere with each other and render the database invalid and/or internally inconsistent. A further cause of integrity violation is invalid updates, which can occur in a traditional file environment as well. The integrity of the database is maintained by means of *validation rules* which are applied to input and update data, and *concurrent access locks and rules* which prevent concurrent transactions from interfering with each other.

Validation
Validation rules will be considered first as they are the simplest. The need for, and provision of, validation rules has existed for many years. Data can be mistyped or just simply be in error on input, and certain mechanisms are available and checks can be carried out to ensure that such errors are detected as far as possible. Some standard mechanisms are: check digits attached to codes, range checks, sequence checks, and consistency checks. For example, Isbn numbers include a modulus-11 check digit and can thus be checked for validity, a person's status can be checked to see if it is in the range of valid statuses, and so on. Details of validation mechanisms and validity checks which can be carried out may be found in most books on data processing.

Concurrent access control
Concurrent access control is a somewhat more difficult task. The classic concurrent update problem situation may be outlined as follows:
Consider two users, A and B, both of whom wish to update an item in record X. The following sequence of events occurs:
A reads X (item value = 150)
B reads X (item value = 150)
A adds 20 to the item and rewrites X to the database
B deducts 10 from the item and rewrites X to the database.
This particular sequence of events, in which A's and B's updates interact with each other, produces an item value of 140 at the end when it should be 160. This is because A's update has been completely destroyed by B's update.

One way of preventing this from happening is to permit serial execution of transactions only. In this case, A must process his complete transaction before B is allowed to start his (or vice versa, since the end result after both transactions have been processed will be the same and will be correct, regardless of the order of processing the transactions). However, this solution completely removes one of the advantages which a database approach is supposed to have over a traditional file approach, and that is shared access to data. The objective of concurrency control, therefore, is to enable transactions to run concurrently as far as possible, but controlled in such a way that the effect is the same as it would have been if they had been run serially; this is referred to as *serializable execution* and is defined by Bernstein as follows:

"An execution is *serializable* if it is computationally equivalent to a serial execution, that is, if it produces the same output and has the same effect on the database as some serial execution." (Bernstein 1981a)

One way of providing serializable execution of transactions is by means of a *locking mechanism*. For example, if A locks X before he reads it, B will not be able to access X until A has released the lock. A can complete his update, before B is allowed to read and update X. Thus concurrent access is controlled and the database remains valid. Locks may be classified as read (retrieve) or write (update) locks, and in some systems there is a provision for them to be held for exclusive, protected or unrestricted use. They may be applied to different types of object (relations, cosets, records, data items, etc.). In some situations (e.g. 'read-only' situations) no problem can arise if two or more users access the same data object concurrently. It is only when updates are to be carried out that concurrent access can cause a loss of database integrity. Concurrent access rules are therefore provided to determine which combinations of read/write locks are permissible, so that as many transactions as possible can run concurrently. The overall objective in the design of a concurrent access mechanism is to obtain maximum possible concurrency (and hence utilisation of resources) and minimum possible delay in processing transactions. In the simple case of read/write locks only, the following table might be used to control access:

Object already locked for:-	User allowed to lock for	
	Read	Write
Not locked	Yes	Yes
Read	Yes	No
Write	No	No

In the case of locks for exclusive, restricted or unrestricted use, more elaborate concurrent access rules are necessary. For example, if an object has been locked for exclusive use, no other user will be allowed to access that record while it is locked; if it has been locked for protected retrieval, another user may be allowed to lock it for protected or unrestricted retrieval but not for update; while if it has an unrestricted lock on it, another user may be allowed also to put an unrestricted lock on, but not a protected or exclusive lock. These are just some of the possible combinations for which rules would be provided.

Deadlock detection and prevention

The main problem which has to be overcome with locking mechanisms is that of *deadlock*. This can arise when two or more users require access to more than one object for a transaction, and each has locked one of the required objects but requires another which the other user has locked. For example:

A has locked X and requires Y
B has locked Y and requires X

Neither can do anything — deadlock. Thus concurrent access mechanisms usually incorporate techniques either for deadlock prevention or deadlock detection.

In the case of deadlock detection, once deadlock has been detected one of the transactions must be backed out to release the necessary locks and enable the other transaction to continue. The backed out transaction is then restarted once the locks have been released by the other transaction.

Deadlock can be prevented, however, if users and applications are required to lock all required objects at the start of a transaction. In this case a user will either have locks on all the required objects and his transaction can therefore be processed to completion; or alternatively he will not have any locks at all and will need to wait until the objects which are locked have been freed. The success of this mechanism depends on the *locking granularity*. Locking granularity relates to the level of object for which locks may be specified (e.g. file/relation, coset, record, or data item/attribute). If locks are at file/relation level there is more chance that other users and applications will be 'locked out' and have to wait, and hence the degree of concurrency will be low and resources underutilised. If, however, locks are at record level (or even data item level) more users will be able to access the database concurrently, but the management of locks will require more storage space and time overheads due to the larger number of locks which are involved. A variety of locking levels may actually be provided in a DBMS, from a single record to many relations or files; both System R (Chamberlin 1981) and DB2 (Cheng 1984), for example, provide various levels of locking granularity.

Acquiring all the locks required for a transaction before releasing any is referred to as a *two-phase locking protocol*. Although this protocol ensures database integrity, it only ensures a deadlock-free environment if all the locks are acquired in a single step (so that either all or none are acquired as discussed above). This strategy does not necessarily produce the optimum degree of concurrency, though, and alternative deadlock prevention mechanisms are available. Locking and deadlock prevention are discussed in detail in Date (1983), and concurrency control in Codasyl systems is discussed in Olle (1978).

'Optimistic' concurrency control

Locking may be considered to be a pessimistic concurrency control mechanism, since it assumes that there will always be transactions requiring access to the same objects at the same time. An alternative approach suggested by Kung & Robinson (Kung 1981) is based on an *optimistic* view which assumes that conflicts will only occur very rarely. Two mechanisms are proposed which do not use locks and hence cannot give rise to deadlock situations. The retrieval of data from the database is allowed to be carried out without restriction; only updating the database is restricted. Updating consists of three phases. In the first phase, objects are retrieved without restriction and local copies of them are updated as required by the transaction. In the second phase, called validation, a check is made to see whether the update would cause a loss of database integrity if it were carried out on the database; this might occur, for example, if some other transaction has retrieved or updated the same object concurrently. In the third phase, which takes place only if the validation phase is satisfactory, the updates are made permanent in the database. If the validation phase fails, which is assumed to be a rare occurrence, the transaction is backed out (using the transaction log referred to in section 5.5.1) and restarted.

Two validation algorithms are described in Kung (1981). They involve comparing the set of objects retrieved and/or updated by concurrent transactions and comparing the timing of the operations, in order to determine whether there are objects in common between the transactions and if so whether the order of processing the objects has invalidated the transaction being checked. Alternative validation schemes for optimistic concurrency control mechanisms have also been suggested (Unland 1983). The objective of optimistic concurrency control is to increase the degree of concurrency as compared with locking concurrency control mechanisms.

Timestamping

Locking mechanisms have so far dominated the concurrency control scene in centralised DBMSs, but an alternative which is gaining popularity, in particular in a distributed database environment, is *timestamping*. Timestamps may be used on their own without locks, or in conjunction with locks to avoid deadlock situations. A timestamp is a unique number assigned to a transaction or a data object. It may be taken from the internal clock of the computer or it may be a serial number maintained by the DBMS. The basic principles of timestamping will be mentioned here and briefly reconsidered in the next chapter in relation to its use in a distributed environment.

With a timestamping mechanism, each new transaction is given a timestamp before it commences its processing. When it wishes to update a data object, the system checks to see if a conflict situation exists. If there is no conflict, the transaction continues; the relevant data object is updated and its timestamp is changed to that of the current transaction.

A conflict situation may exist if a transaction tries to update a data object which has a timestamp greater than that of the transaction (i.e. the object has already been updated or read by a transaction which started after this one). In such a situation, the transaction attempting the update would be backed out and restarted with a new timestamp assigned to it. Timestamping mechanisms require that updates are only made permanent in the physical database at the end of a transaction. Thus backing out a transaction does not require any changes to be made to the physical database, only to the copies of objects held in temporary storage.

Deadlock cannot occur with a simple timestamp mechanism such as the one above, but one disadvantage of timestamps is that repeated backing out and restarting of transactions may occur. A number of variations of the basic timestamping mechanism have been suggested, which are aimed at minimising the amount of backing out and restarting of transactions. A further disadvantage of timestamps is the storage space required for maintaining them. However, they can be stored in separate tables (rather than as part of the stored objects themselves), and it is then only necessary to store the timestamps for the objects most recently accessed. All data object timestamps which are less than all the current transaction timestamps can be considered to be zero and dropped from the table, since a conflict can only exist if any data object timestamps are greater than transaction timestamps.

Timestamping is discussed in more detail in Kohler (1981) and Bernstein (1981a), although primarily in relation to distributed database systems.

Comment on concurrency control

It goes without saying that there are overheads to concurrency control, and in designing a mechanism, care must be taken that it is not so complex that more time is spent in concurrency control than in processing transactions!

5.6 Summary

This chapter has taken a close look at database management systems. First, the main facilities which should be provided by a DBMS were discussed and a selection of currently available systems were listed. Implementation aspects were then discussed. First, the organisation and storage of data in different types of database — relational, binary relationship, network, and hierarchical — were considered, and this was followed by a discussion of techniques for processing queries on these databases. The subject of database protection was finally discussed, including the ways in which the reliability, security and integrity of the database may be maintained.

CHAPTER SIX

Distributed Database Systems

6.1 Introduction

Interest in distributed database systems initially arose from large decentralised companies who wished to decentralise their computing facilities. Early attempts were somewhat primitive and barely deserved the label 'distributed database system', but during the past 10 years there has been significant research effort aimed at providing sophisticated systems. The impetus for the increased research effort over recent years has come to a large extent from the great advances in data communications which have led to the widespread availability of cost-effective wide area and local area networks (WANs and LANs). These have made it economically feasible to transfer messages (queries, responses, mail, etc.) from computer to computer, at different locations. Distributed database technology therefore represents the merging of two major technologies: database technology and data communications technology.

A distributed database system (DDBS) poses far more problems than a centralised one and this chapter addresses itself to these problems, in addition to introducing the concepts and features underlying such systems. It concentrates on the database aspects of DDBS rather than the data communications aspects although the latter feature in some of the discussions. It is not possible in one chapter to do more than just outline the main concepts and issues, and provide a few examples. The objective therefore is to provide a basic understanding of this important field of distributed database systems. Readers are referred to Ceri (1984) for more comprehensive coverage, and to the various references provided below for details of specific systems and techniques.

6.2 Major Issues in Distributed Database Systems (DDBSs)

The major issues in relation to distributed database systems are introduced in this section and then each one is discussed in detail in the remaining secions of this chapter.

One issue is whether distributed database systems are economically and technically viable given the current state-of-the-art, and if so under what circumstances should a distributed database approach, rather than a centralised database approach, be adopted. The advantages and disadvantages of the two approaches are considered in section 6.3.

A second issue relates to the data communications network architecture and the associated DDBS software architecture. A number of options are possible. The network architecture and DDBS software architecture are, to a certain extent, independent of each other, but not entirely. Furthermore, the decisions regarding both types of architecture may be governed by the nature of the company adopting the DDB approach. The options available are outlined in section 6.4.

A third issue is fundamental to the design of the software. It is the degree of heterogeneity in the system. A DDBS may consist of identical DBMSs at the nodes in the communications network, but it can also be designed to support a variety of different DBMSs. How different they are (i.e. the degree of heterogeneity) affects both the design and the complexity of the resulting DDBS. In section 6.5 the varying degrees of heterogeneity are first discussed and then generalised software architecture for a heterogeneous DDBS is presented in detail. A brief review of some prototype systems is also provided, to illustrate the different software design approaches.

A fourth issue concerns the distribution of the database itself. Relevant questions to be answered include: 'Should the data be replicated at different nodes?' and 'How should the database be partitioned and distributed?' The background to these questions is discussed in section 6.6, and the possibilities outlined.

A further issue relates to data models, languages, and protocols. This is a major issue with heterogeneous DDBS and requires careful attention. Mapping between different data models and translation between different languages is discussed in section 6.7.

An important issue with any type of distributed computing system is coordination and control of processing. The different aspects of this in relation to a DDBS are considered in section 6.8, in particular the coordination and control of query processing, and the synchronisation and control of database updates.

Six major issues in DDBS have been identified. In summary, the questions they pose are:
- under what circumstances should a DDBS approach be adopted?
- what communications network and software architecture combinations are available, and for what situations are they appropriate?
- what is the effect of heterogeneity on DDBS design and implementation?
- how should the data be distributed?
- what data models, languages and protocols are appropriate in a DDBS environment?
- what coordination and control problems are specific to a DDBS environment, and how might they be solved?

The following sections attempt to provide the background for answering these questions.

6.3 Centralised Database versus Distributed Database

The decentralisation of computing facilities does not necessarily imply the existence of a distributed database system. Three main decentralised computing scenarios may be identified, only one of which involves a DDBS.

The first involves a centralised database. A central node holds the main database and the local nodes are sent copies of the relevant data for local use. This transmission of data from central to local node might take place at the beginning of each day, with updates to the data being saved locally and sent to the central node at the end of the day for overnight updating of the central database. Queries regarding non-local data might be processed via remote terminal access to the central database.

A second scenario involves local databases, but these are not integrated. Queries regarding non-local data may require transmission of requests to another node, with someone at that node being responsible for answering the query and transmitting the result back. Alternatively, the local node may access another node's database via remote terminal facilities. The former situation is most likely to exist if the nodes support different DBMSs, while the latter is possible if they support the same DBMSs or users are conversant with the different systems.

The third scenario requires a distributed database system. All nodes support their own local DBMSs which manage the local databases. The basic difference between this scenario and the previous one is that the local DBMSs are able to 'talk' to each other via special purpose software which integrates the systems — the DDBS. The various local databases appear as a single integrated database to the local user, and queries involving data at other nodes are automatically processed by the DDBS.

The first scenario may be referred to as a *centralised database approach*, the second as a *decentralised database approach*, and the third as a *distributed database approach*. Variations on these themes exist, of course. For example, a mixture of the decentralised and centralised approaches may exist if a central database is maintained, but local nodes also have their own databases and some local autonomy.

In the rest of this section the choice between the centralised and distributed approaches will be considered. In order to make this choice, it is necessary to weigh up the advantages and disadvantages of the two approaches.

Advantages of a centralised database approach

The advantages of a *centralised approach* are first discussed.

Economies of scale accrue from centralisation when hardware, software and operations are taken into account. Centralised computing equipment running a single DBMS, with access from remote nodes via terminals and data communications lines, is generally cheaper and easier to maintain than computers at each node in the network running their own DBMSs. From the viewpoint of control of the database, centralised control is much simpler with only a single database and a single node for updates. One of the advantages of the database approach as compared with the traditional file approach mentioned in Chapter 1 was that of centralised control. The distributed approach may be seen as a step backwards, unless distributed control is adequately executed. Coordination and control in a DDBS environment has been the subject of much research, due to the many problems associated with it.

A further advantage of a centralised database is that all the data is in one place, and is modelled according to one conceptual basis (relational, network, hierarchy, binary relationship, etc.). Access to single logical data objects (e.g. records, relations) is relatively easy. Everything is homogeneous and compatible. With a distributed database single logical objects may be distributed across many nodes, and may even be replicated at different nodes. Collecting together the data relating to a complete relation or coset, and ensuring its consistency and integrity in a distributed update environment is not a trivial task. Furthermore, different nodes may run database systems which support different conceptual bases, and hence mappings between them and translation between the languages which manipulate them may be necessary.

Advantages of a distributed database approach

The value of the advantages of a *distributed database approach* will vary from company to company, but there can be significant advantages. A decentralised company with a centralised database is vulnerable in two directions; firstly, hardware/software failure at the central node, and secondly, communications failure between a remote and the central node. If the database is distributed, then remote nodes can still be partially operational even if there is a central node or communications failure, so long as the data required to support the main data processing activities at a node is held locally. How the data is to be distributed amongst the nodes requires careful consideration.

One important cost advantage of the distributed approach as compared with the centralised approach is the reduction in the cost of data communications. This could be very significant in a large company if large volume data transfer to nodes would otherwise be necessary. The distributed approach should also avert a possible communications bottleneck, which might arise in the centralised case if data communications lines become clogged by large amounts of traffic. A further advantage of reduced data transfer is faster processing. Delays are inevitable in transferring data between nodes, not only due to line speeds but also due to the need for occasional retransmission due to errors/faults on the line; hence the greater the amount of processing done on local data, the faster it is likely to be.

A final possible advantage concerns the hardware. If the different divisions in a company are not only geographically distributed, but also have very diverse processing requirements, a distributed approach will have the advantage of enabling each division to have computing equipment tailored to its own specific requirements. Flexibility is increased; new nodes can be added to the network without disrupting the existing nodes, as well as existing nodes being able to upgrade their equipment as required, with relative ease.

Currently, the distributed database approach is likely to be most appropriate and cost effective in a wide area network environment, for companies which are merging and already have their own separate computing equipment and database software, and for companies in which different divisions are both geographically distributed and relatively autonomous. But continuing research and development in distributed database systems is likely to result in more economic systems, and it should be noted that the design and development of DDBS for local area network environments is already under way.

6.4 Communications Network Architecture for DDBSs

Two main types of network architecture may be identified: *hierarchical* (or star) and *horizontal* (or ring). Hybrid architectures (a mixture of the two types) are, of course, also possible.

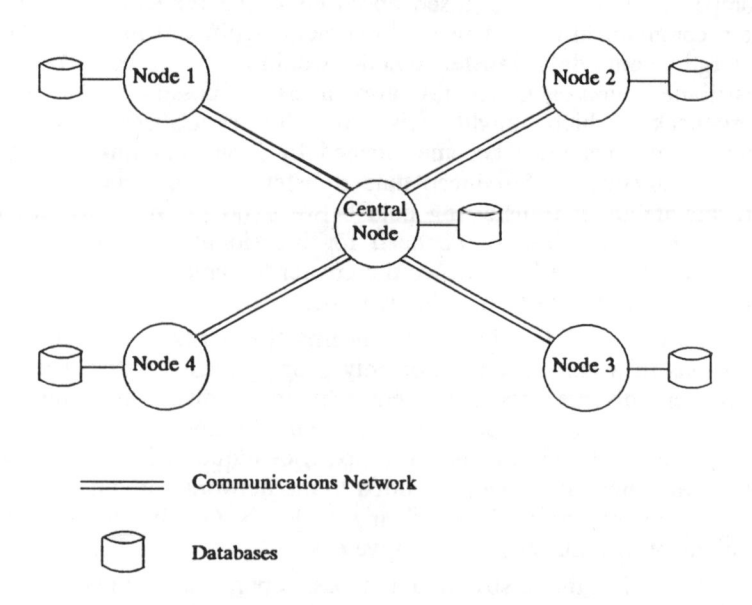

Hierarchical network architecture

The *hierarchical* type of network architecture is illustrated in Figure 6.1 and is based on a central node (top level) with subordinate/local nodes (lower level) attached to the central node.

Figure 6.1 Hierarchical Network Architecture

Viewed from above (as in the diagram) the architecture looks rather like a star. All data communications between nodes is via the central node. Hierarchical network architecture suggests centrally controlled DDBS software architecture; since all inter-node transfers must be channelled via the central node, it is both logical and sensible for the distributed database system coordination and control software to reside at the central node. It is not, however, essential for the DDBS software to be centrally based.

This type of architecture may be relevant to a company with a controlling head office and subsidiary branches. The advantage is that the head office has complete control of what goes on between nodes. One disadvantage is the complete isolation of nodes when the central node is unavailable for some reason. This need not be much of a problem, though, if most of the work at a branch relates to its own branch data. A further disadvantage is that all DDBS messages must be channelled via the central node which may give rise to a communications bottleneck.

Horizontal network architecture

The *horizontal* type of network architecture is illustrated in Figure 6.2.

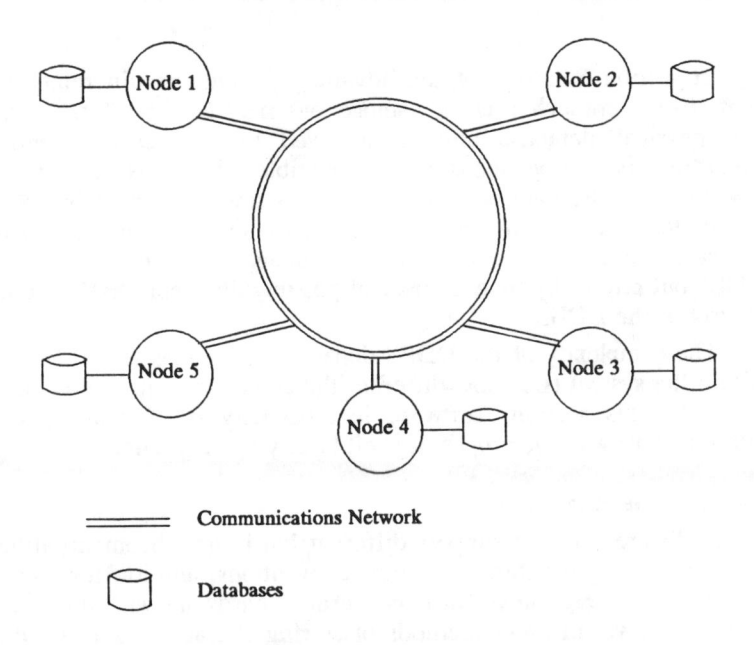

Figure 6.2 Horizontal Network Architecture

All nodes are at the same level, with each node able to communicate directly with all other nodes. The arrangement of nodes when viewed from above resembles a ring — all nodes are 'equal'. Although the communications network is shown as a ring in the diagram, any appropriate communications hardware may be used; for example, British Telecom's PSS (Packet Switched System), the Cambridge Ring Local

Area Network, etc.

Horizontal network architecture imposes no constraints on the DDBS software architecture. Software for coordination and control of the DDBS may equally well reside at a single node (acting as a central node as far as the software is concerned) or be replicated and distributed, enabling any node to take control when relevant.

6.5 DDBS Software Architecture

6.5.1 Homogeneous and Heterogeneous Systems

In section 6.3, one of the advantages mentioned in relation to the centralised approach was its homogenous nature. The data is stored in one physical database and is managed by one DBMS, and hence everything is homogeneous and compatible. In a distributed database environment, the data is conceptually in a single database but physically distributed over a number of different databases. Similarly, from the software viewpoint, the database is managed conceptually by a single DDBS but physically by a number of possibly different DBMSs, under the control of the DDBS.

The complexity of the DDBS depends on the degree of heterogeneity within the system (i.e. how different the components in the whole system are). In this section, software heterogeneity is of primary concern, although hardware heterogeneity will briefly be mentioned.

Hardware heterogeneity

If different nodes support different hardware, incompatibilities may arise in data representation, naming conventions, and low level protocols. As far as *data representation* is concerned, hardware with different word sizes will have different methods of storing character data and different maxima for numeric data. However, if all messages (queries, data, etc.) are transmitted from node to node as a sequence of characters in byte form, the only real problem is what the DDBS software should do if it receives a number in character form which, when converted to binary form, is too large for the hardware at the node to represent. This is not a major problem and can be solved by various means, including the provision of a recognised DDBS error. *Naming conventions* for files may be different on different hardware. Again this is not a major problem since it only affects the naming of message files passed from node to node; the controlling software for data transfers can have access to a table containing the naming conventions associated with each node, and can hence ensure that an appropriate name is allocated to a message file when the file transfer protocol is set up. The third possible incompatibility due to hardware is that of *low level protocols*. However, this problem has been virtually removed by the introduction of protocol standards for data communications, in particular the layered protocol approach of the OSI Reference Model (which will be discussed briefly in subsection 6.7.2).

Software heterogeneity

The next consideration in this subsection is software heterogeneity. Distributed database systems may be classified into three main groups according to the degree of heterogeneity; these are: *monotype homogeneous*, *monomodel homogeneous*, and *heterogeneous*.

A *monotype homogeneous* DDBS is one in which the DBMSs at each node are identical, i.e. they are all Ingres, or all MDBS III, or all DB2, etc. In this case, the DBMSs at the nodes support the same conceptual data model, 'speak' the same language, and provide the same facilities and system characteristics. No data model mapping or language translation is necessary; only coordination and control of the processing of distributed messages is necessary. The DDBS in this case is at the lowest level of complexity.

A *monomodel homogeneous* DDBS is one in which the DBMSs at each node are not identical, but they all support the same conceptual model. For example, some of the nodes may use Ingres, some may use DB2, and others may use Oracle — these are different DBMSs but all are relational. They will not necessarily 'speak' the same language, nor provide the same facilities and system characteristics; but there will be a high degree of similarity, data model mapping will not be necessary, and language translation should be relatively simple, since all the languages will be designed to manipulate relations (or cosets, if the DDBS has a homogeneous Codasyl base). The DDBS in this case is a little more complex since some language translation will be necessary, in addition to coordination and control.

A *heterogeneous* DDBS is one in which not only are there different DBMSs in the system, but also different conceptual models are supported. There may be relational Ingres or Oracle at some nodes, Codasyl-based IDMS or MDBS III at some nodes, and maybe even the logic-based Prolog at other nodes. In this situation, the degree of complexity of the DDBS software will be quite high.

Some classifications of DDBS only distinguish between homogeneous and heterogeneous systems, in which case 'homogeneous' is generally equivalent to 'monotype homogeneous' as defined above, and all other systems are classified as heterogeneous. In fact, most research prototypes and systems under development are either monotype homogeneous or heterogeneous. It is however useful to be aware of the distinction since it affects the complexity of the software. This is discussed further in Spaccapietra (1980) (but note that Spaccapietra uses the term 'monotype' in place of monotype homogeneous, and 'homogeneous' in place of monomodel homogeneous).

A further type of DDBS should be mentioned. This is a *multi-database* system. A multi-database system is one which aims to provide a unified and integrated interface to separate databases at different nodes or the same node. This type of system will not be discussed specifically here since a number of the problems associated with such systems are common to the problems of heterogeneous DDBS. More information about such systems may be found in Litwin (1983).

In the remaining part of this section, a generalised software architecture for a heterogeneous DDBS will be presented (subsection 6.5.2) and some prototype DDBSs will be introduced (subsection 6.5.3), while the sections which follow will be mainly concerned with different aspects of the design and implementation of a DDBS.

6.5.2 Generalised Software Architecture for a Heterogeneous DDBS

The objective of this subsection is to identify the tasks to be carried out by the main software components of a heterogeneous DDBS. Whereas monotype homogeneous systems only require software for coordination and control of the processing of DDBS messages, heterogeneous systems also require data model mapping and language translation software, and are hence much more complex.

To put this additional complexity into perspective, it is worth considering how a user, without the aid of a DDBS, might access a database at a remote location which is managed by a different DBMS from the one which the user normally uses. The user must know the location of the database to which he requires access, the protocol for communicating with the computer at that location, and the remote DBMS query language and data formats. If his query involves data at many remote locations, he must decompose it into subqueries, express each of them in the relevant remote query languages, and arrange for the responses from each location (the subresponses) to be temporarily stored. When all responses have been received, he must either manually compose the query response by reference to the separate subresponses, or alternatively write a program to compose the response. The subresponses will, of course, be in different formats and it may be necessary to convert them to a standard format before the response to the query is composed. All this is time consuming and highly error prone. When such remote access requirements are frequent, the advantages of a DDBS are obvious.

An important feature of a heterogeneous DDBS, which provides the basis for integrating the different DBMSs, is the global language for communication between nodes; this includes message protocols, together with languages and formats for specifying queries, responses, errors, etc. The existence of a global language means that for each node supporting a different DBMS, a language translator is only required to and from the global language, rather than to and from every DBMS language supported by other nodes. This is discussed further in section 6.7.

There are many variations on a theme as far as software architecture is concerned; a generalised architecture will therefore be presented. Figure 6.3 illustrates generalised software architecture with respect to query processing in a heterogeneous system. It shows the major software modules involved. The coordination and control software is referred to here as the *DDBS Nucleus*, since it is at the 'centre' of the DDBS, while the mapping and translation software is referred to as the *DDBS Interface*, since it acts as an interface between the local DBMS and the global DDBS. At the user/application end, the interface is more specifically referred to as the *query interface*, while at the local database end it is known as the *data interface*.

A node may contribute to the DDBS as a *query node* supporting the query interface, as a *data node* supporting the data interface, or as both a query and data node. The Nucleus may be completely centralised, in which case the node supporting it may be referred to as the *global node*. Alternatively, the Nucleus may be distributed to all query nodes enabling them to coordinate and control the processing of their own queries. (The latter case implies the horizontal network architecture shown in Figure 6.2, while the former case may be implemented on either a hierarchical or a horizontal network architecture). Figure 6.3 shows the Nucleus residing at the query node. The architecture will be discussed by working through Figure 6.3 from the point at which the user enters his query to the point at which he receives his response.

The DDBS Query Interface

The user expresses his query in some external query language (e.g. SQL, Quel, QRS) which may be the language of his local DBMS or a special DDBS external query language. The query is passed to the DDBS Query Interface where the external/global query translation module translates it into the global language. For this purpose reference will need to be made, either directly or indirectly, to the local external schema and also to a schema which describes the data model of the complete distributed database — this is referred to as the *global conceptual schema*.

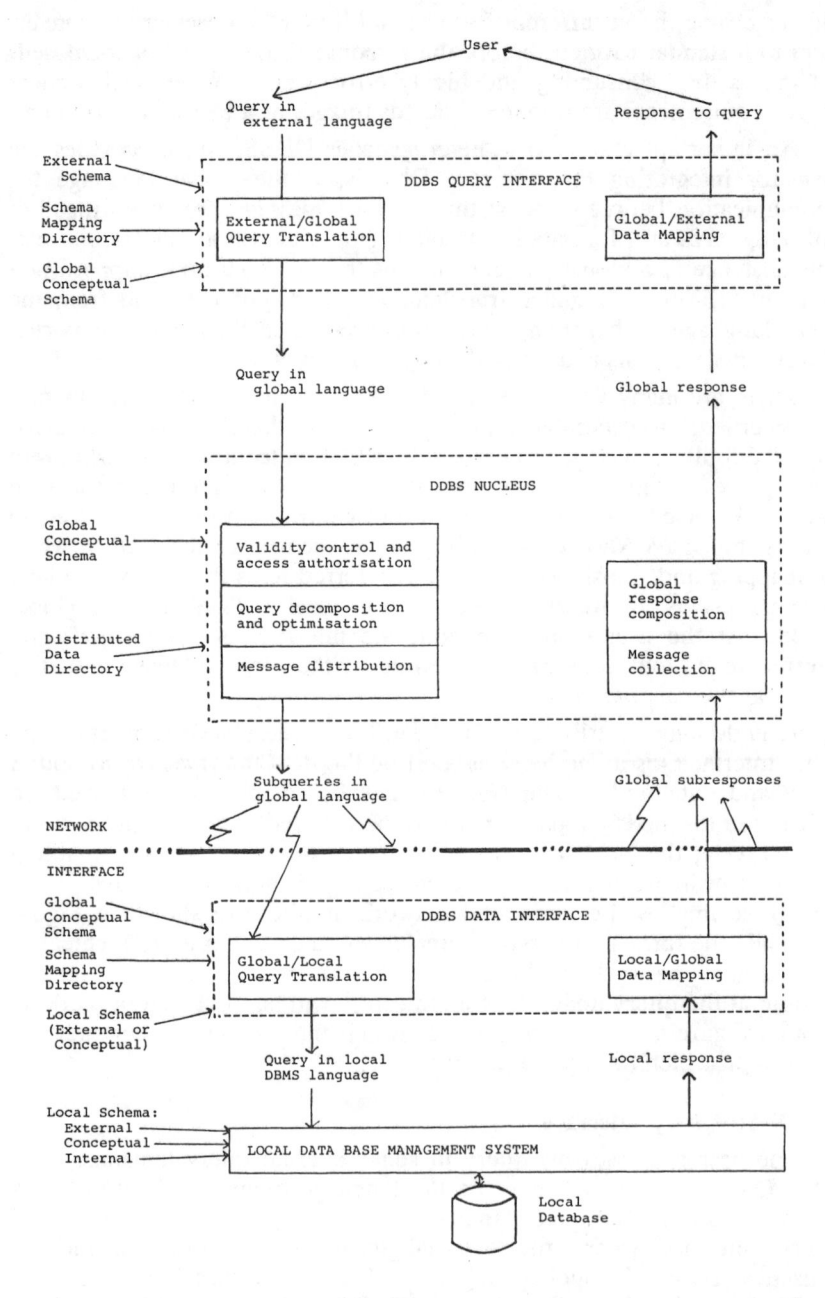

Figure 6.3 Generalised Software Architecture for Query Processing in a Heterogeneous DDBS

The translation may be carried out by means of rules applied directly to elements in the two schema, or alternatively it may be carried out by means of a special *schema mapping directory* which will have been derived from the two schema mentioned above. The resulting translated query will be expressed not only in the global language but also in terms of the global data model rather than the local data model, which may have a completely different conceptual basis.

If the DDBS Nucleus is distributed to query nodes, the next stage will take place locally, otherwise the query will be 'parcelled up' to form a DDBS message, using the appropriate protocol. This involves adding information to identify each DDBS message, for example, the type of message (query, response, etc.), a unique identifier for the message, the source of the message, and the destination (this is discussed further in subsection 6.7.2). The DDBS message is then sent via the data communications network to the global node for further processing.

The DDBS Nucleus (Query Modules)

One task of the Nucleus is to verify that the initiator of the query is authorised to access the distributed database, or at least that part of it to which the query relates. Some initial checking of the query is also necessary even though it has been produced by a software module, since software bugs cannot be ruled out! These are the tasks carried out by the validity control and access authorisation module.

A major task of the Nucleus is query decomposition and optimisation. In Chapter 5, these were discussed in relation to centralised DBMSs. In a DDBS environment, further decomposition is necessary since a complete logical relation (or coset in the case of Codasyl databases) may exist only as a set of fragments, with different fragments held at different nodes in the network. A *distributed data directory* must exist to provide information regarding data fragmentation and distribution. This will be used in the query decomposition process to enable a set of subqueries to be produced for distribution to nodes in the network as relevant. Data fragmentation is discussed in the next section, while query decomposition to reflect data fragmentation and distribution is discussed in section 6.8, together with query optimisation.

Some nodes in the network may be sent one subquery, some more than one, and others none. Before the subqueries can be sent to the relevant nodes, however, some further processing is required. The message distribution module of the DDBS Nucleus is responsible for creating a DDBS message for each subquery using the appropriate protocol, sending the subqueries to the relevant nodes, and creating message log information for control purposes when subresponses (responses to subqueries) are received back.

The DDBS Data Interface

When a node in the network receives a subquery, the DDBS Data Interface must translate the query in the opposite direction — from global language to local language. At any specific node, the local language may or may not be the same as the external language used for specifying queries. It is likely to be different in particular if a natural language or graphical interface is provided for end-users. The local language in the DDBS context is most likely to be a formal query language or high-level procedural language (e.g. SQL or a language based on relational algebra), or some internal equivalent using symbolic notation. The translated query is processed in the normal manner by the local DBMS and a local response will be produced as a result.

The local response will be in a format provided by the local DBMS and relate to objects in the local data model. It must be mapped into the global format and be related to objects in the global data model. This task is carried out by the local/global data mapping module of the DDBS Data Interface. The subresponse is then passed back to the node which sent the subquery, after it has been made into a DDBS message.

The DDBS Nucleus (Response Modules)

One of the DDBS coordination and control tasks is that of message collection. At any one time, in particular in the case of a centralised Nucleus, subresponses relating to a number of different global requests (queries, update requests, etc.) may be outstanding. Whereas subqueries relating to a specific request are all sent out together, the relevant subresponses will be received back over a period of time and may be interspersed with subresponses relating to different requests. Some subresponses may not be received at all if a particular node is out of action for some reason. By means of the message log created by the message distribution module, related subresponses will be collected together and either when all have been received or a time limit has been reached, appropriate information will be passed to the response composition module.

The response composition module produces a single global response from the information received from the message collection module. The actual tasks carried out by this module depend on whether the query decomposition process distributes all the processing or only processing which can be carried out at single nodes (see subsection 6.8.1). In the simple case where all processing is distributed, the information received by this module might be the complete response to the query, or an error message, or a partial response together with some message log information. If, on the other hand, only those subqueries involving single nodes are distributed, the responses to those subqueries will be passed to this module, and it will need to apply the remaining subqueries (representing multi-node operations) to the data contained in these subresponses, in order to produce the final single response. In this case, the module acts like a DBMS but it processes data in a temporary database of subresponses.

When the single global response is eventually passed to the DDBS Query Interface, it is mapped into a suitable format for presentation to the user.

DDBS updates

Some variations to the software architecture of Figure 6.3 are required for other types of DDBS request, such as updates. Update requests still need to be translated, decomposed, optimised, distributed, etc., but whereas a partial answer to a query might be acceptable a partial update is completely out of the question. It is important to ensure that all updates relating to a particular request are applied; furthermore, the updating process needs to be synchronised at the different nodes to ensure that the updates are applied in the correct sequence and without interference from other updates. Thus, for updates, the DDBS Nucleus will contain an additional 'module block' for update synchronisation and control. Various techniques have been suggested for update synchronisation and control in a DDBS environment, and some of these will be considered in section 6.8.

6.5.3 Major Features of Some DDBSs

To illustrate the different approaches to DDBS, the main features of a few of the research prototypes will be briefly discussed in this subsection. The following systems will be considered: SDD-1, R*, Porel, Sirus-Delta, Multibase, and Proteus; other systems also exist but these will be sufficient to illustrate the range of approaches. SDD-1, R* and Porel are all homogeneous monotype systems. They do not therefore require language translation modules in the DDBS Interface; only a simple interface is needed to handle the DDBS messages and, in some systems, to carry out local optimization on subqueries. Sirus-Delta, Multibase and Proteus are heterogeneous systems. All require language translation modules at the local DBMS end of the system, and, with the exception of Multibase, also at the user end.

In the papers describing the systems, they are split into modules and components in many different ways and different naming conventions are used. It is therefore difficult to compare the systems without an overall unified view. The objective here is to highlight the similarities and differences between the systems, and in order to do this, common terminology is used to provide a unified view as far as possible. No attempt is made to describe the actual modular structure of the systems; this is provided in the references supplied.

SDD-1

SDD-1 (Rothnie 1980) is based on an existing centralised relational system, the Datacomputer DBMS. It was the first large distributed database project and has provided a testbed for techniques and strategies for the different components of the Nucleus, in particular query processing and concurrency control. Queries (transactions) are expressed in a semi-procedural language called Datalanguage, and are decomposed into relational algebra expressions in the form of an operator tree, from which single node subqueries are derived; the subqueries are referred to as 'reducer programs' since they reduce the size of relations to be transmitted to other nodes by carrying out selections, projections, and semijoins (partial joins) on relations. A main processing node is selected on the basis of minimum data transmission cost and the nodes return their subresponses to the main processing node which carries out the bulk of the processing and passes the query result to the originating node (unless it is that node). Thus, a single node (not necessarily the query node) carries out all the multi-node operations.

One of the most significant contributions from the SDD-1 project has been the research into synchronisation and concurrency control algorithms, which will be referred to again later.

R*

R* (Williams 1982) is also based on an existing relational system, System R (which has already been mentioned in previous chapters). It contains the same underlying architecture and features as System R, with additional system modules to support the DDBS. The SQL language is used both globally and locally, but has been extended to support DDBS aspects such as data distribution. Unlike SDD-1, multi-node operations in queries may be carried out at different nodes, the choice for each multi-node operation depending not only on data transmission costs, but also on the access paths (indexes, etc.) available at the relevant nodes, and the node at which the final result is required.

One of the major aims of the project was to maintain the autonomy of the local nodes. The node at which the query originates becomes the Master Node for the query and is responsible for global query optimisation and coordination of query processing by means of a global execution plan. (The other nodes involved in the query are referred to as Apprentice Nodes.) The autonomy of the local nodes is maintained by the Master Node sending them the original SQL statement (rather than a subquery derived from it) plus a global execution plan worked out for each node; it is then left to the local node to work out its own local execution plan within the constraints of the global plan.

Porel

Porel (Neuhold 1982) was designed from scratch as an integrated DDBS. A relational approach was chosen to provide flexibility in relation to data distribution. Relational algebra was chosen as the basis for the internal language of the Porel Relational Base Machine (a software database machine), with an SQL-like language for end-users. Like R*, the query node is responsible for query optimisation and coordination of processing, and multi-node operations may be carried out at different nodes, but unlike R*, the query node decomposes the original query and sends each local node a specific subquery derived from the original query.

Sirius-Delta

Sirius-Delta (Litwin 1982) was designed as a heterogeneous system, and as such it contains a global query language, referred to as the 'pivot' language, which is based on relational algebra. There are two main DBMSs currently supported by the heterogeneous DDBS project: the relational Sirius-Delta DBMS, and a DBMS package for micros, called Phlox, which supports a network data model and procedural language (as well as a relational interface). (There are also other related Sirius projects, e.g. a multi-database project, but these are not considered here.) Since Sirius-Delta is heterogeneous, it contains the full DDBS Interface, including query translation and data mapping modules for query nodes and data nodes. Apart from the additional processing necessitated by the heterogeneous environment, query processing is carried out in a similar manner to Porel. The query node is responsible for decomposing and optimising the query, together with the coordination of its processing, while multi-node operations are distributed to appropriate nodes.

Multibase

Multibase (Smith 1981, Landers 1982) was designed to provide a single user interface to a number of different, already-existing DBMSs and databases. It was designed both as a heterogeneous system and as a multi-database system. The user specifies his query using the functional language Daplex which supports the Functional Data Model (FDM) (Shipman 1981). This is also the global query language and hence no language translation is necessary at the query node. The query node is in fact a special Multibase node which coordinates and controls query processing, including carrying out response composition tasks, as necessary. It contains an internal DBMS supporting all the Daplex facilities so that it can manipulate subresponses and compose the response to the user. In its permanent database, it holds data not available at other nodes and any data needed to resolve incompatibilities between nodes.

Proteus

Proteus (Atkinson 1984) was designed as a heterogeneous system interfacing to a number of different, already-existing DBMSs. However, unlike Multibase, it enables users to query the distributed database using the query language available at their local node. Thus, both query and data nodes provide language translation facilities (and, of course, data mapping as necessary). Coordination and control of query processing in the initial version of the system takes place at a central node, the Switch Node, and all communication between nodes is via this central node. Query processing in the initial version is similar to that of SDD-1 but with all the multi-node operations processed at the central node. However, the system was designed in such a way that the Nucleus functions could be distributed; the central node was primarily created as an aid to implementation at the research prototype stage. The global query language, NQL, is based on relational algebra, with extensions to support special DDBS facilities and local DBMS facilities; the extensions include a grouping operator, operators for individual data item computation, and provision for multiple result relations. The global data model used in Proteus, the ACS (Abstracted Conceptual Schema), was designed by Stocker et al (Stocker 1983) specifically for use as a global conceptual model in a heterogeneous DDBS. It is a set-oriented model which not only supports a relational view of data but also enables functionalities and constraints amongst the data to be specified; it also supports categorization (subsets) and other additional semantic aspects.

Summary of query processing features

The query processing features of the systems considered above may be summarised in relation to the generalised software architecture of Figure 6.3 as follows:

SDD-1:
    Monotype homogeneous.
    Simple DDBS Interfaces at query and data nodes.
    Query modules of DDBS Nucleus at query nodes.
    Response modules of DDBS Nucleus at data nodes.

R*:
    Monotype homogeneous.
    Simple DDBS Interfaces at query (Master)
        and data (Apprentice) nodes.
    Modified DDBS Nucleus at query nodes (no subqueries created).
    Some Nucleus-like functions at data nodes
        (e.g. query decomposition and optimisation).
    Response composition distributed to data nodes.

Porel:
- Monotype homogeneous.
- Simple DDBS Interface at query nodes.
- DDBS Nucleus at query nodes.
- Response composition distributed to data nodes.

Sirius-Delta:
- Heterogeneous.
- DDBS Interfaces at query and data nodes provide language translation and data mapping.
- Query modules of DDBS Nucleus at query nodes.
- Response composition distributed to data nodes.
- Relational algebra-based global query language.

Multibase:
- Heterogeneous.
- Special Multibase node containing DDBS Nucleus and acting as query node (no language translation necessary because a common language is used).
- DDBS Interfaces at data nodes provide language translation.
- Multibase node performs all Nucleus functions.
- Daplex used as global query language as well as end-user query language.

Proteus:
- Heterogeneous.
- DDBS Interfaces at query and data nodes provide language translation and data mapping.
- DDBS Nucleus at central (switch) node, but can be distributed, and performs all Nucleus functions.
- Relational algebra-based global query language.

Multibase and Proteus software architectures most closely match the generalised architecture of Figure 6.3. Multibase differs only in that it has a single query node and no language translation requirement at that node. Proteus differs in that the Nucleus resides at a central node in the research prototype.

6.6 Data Distribution

In a centralised system, the database is held at a single location. Each relation, coset, etc., is managed as a single logical object by the DBMS. In a distributed system, regardless of whether it is heterogeneous or not, single logical objects may be split up into fragments held at different nodes in the network. The implications of this as far as query decomposition is concerned will be considered later. In this section, the different ways in which the database may be distributed across nodes in the network are considered.

Three different types of data distribution may be identified: *replication, partitioning*, and *fragmentation*. These may occur in isolation or in combination.

To illustrate the different types, the university library database will again be used as an example. The university will be assumed to consist of four buildings, a Social Sciences Faculty building (S), a Natural Sciences and Maths building (N), a Humanities and Arts building (H) and a Library and Administration building (L). Each building has its own computer and DBMS and they are linked by means of a local area network. The DBMSs will be assumed to be relational.

Replication

If a *fully replicated database* is established, all the relations in the library model would be replicated at each of the four nodes: S, N, H and L. In this extreme case, queries would not need to be distributed at all, while updates would be broadcast to each node without any need for decomposition (synchronisation of updates and concurrency control would still be necessary though). In practice, this extreme case is unlikely to be found. It is more likely that either none, or only part, of the database will be replicated. *Partial replication* may be used as a means of reducing (though not eliminating) the need for queries to be distributed. If some of the data is mainly required by a single node, while the remainder is required by all nodes, then partial replication is a possibility. For example, Book, Loan, Reservation, Person and Status relations may mainly be required by node L, while Catalogued-Book is required by all nodes; Catalogued-Book could therefore be replicated at each node. This is a rather trivial example, but suppose a separate administration node (A) exists, then Book, Loan and Reservation might be held only at node L, Person and Status only at node A, and Catalogued-Book might be replicated at the other three nodes as well as being held at node L.

Partitioning

In a *partitioned* database, no replication exists. All data is divided between the nodes in logical units. Suppose only one of the faculty buildings houses a computer to be shared by all faculties, and a separate administration node exists, the database might be partitioned as follows: the faculty node holds a single copy of the Catalogued-Book relation, the library node holds Book, Loan and Reservation, and the administration node holds Person and Status. When a database is partitioned, each partition (which may be a single relation (or coset type), or may be a set of relations, etc.) is held at the node with the highest activity with regard to that partition. Other nodes requiring access to data in a partition held at another node would need to send a request (query, update, etc.) to the DDBS.

Fragmentation

In a *fragmented* database, at least one of the logical objects is split into fragments. A fragmented database may also be partitioned, or partially replicated. In relational terms the fragments may be *horizontal* (representing relational algebra selection operations) or *vertical* (representing projection operations), or a combination of the two. The following notation will be used to represent fragmented relations:

R[i]   horizontal fragment i of relation R
R[,j]   vertical fragment j of relation R
R[i,j] vertical fragment j of horizontal fragment i of relation R

In the library example (assuming once again that each faculty building has its own node), Catalogued-Book might be fragmented as follows:

CB[1]: all tuples with a Social Sciences Classmark
        selected from Catalogued-Book
CB[2]: all tuples with a Natural Sciences or Maths
        Classmark selected from Catalogued-Book
CB[3]: all tuples with a Humanities or Arts Classmark
        selected from Catalogued-Book

CB[1], CB[2] and CB[3] would, of course, be held at nodes S, N and H respectively; they are all horizontal fragments.

An alternative possibility for the Catalogued-Book relation incorporates both horizontal and vertical fragmentation. It is likely that the faculty nodes will only be interested in the Author, Title and Classmark attributes in the catalogue. Hence Catalogued-Book might be vertically fragmented as follows:

CB[,1]: Isbn, Author, Title, Classmark
        projected from Catalogued-Book
CB[,2]: Isbn, Publisher, Year
        projected from Catalogued-Book

(Note that Isbn appears in both vertical fragments to provide a primary key.) The first vertical fragment might be horizontally fragmented via a selection on the Classmark attribute as indicated previously, to produce:

CB[1,1]: Social Sciences fragment, held at node S
CB[2,1]: Natural Sciences and Maths fragment,
         held at node N
CB[3,1]: Humanities and Arts fragment, held at node H
with CB[,2] left as a complete vertical fragment,
              held at node L.

Comments on data distribution

The basic objective in the selection of a data distribution policy should be to hold as much as possible of the locally required data at the local node while at the same time minimising replication and data communication costs. It should be pointed out, however, that not all DDBSs will necessarily provide the full range of data distribution options, partitioning and horizontal fragmentation being the most likely to be available.

As a final comment it should be noted that partitions and fragments are rather like user views (discussed in sections 3.7 and 4.8). The distributed data model can therefore be described in much the same way as user views are described. This description, which may be referred to as the *fragmentation schema*, will form part of the distributed data directory (see Figure 6.3), which will also include information regarding the nodes at which each partition or fragment is held, known as the *distribution schema* (or *allocation schema*).

6.7 Data Models, Languages and Protocols in a DDBS

The primary concern of this section is the *global language* which unifies the DDBS. In subsection 6.5.2, in the discussion on software architecture, it was indicated that a global language would exist for communication between nodes in a heterogeneous system, and this would include message protocols, together with languages and formats for specifying queries, responses, errors, etc. In any DDBS, protocols must be established for message identification, but it is only in a heterogeneous system that a global query language, and response and error formats, etc., need to be designed. The global query language, in particular, is a major design issue.

In this section, specific consideration is given to design decisions regarding the global data model and query language, and to message protocols.

6.7.1 The Global Data Model and Query Language

The *global query language*, together with the underlying *global data model*, will be considered first. (The term 'query language' is used loosely here, as in Chapter 4, and will be assumed to contain update as well as retrieval facilities.) The provision of a global query language in a heterogeneous DDBS means that only one language translator is necessary for each DBMS language in the system. The language acts as a 'pivot language' and in fact is sometimes referred to by this name (cf. Sirius-Delta). Unless it is used for purposes other than internal to the system, it does not need to be a user-oriented language. Without a global query language, each DBMS language would need a translator to and from every other language in the system.

The important issue is: What is a suitable global query language? Each DBMS language is designed to support its own data model and consequently has limitations with regard to its ability to support other data models. A global language should be able to support a data model which embraces the semantic concepts of all the types of data model in the DDBS. If it cannot do this, it will not be possible to provide complete translations for all the DBMS languages. In practice, compromises are necessary, since as yet there does not exist a fully comprehensive data model and associated language (it is, of course, arguable whether they could ever exist, bearing in mind the complexities of the real world).

Thus, any existing data model and language considered for the global role in a DDBS may be relatively rich in semantics but may not be able to support absolutely every semantic aspect of all the DBMS data models. Those aspects which cannot be supported require attention; one possibility is to enhance the syntax of the language as relevant.

An alternative to using an existing model and language is to design a new data model and language specifically for use in this DDBS global role. Ease of mapping to and from other languages is a basic requirement, together with the possibility of applying query optimisation techniques (discussed later), but since the model and language are only to be used internally, no end-user aspects need necessarily be considered in their design.

Referring back to the systems introduced in subsection 6.5.3, it may be remembered that an existing data model and language, FDM and Daplex, are used in Multibase at the global level, while in Proteus the global data model, ACS, was designed specifically for the purpose, and the language, NQL, although based on relational algebra, was enhanced to support the functions required of a global query language. NQL was designed for internal (global) use only and is not intended as a user-oriented language.

Selecting a suitable global data model and language cannot eliminate all language translation problems. There may still be problems in translating a query from global to local representation, when the underlying global model is semantically rich and the local model is not. Those parts of a query or subquery which cannot be translated into a particular local language must be removed and treated as exceptions either at the DDBS Data Interface level or at the query decomposition stage of the DDBS Nucleus. In the former case, some processing and reprocessing of data in an 'exception handling' module at the data node may be necessary. In the latter case a subquery scheduled for a particular node may be further decomposed into a set of subqueries which can be translated completely by the node, together with a special subquery (or set of subqueries) to cater for the parts of the original subquery which cannot be handled locally. In Sirius-Delta, for example, if some operations of the Sirius pivot language (the global language) do not exist in the local language, programs to execute the missing operations are added to the Sirius equivalent of the DDBS Data Interface. In Multibase, some incompatibility problems are resolved by means of an 'auxiliary schema' and internal database, held at the Multibase node, enabling that node to carry out any necessary further processing of subresponses by reference to its internal database; the internal database may hold data not available at other nodes as well as data needed to resolve incompatibilities.

Many investigations have been carried out into the problems and possibilities of mapping between different data models and different languages. The discussion and presentation of the different data models in Chapters 3 and 4 of this book were designed to highlight the similarities and differences between the different approaches; however, only simple examples were provided. It must be stressed that data model and language mapping is complex, if complete (or nearly complete) mappings are required. Some examples of research in this area include: mapping between Niam and ACS data models (Flynn 1985), integrating network and relational data models (D'Appollonio 1985), mapping between relational and functional schema, and designing relational and functional interfaces to Codasyl databases (Gray 1984), and translation of relational queries into Codasyl DML and vice versa (Katz 1982a, 1982b).

As a final comment on global data models and query languages, it may have been noticed that the relational approach dominates in the DDBS research prototypes, regardless of whether they are homogenous or heterogeneous systems. This is due to the great body of knowledge which already exists with regard to relational models and languages, and also due to the greater flexibility of this approach as compared with network and hierarchical models. It is anticipated, however, that future research in DDBS will concentrate more on logic-based and functional model approaches, since they offer even greater opportunities for efficient and effective query processing in a heterogeneous distributed database environment.

6.7.2 DDBS Message Protocols

When a message needs to be transmitted from node to node in the network it is important that it should have some means of identification by the recipient. This identification is generally provided at the beginning of the message in the form of a 'header'. The actual message transmitted, therefore, commonly has the following structure:

DDBS Message

| Header | Message (Query, Response, etc.) |

The header by itself is not sufficient to identify the message; its format must be recognisable to the recipient and hence a standard protocol for headers must be designed and used.

What has been said above relates only to the message as seen by the DDBS. To the communications network, the complete DDBS message, including the header, is a single block of data to be transmitted. This block of data also requires a header as a means of identification to the communications network. For example:

Communications Network Message

Comms Header	DDBS Message
	DDBS Header	Message

The communications network itself generally consists of a hierarchy of layers, each of which is responsible for a particular aspect of the data communications process and has its own header and protocol. A commonly accepted network design is the Open Systems Interconnection (OSI) Reference Model developed by the International Standards Organisation (ISO), which consists of seven layers.

At the bottom is the *physical layer* which is concerned only with the transmission of raw bit streams between two machines. Next is the *data link layer* which divides the bit stream into 'frames', each of which includes a checksum or some similar mechanism for the detection of transmission errors; this layer is responsible for handling frame transmission errors transparently if possible. The frame becomes a 'packet' when it has had its data link layer header (and trailer) stripped off and has been passed to the *network layer* for routing to the destination address. The *transport layer* is responsible for ensuring that a complete message, which may consist of a number of packets, arrives at the destination correctly; it provides a network-independent transport service to the session layer. The *session layer* establishes and maintains connections between hosts or processes, while the next layer, the *presentation layer*, carries out transformations on the data including conversion to and from network standards for terminals and files. The last layer, the *application layer*, is 'user' defined. A tutorial on network protocols, including a discussion of the OSI layers, may be found in Tanenbaum (1981).

In general, a data communications network which supports the ISO OSI Reference Model provides standard protocols and facilities for the six layers up to and including the presentation layer. The DDBS operates at the level of the application layer (as a 'user') and communicates directly with the presentation layer which (amongst other things) provides a file transfer facility. The DDBS need not concern itself with any of the other layers.

When a message is first received at a node, the 'Comms Header' (illustrated in the diagram above) will actually include all of the headers for the bottom six OSI layers. When it is processed by each successive layer of the network, the relevant header is stripped off. By the time the message reaches the DDBS, it has been reduced to the DDBS Message structure indicated at the beginning of this subsection. The DDBS then strips off the DDBS header and uses this to determine what to do with the actual message.

To provide some indication of the information required in a DDBS header, an example from the Proteus DDBS will be provided. A Proteus header consists of the following items:

- message class letter (e.g. Q for Query)
- destination site and system
- source site, system and sequence no.
- originating site, system and sequence no.
- version no.
- date (yymmdd format)
- time (hhmmss format)
- software module or person responsible for message

For example:

```
Q
KENT MDBS
NETWORK PROTEUS 350
ABERDEEN ASTRID 67
1
850319  143000
MULTIPLEXER
*
```

The * at the end of the header is used to separate the header from the message itself, and provides the possibility of extending the header (if additional header information needs to be added at some later stage in the development of the Proteus system).

The example header above is for a query message (class=Q). It indicates that the message itself is a query, and that the original query came from the ABERDEEN query node via the ASTRID database system. It has been processed by the DDBS Nucleus, called PROTEUS, at the NETWORK central node, and this particular message will therefore be the relevant subquery for the KENT data node, to be processed by the MDBS database system at that node. Sequence numbers are unique within a node but not across the complete DDBS. They enable a node to uniquely identify responses to a message which it has sent; for example, the KENT response to the subquery with the above header will contain the source and originating site information from the header, thus enabling the central node to identify the subquery and the original query to which the response applies. All the names used in the header (e.g. KENT, NETWORK, ASTRD, etc.) are globally recognised names (part of the header protocol).

6.8 Coordination and Control — The DDBS Nucleus

As indicated in a previous section, the main modules of the DDBS Nucleus are those concerned with query decomposition and optimisation, response composition, and update synchronisation and control. These tasks will be discussed in the subsections which follow. Query decomposition will be covered first, followed by query optimisation. Reference will also be made to the task of response composition in these two subsections. Finally, techniques for the synchronisation and control of distributed updates will be considered.

6.8.1 DDBS Query Decomposition

In Chapter 5, query processing was discussed and some techniques and strategies in relational, binary relationship and network database systems were considered. Query processing in a distributed database environment is to be discussed in this subsection. An example based on a relational query will be used for illustrative purposes, since most of the existing DDBSs are relational. The query tree decomposition technique and object graph (introduced in subsection 5.4.1) will be extended to support queries over fragmented and distributed databases.

The query used in subsection 5.4.1 will be changed slightly in order to provide a better example for a DDBS environment. The requirement will be to find the title, year of publication and book number for all books by J. Austen which are on loan and due back after 31.12.85. This query would be decomposed to produce the query tree in Figure 6.4.

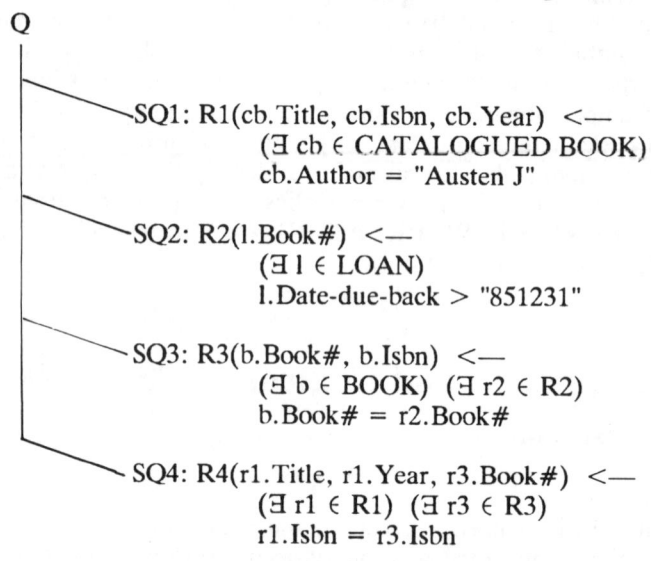

```
Q
 ├─ SQ1: R1(cb.Title, cb.Isbn, cb.Year) <—
 │       (∃ cb ∈ CATALOGUED BOOK)
 │       cb.Author = "Austen J"
 │
 ├─ SQ2: R2(l.Book#) <—
 │       (∃ l ∈ LOAN)
 │       l.Date-due-back > "851231"
 │
 ├─ SQ3: R3(b.Book#, b.Isbn) <—
 │       (∃ b ∈ BOOK) (∃ r2 ∈ R2)
 │       b.Book# = r2.Book#
 │
 └─ SQ4: R4(r1.Title, r1.Year, r3.Book#) <—
         (∃ r1 ∈ R1) (∃ r3 ∈ R3)
         r1.Isbn = r3.Isbn
```

Figure 6.4 The Example Query in Query Tree Form

In a DDBS environment further decomposition is necessary to take into account any fragmentation of the database and the distribution of relations and fragments at remote nodes. In addition, unless multi-node operations are all carried out at a single node, the allocation of these operations to appropriate nodes must also be taken into account. A graphical technique for representing these decomposition stages is presented in Mahmoud (1979). Four related query graphs are produced: system view, partitioned view, distributed view and coalesced view. A slightly modified version of Mahmoud's technique will be presented here.

System view query graph

The first graph — the system view — is an object graph representing the global view of the query and is reproduced directly from the query tree. The graph relating to the query tree in Figure 6.4 is shown in Figure 6.5.

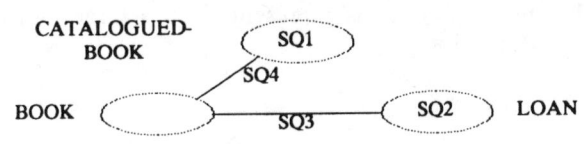

Figure 6.5 System View Query Graph

The nodes of the graph (ellipses) represent complete relations or single-relation subqueries from the tree, while the edges represent the two-relation subqueries and are labelled accordingly.

Fragmented (partitioned) view query graph

The next graph — the fragmented view — reflects the fragmentation of the database. In this graph, subqueries involving fragmented relations are decomposed further into sub-subqueries as relevant. It will be assumed that there is horizontal and vertical fragmentation of the Catalogued-Book relation as discussed in section 6.6. The following fragments therefore exist:

CB[1,1]: Isbn, Author, Title and Classmark attributes for all books with a Social Sciences Classmark
CB[2,1]: as above for all books with a Natural Sciences or Maths Classmark
CB[3,1]: as above for all books with a Humanities or Arts Classmark
CB[,2]: Isbn, Publisher and Year attributes only

All these fragments are involved in the subquery SQ1. Tuples from the first three fragments, which satisfy the condition: Author = "Austen J", must first be selected and 'unioned' together. This is not sufficient to produce the result of SQ1, however, since these fragments do not contain the attribute Year which is required in the target list. This can only be obtained by joining with the fourth fragment on the common attribute Isbn. Thus, SQ1 is decomposed into the following sub-subqueries:

SQ1.1: R1.1(cb.Title, cb.Isbn) <—
        (∃ cb ∈ CB[1,1] ∨ CB[2,1] ∨ CB[3,1])
        cb.Author = "Austen J"

SQ1.2: R1.2 = union (all R1.1)

SQ1.3: R1(cbf.Title, cbf.Isbn, cb.Year) <—
        (∃ cbf ∈ R1.2) (∃ cb ∈ CB[,2])
        cbf.Isbn = cb.Isbn

The fragmented view query graph, in which the SQ1 ellipse is replaced by a subgraph representing SQ1.1, SQ1.2 and SQ1.3, is shown in Figure 6.6. The union (SQ1.2) is represented by a large ellipse enclosing the separate SQ1.1 ellipses.

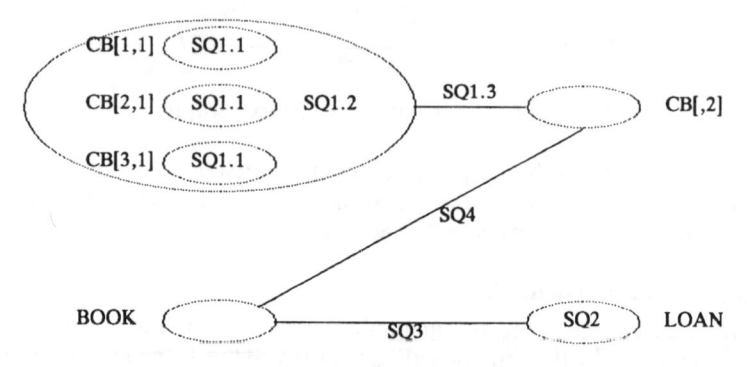

Figure 6.6 Fragmented View Query Graph

Distributed view query graph

The third query graph — the distributed view — reflects the distribution of relations and fragments at remote nodes; it could be thought of as the nodal view. In this view all the multi-node operations are shown external to the nodes in the network, while single-relation subqueries and single-node joins are shown internal to the nodes. In the example, it is assumed that the fragments CB[1,1], CB[2,1] and CB[3,1] are held at the SS, NS and H nodes respectively, while the fragment CB[,2] and the relations Book and Loan are held at the L node. The distributed view query graph is shown in Figure 6.7. The rectangular boxes represent the different nodes, and enclose subgraphs which represent the parts of the query to be processed at those nodes. The unnamed ellipse, external to the nodes, indicates an empty relation implicitly containing the same attributes as R1.1 (the result of SQ1.1); this is used as the basis for the union operation of SQ1.2.

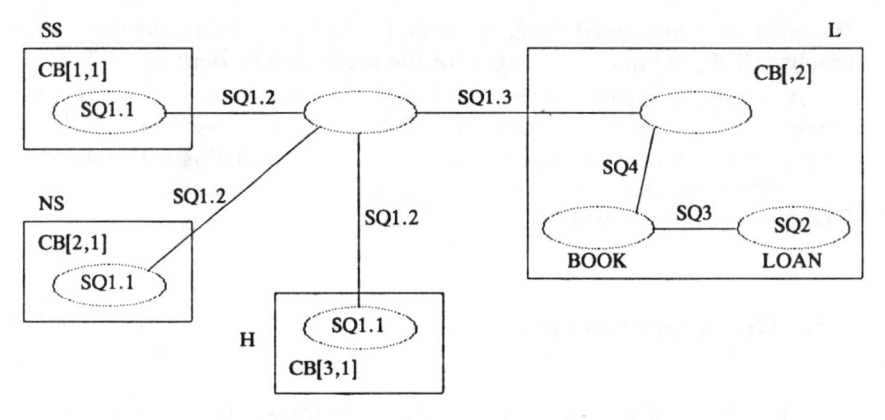

Figure 6.7 Distributed View Query Graph

Coalesced view query graph

If all the multi-node operations are to be processed at a single node, it is now only necessary to extend an existing node box to enclose the external operations; the node would be selected on the basis of least cost for transmission of data to it, or some other criterion (or combination of criteria) such as the location of the final result. On the other hand, if the multi-node operations are to be distributed to different nodes to minimise some function of overall processing time, data transmission costs and other costs, a further graph is necessary to reflect this distribution of the response composition task. The graph in Figure 6.8 is a modified version of Mahmoud's coalesced view.

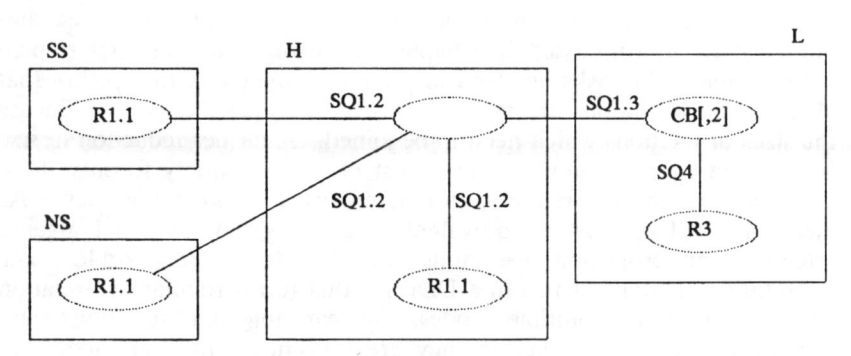

Figure 6.8 Coalesced View Query Graph

In this graph, the single-node subqueries (SQ) are replaced by the corresponding results (R). It is assumed that the minimisation of the cost function has resulted in the selection of node H to process the union operation (SQ1.2) and node L to process the join with the vertical fragment of Catalogued-Book held at L (SQ1.3). From the final two graphs, all the subquery messages for the nodes can be derived.

A similar sequence of graphs can be produced from the operator graph presented briefly in subsection 5.4.1, which is based on relational algebra operators as compared with the relational calculus expressions of the query tree and object graph. Operator graph decomposition of a DDBS query is described in Ceri (1984).

6.8.2 Query Optimisation

The objective of *query optimisation* is to transform a query into an equivalent form which is cheaper and faster to process than the original form. Optimisation was discussed in Chapter 5 in relation to centralised database systems; in this subsection it will be discussed in relation to distributed database systems. There are different degrees of optimisation, and, of course, a cost attached to applying the various optimisation techniques which must be balanced against the benefits. It is in a DDBS that query optimisation can produce really significant benefits in the form of smaller volumes of data to be transmitted to other nodes, the elimination of non-relevant nodes from the processing of a query, and more efficient division of the processing tasks between the different nodes. Various types of query optimisation are mentioned below.

Promoting selections and projections

The process of decomposition of a query to the query tree and graphical forms (discussed in Chapter 5), incorporates the first step in optimisation. The tasks involved in producing the query tree ensure that all selection conditions are processed as early as possible, thus reducing the sizes of relations which need to be joined. A further reduction in size is obtained by restricting the target list of each subquery to only those attributes which are required for later two-relation subqueries. As mentioned before, this is equivalent to carrying out relational algebra selection and projection operations before joins, where possible. The important advantage of this in a DDBS is that if a particular two-relation subquery involves multiple nodes, by carrying out selections and projections on relations before they are transmitted to other nodes for further processing, the cost of transmission is reduced.

The semijoin operation

An additional operation can also be carried out at single nodes to reduce the amount of data to be transmitted to other nodes. This is the *semijoin* operation (which was mentioned in subsection 6.5.3 in relation to the SDD-1 system and is discussed in detail in Bernstein (1981b)). When a multi-node join is necessary, one of the two nodes involved will need to transmit data to the other node. The idea behind the semijoin is to ensure that the minimum amount of data is transmitted. A semijoin of two relations A and B is equivalent to the join of A and B followed by the projection of only the attributes of A from the result. That is:

semijoin A,B =
{ join A,B;   project * (attrA) }

where * indicates the result of the join
and 'attrA' indicates the attributes of A.

If A resides at node X and B resides at node Y, the procedure is as follows:
1. node Y projects the join attribute from B and sends this to node X (this will be a relatively small single-attribute relation).
2. node X carries out the semijoin of A with the relation sent by node Y (this will produce only those tuples in A which are needed for the join with B and hence will be smaller (possibly substantially so) than A; node X then sends this to node Y.
3. node Y carries out the join.

The use of semijoins does not always result in cost savings, but in cases involving large relations with only a few tuples in the resulting join, the savings can be substantial.

Simplification

A reduction in the cost of processing a query can also be achieved by *simplification*. One example of simplification in a DDBS query is the elimination of a subquery which will always yield a null response at a particular node due to the data fragmentation rule for that node. For example, if a query contains a selection on the Classmark attribute, which is used to determine the horizontal fragmentation of the Catalogued-Book relation, the value or range of values in the Classmark selection condition can be compared with the fragmentation conditions to determine those fragments which are relevant to the query. Subqueries in the partitioned view query graph relating to non-relevant fragments can be removed, thus simplifying the query.

Amelioration

It is also possible to add conditional expressions to queries to reduce the size of relations to be used in join operations. This is one of the techniques known as *amelioration*, and involves the use of semantic constraints (if they are available in the metadatabase). If, for example, it is required to find the names of all people with loans due back after a particular date which is more than four weeks in the future and it is known that only staff members can borrow books for more than four weeks, the condition: person.status = "staff" can be added to the query to reduce the size of the Person subrelation to be joined with the Loan subrelation. (A subrelation is the result of applying a subquery to a relation.)

Selection of processing nodes

A final form of optimisation to be considered here relates to the choice of processing node or nodes for the multi-node operations in a query. Various alternatives will exist, each requiring transmission of data from other nodes to the processing node(s). The estimated costs of the various alternatives are calculated and the least cost alternative is chosen. The main problem with this is the need for statistical information about the database, since it is not until the query is actually processed that the exact size of the relations or subrelations to be transmitted is known. Only expected costs, based on statistical estimates of, for example, the number of tuples satisfying a particular selection condition, can be calculated at the query decomposition and optimisation stage. Thus, the success of this form of optimisation, reflected in the coalesced view query graph, depends on the existence of appropriate database statistics.

The above forms of optimisation, together with many other techniques are discussed in detail in Jarke (1984b).

6.8.3 Update Synchronisation and Concurrency Control

Concurrency control has already been discussed in relation to centralised database systems (subsection 5.5.3). It should be remembered that concurrency control is only relevant when database updates may occur concurrently with other transactions; it is only when changes are being made to the database that, without control, inconsistent information may be retrieved from the database or incorrect data written to the database, due to 'interference' from other updates. Additional control problems exist in a DDBS due to the distribution of database updates to remote nodes. As mentioned in an earlier section, in order to maintain database integrity it is important to ensure that all the updates at remote nodes relating to a particular request are applied to the database (partial updating must not occur); it is also important to ensure that concurrent update requests are applied in the correct sequence (i.e. the execution of a set of transactions must be serializable). In the former case a two-phase commit protocol is generally adopted for update synchronisation, while in the latter case various controls based on locking and/or timestamping may be used.

Update synchronisation

The *two-phase commit protocol* is commonly used to synchronise the processing of updates in a distributed database environment; it consists of a 'prepare-for-update' phase and a 'commit-or-abort-update' phase. In the 'prepare-for-update' phase which starts after the update request has been decomposed, update subrequest messages are distributed to relevant nodes. Upon receipt by each node, the update is carried out on copies of the relevant database objects held in 'secure storage' (i.e. in storage for which recovery facilities are available in the event of some failure). If the local node carries out this updating successfully, it returns a 'ready-for-update' response to the node controlling the update. This ends the 'prepare-for-update' phase and at this stage, the permanent database has not been updated. If all nodes have sent a 'ready' response, this means that the global update can be completed successfully using the updated copies of objects in secure storage, even if there is some failure at a node. If a failure does occur, that particular node's update can be carried out upon recovery. The 'commit-or-abort-update' phase then begins, a 'commit-update' message being sent to relevant nodes if all are ready, or an 'abort-update' message otherwise. In the 'commit-update' case, the nodes copy the updated objects to the permanent database and return an 'acknowledgement' response to the controlling node. This completes the update. The controlling node then produces an appropriate global update response to be passed to the node requesting the update.

Concurrency control

The two-phase commit protocol discussed above provides the means by which the local processing of a global update request at the various nodes may be coordinated to ensure that the effect is a single global update transaction on a single database. But DDBS requests are not processed in isolation. The DDBS may receive a number of concurrent requests whose execution, as in the centralised database situation, must be controlled to avoid interference with each other. But because the database is distributed and managed by separate local systems, concurrency control is more complex.

The work of Bernstein et al on SDD-1 (Bernstein 1980) has provided a major contribution to the field of concurrency control in general and deserves special mention. In SDD-1, transactions are grouped into classes according to their read- and write-sets (i.e. the subsets of the database which the transactions read from, or write to). Concurrent transactions only conflict if the read- or write-set of one intersects with the write-set of another. By means of a technique referred to as 'conflict graph analysis', transactions which are likely to conflict can be identified and controlled, while other transactions can be allowed to run with little or no control, thus increasing the amount of concurrency possible in the system. Conflict graph analysis is a general technique which can be used as a preprocessing step to determine which transactions need to be controlled; it is independent of the actual concurrency control technique used in a particular system.

Various concurrency control techniques have been designed. Some involve locking mechanisms, and others use some form of timestamping. In some the control is centralised at a single node, and in others the control is distributed to the nodes involved in the transaction. Comprehensive surveys of different techniques may be found in Bernstein (1981a) and Kohler (1981); the main types will be outlined here.

Techniques which provide some form of centralised control include: centralised two-phase locking, primary copy two-phase locking, and circulating control token.

Two-phase locking was discussed in section 5.5.3 (it should not be confused with the two-phase commit protocol discussed above). In its simple form, all objects in a transaction are locked before any are unlocked, although locking need not be carried out in one step. In the *preclaim* form of two-phase locking, all locking is carried out in one step at the start of a transaction; this avoids deadlocks but concurrency is reduced (i.e. fewer transactions can run in parallel).

Centralised two-phase locking is a modified form for a distributed database environment. A centralised scheduler is used at the controlling node; it maintains a global lock table and locks are obtained for a transaction from the scheduler. *Primary copy two-phase locking* is a version which supports replication of database objects. One copy of each replicated object is designated as the primary copy, and before a transaction is allowed to lock any copy, the primary copy must be locked. This avoids concurrent updates of different copies of the same object.

In the *circulating control token* technique, no locking is necessary. Nodes are implicitly linked to form a virtual communication ring on which a unique control token circulates. An update can only be initiated by a node when it possesses the control token; then when the update is complete the token is passed on to the next node on the virtual ring. The disadvantage of this technique is that no concurrent updates are possible. A modified version which permits concurrency has been suggested but it is not really suitable for an interactive update environment; the database is divided into sections (logically, not physically), and the control token consists of a set of tickets, one for each database section, which can be allocated separately to different nodes.

Techniques which provide decentralised control include: timestamping, and majority consensus (or voting).

Timestamping was introduced in section 5.5.3 in relation to centralised systems. A *timestamp* is a unique number assigned to a transaction or a data object; in a DDBS it may be a unique time from a 'global clock', or a local time concatenated with the identifier of the local node to ensure global uniqueness. Various timestamping mechanisms have been proposed, which are aimed at avoiding backing out transactions as far as possible. Backing out and restarting is, of course, a more serious problem in a distributed system as compared with a centralised one. One alternative to the basic method is for local nodes to buffer read and write (update) requests so that they can be processed strictly in timestamp order and so that no backing out is necessary. For this to work, each node must have some means of knowing which requests it will need to buffer, and when it is safe to execute a buffered request. The fact that some requests must wait, however, can give rise to a deadlock situation. Various different timestamp mechanisms are discussed in Kohler (1981), Bernstein (1981a).

A concurrency control mechanism based on the timestamping approach mentioned above is used in SDD-1 (Bernstein 1980). However, it should be noted that the SDD-1 mechanism is more sophisticated than that described above and includes additional techniques to avoid deadlock situations.

The final decentralised control mechanism to be considered here is the *majority consensus* (or *voting*) technique which may be used with locks or timestamps, and applies to replicated objects. The node updating a replicated object, issues a 'prepare-for-update' message to nodes containing copies; if the majority acknowledge with a 'ready-to-update' response (i.e. they vote for the update), the node goes ahead with the update. Nodes involved in the update will vote for the update if they are able to lock it or there is no timestamp conflict, otherwise they will vote against it.

Before ending this subsection, it should be mentioned that while concurrency control in a monotype homogeneous DDBS is more complex than in a centralised system, it is even more complex in a heterogeneous DDBS since each DBMS will have its own local concurrency control mechanism. For this reason, some heterogenous prototypes (e.g. Multibase and Proteus) do not currently permit global updates (only local updates, which are not under the control of the DDBS Kernel, are allowed).

6.9 Summary

In this chapter, the major issues in distributed database systems have been identified and discussed. Important aspects of a DDBS are the software architecture, the global data model and global language (in heterogeneous systems), query processing (including decomposition of the query to reflect the partitioning and distribution of the database, and also optimisation of the query), update synchronisation, and concurrency control. All these aspects have been discussed. In addition, some prototype systems have been reviewed briefly, in order to compare and contrast the different software design approaches.

Distributed database systems are not yet in widespread use, since performance problems still need to be overcome. However, much research is currently being undertaken in the DDBS field, and the growing use of data communications networks, both wide area and local area, is providing further impetus for this research.

CHAPTER SEVEN

New Directions

7.1 Introduction

Important advances in both hardware and software are having an impact on database technology. Some of the ideas behind these advances have been around for a long time but have not been realised in commercial systems due to problems such as cost, hardware limitations, lack of generality, etc. In many cases, these problems are fast being solved and we may therefore look forward in the not too distant future to exciting new database products. These new database products should be more *user-friendly*, *'intelligent'* and *responsive*.

Future systems should achieve greater intelligence by supporting data models with much enhanced semantics. Furthermore, the use of such systems should be greatly facilitated by the availability of interfaces which are more user-oriented, in particular ones which exploit the latest graphics technology. And finally, by exploiting new hardware specifically designed to support databases, the systems should provide faster access to data than is currently possible.

These aspects are discussed in this chapter, and the chapter ends by presenting a possible architecture for an intelligent knowledge based system.

7.2 From Databases to Knowledge Bases

7.2.1 Introduction

Current database management systems are limited in their support for data model semantics, as was pointed out in Chapter 3. The effects of such limitations are many. They include the following:
- some conceptual information will be represented in the DBMS data model in an unnatural way;
- some conceptual information may be omitted completely from the DBMS data model;
- conceptual information will be split between the database and the programs which use the database;
- the application designer has the responsibility of ensuring that certain semantic constraints are not violated;
- semantic constraints may be violated by interactive users, since the DBMS has no means of checking constraints which it does not automatically support;
- the inference/deductive capabilities of the DBMS are limited or non-existent.

These are not the only reasons, however, why much current research effort is being devoted towards the design of systems to support rich semantics. Other developments have also provided the impetus for such research. Recent interest in *expert systems* has resulted in a pooling of knowledge amongst artificial intelligence (AI) experts and database experts. Research effort in the field of *heterogeneous distributed database systems* has involved the search for a global conceptual model which can support rich semantics (as discussed in Chapter 6). Interest in *speech understanding* and *natural language interfaces* has also contributed to this area.

Support for rich semantics will transform database management systems into *knowledge base management systems* (*KBMS*), and the key to that support is the *metadatabase*. The current situation regarding metadata and data dictionaries will be discussed in the next subsection, and this will be followed by a discussion of the changes which are necessary to support a knowledge base, as distinct from a database.

7.2.2 Metadata and Data Dictionaries

Metadata was briefly discussed in Chapter 2, together with the concept of a *data dictionary* as a repository for the metadata. A range of data dictionary systems (DDS) are currently available. They are also sometimes known as 'dictionary/directory systems', the dictionary part relating to logical aspects and the directory part relating to physical aspects, but the term 'data dictionary' will be used here to include both aspects.

In this subsection, a brief guide to the different categories of DDS will be provided, together with an indication of the type of information currently supported by DDSs. The intention here is to lay the foundation for the discussion of knowledge base requirements in the next subsection. Readers who are interested in finding out more about data dictionary systems will find a useful survey, including features of some existing systems, in Allen (1982).

Currently available data dictionary systems may be split into three main categories: independent, interfaced, and embedded. These categories will be briefly described.

The *independent DDS* is independent of any DBMS, and there is no automatic link to a DBMS. The data dictionary itself is used as a central repository for the metadata collected during data investigation and the other stages of database development (discussed in Chapter 2). The DDS can also be used to generate database schema from its stored metadata for use in specific DBMS, by means of appropriate data description language templates. Such DDSs are used not only in DBMS environments but also in traditional file environments.

The *interfaced DDS* acts like an application system as far as the DBMS to which it is interfaced is concerned. The data dictionary itself is stored and managed by the DBMS as a separate database, independent of the database to which it is related. The DDS carries out a limited form of integration of metadata with data. This type of system is usually provided as an 'add-on' to an existing DBMS — the DBMS is produced first, and the DDS is added later to enhance the DBMS capabilities.

The *embedded DDS* is completely integrated and is part of the DBMS. The DBMS is designed from the outset to support data dictionary facilities. It is this third category of DDS which is important for the future development of knowledge based systems.

However, currently available data dictionary systems provide facilities which are oriented towards support for standard record-based DBMSs

only. Typical of the type of information stored in a data dictionary is the list below:
- . identification information for data objects
    - name, synonyms, description, etc.
- . representation information
    - attribute type, length, where it originates, etc.
- . relationship information
    - name of relationship, objects related, access path, etc.
- . statistical information
    - frequency of access to objects
    - performance statistics
    - frequency distributions showing the number of occurrences of each object type over time
- . control information
    - authority, passwords and other access control data
    - validation data (range, uniqueness, valid values, etc.)
- . functional information
    - application programs which access the objects
    - functions performed on the objects
    - representation in application programs
    etc.

Although adequate for conventional DBMS, current DDS facilities are inadequate for use in a knowledge based system. However, they do provide a starting point, since a knowledge base must contain the information indicated above, as well as much additional metadata.

7.2.3 The Knowledge Base and KBMS

At the beginning of this section the semantic limitations of existing systems were summarised, and it was mentioned that the key to support for rich semantics is the metadatabase. This subsection will aim to identify the important requirements of a knowledge base and its supporting system.

In Chapter 2, a conceptual modelling notation was introduced which enables data models rich in semantics to be constructed. In Chapter 3, however, it was shown how existing DBMSs are in general very poor in their semantic support and the only way of overcoming this problem at the present time is to build the additional semantics into application programs which use the database. This is highly undesirable and violates one of the important objectives of the database approach — that of *data independence*. The application designer should not be responsible for ensuring the maintenance of semantic integrity within the database; the DBMS should be responsible for all data semantics. New DBMSs (or

KBMSs) are thus needed to support data semantics at least as rich as those discussed in Chapter 2.

An important construct which is lacking in most DBMSs, or only available in a primitive form, is the *rule*. In some systems certain types of rule (e.g. simple validity constraints) are permitted, but there is no general rule capability. Prolog, of course, does have such a capability, but it lacks many of the important facilities required for general use in a data processing environment.

Many types of rule need to be stored in a knowledge base. For example, rules are required for:
- defining constraints on domain and attribute values
- defining integrity and consistency constraints
- deriving new data
- defining user views
- categorization (defining subsets)
- specifying the existence characteristic of relationships
- defining partitions and fragments in a distributed data base.

All of the above may be expressed in the form of *predicates*, and this factor is significant in the choice of approach for the KBMS of the future.

However, not all metadata is in the form of rules; some of it can be represented as simple facts. For example, facts may be used:
- to specify the size and type of attributes
- to specify domain associations
- to specify access permissions
- to specify synonyms
- to indicate which application programs use which objects, and other functional information
- to indicate access mechanisms for objects (index, hash table, etc.)
- to associate physical files with logical object types

Some conclusions can be drawn from the observations made so far in this section. Firstly, metadata and data should ideally be integrated into one knowledge base. Secondly, predicates should be supported as a data type, and the KBMS internal language should be based on predicate logic. The KBMS should also be designed to manage binary relationships efficiently. It must be remembered, though, that it will be required to support not only ad hoc queries, but also large volume data manipulation via application programs. In the latter case, an additional requirement of a KBMS is the ability to build conventional records (n-ary relations) from the data stored in the knowledge base.

With these basic features, a system should be able to support a conceptual model which is rich in semantics, to support very high level user interfaces, and to provide building blocks and automated tools for application systems development. (Readers who wish to investigate the subject of knowledge based systems further might be interested in Addis

(1985), in which an extended relational analysis approach is used as a design technique.)

The big question is whether a system with adequate performance characteristics for operational use could be built at the present time. This question will be considered in section 7.4. But first, the question of user-friendly interfaces will be considered.

7.3 Advanced User Interfaces

7.3.1 Introduction

It is true to say that facilities for the casual non-specialist database user are currently very limited. Most database systems do not provide any higher level interface than a formal English-like query language, and users need to know a fair amount about the data stored in the database, including its structure, before they can use the systems.

On the other hand, users' expectations have increased rapidly over the last few years with the proliferation of microcomputers, both at work and in the home. Users are being tempted by the availability of full-screen facilities, including pointing devices such as a 'mouse' or light-pen for screen navigation and control. High-resolution graphics screens are widely available, permitting diagrammatic and pictorial representation of information, use of icons, etc.

In the two subsections which follow two important aspects of advanced user interfaces are discussed: the use of graphics facilities, and personalising interfaces for end-users by means of 'user profiles'.

7.3.2 The Importance of Graphics Facilities in User Interfaces

Interfaces for experienced and specialist users of databases are generally quite adequate, as was illustrated in Chapter 4; most formal query languages provide excellent facilities for such users. However, the casual, non-specialist user is not so well catered for, and it is for such users that the exploitation of graphics technology is important.

In Chapter 4, two graphics-oriented user interfaces were introduced: QBE (Query-By-Example) and Cupid, and one of the advantages mentioned in relation to such interfaces was the possibility of making them very user-friendly by means of sophisticated pointing devices such as touch screens, light pens and mice; the possible use of icons was also mentioned. Other important advantages indicated were the minimisation of typing, the way in which the user is able to construct his query by specifying the component parts in any order, and the 'view' he has of his query during construction. All those points apply only to graphics-oriented interfaces.

Graphics technology can be exploited even further though, and some research work has been aimed in that direction. There are many opportunities for providing graphics-oriented interfaces which are higher level than QBE and Cupid. The main disadvantage of those two systems is that users must know something about the structure of the database which they wish to access. In this subsection, three examples will be given of the possibilities for more user-friendly interfaces for casual users, which do not require anything more than a basic knowledge of the type of data with which they are working. They all utilise graphics and pointing devices, and two of them introduce the notion of *browsing*.

The three approaches considered here are the Foral-LP approach, and two different browsing approaches of SDMS and LID.

Foral-LP

Foral-LP (Senko 1977) is a graphics and light-pen oriented interface, based on the Diam binary relationship system (Senko (1975). The user who wishes to query the database is presented with his particular view of it, by means of a simplified version of the relevant part of the binary relationship data model, which the system displays on the screen. In Foral-LP, the object types are represented by their names, and lines join objects which are related. The reader is referred back to the binary relationship version of the library model in Figure 3.12. Part of such a diagram might be presented to the user in a Foral-LP interface, but with simple lines joining the objects.

In addition to the data model diagram, an operations list is provided at the side of the screen in the form of a menu. This includes such keywords as OUTPUT, WHERE and PROCESS, and such operators and functions as 'equal', 'gtrthn', 'and', 'or', 'sum', 'cnt', etc. The letters and digits (A-Z, 0-9) and the arithmetic operators are also displayed at the top of the screen.

The user specifies his query by touching the appropriate parts of the screen with the light-pen in the required sequence, and a formal version of the query is built up by the system in the process. The user first establishes the 'context' of his query by touching 'OUTPUT' with the light pen and then touching an object (e.g. Isbn). Other objects are selected by tracing a path with the light pen from the object required, through the relevant relationships and associated objects, back to the context object. For example, if the name of a person reserving a particular Isbn is required, the user would touch the following parts of the Figure 3.12 diagram: Name, named, Person, has-reservation-of, Reservation, reserved-by, Catalogued-Book, has-isbn, Isbn (in the case of relationships, the lines are touched, rather than the names).

Selection conditions are incorporated into the query by the user touching the 'WHERE' keyword and then touching objects on the screen as relevant (including the menu of operators and functions). Constants may be built up using A-Z, 0-9 and other characters on the screen, or typed in on a keyboard.

In such a system as the one described above a user is freed completely from the need to learn a syntax (apart from the 'light pen syntax'); everything can be done by pointing (Senko refers to this as 'primitive natural language'). The user does not need to know the structure of the database — it is presented to him graphically. Furthermore, this approach lends itself to additional refinements, to make it even more attractive to the end-user. For example, icons could be used in the Figure 3.12 diagram in appropriate places — a shape of a person could replace the Person object, a picture of a book could replace the Book object, and the outline of a catalogue drawer could replace the Catalogued-Book object.

Two browsing approaches — SDMS and LID

One disadvantage of all the query interfaces presented in this book so far, is that the user has to specify his query completely before it is answered. The SDMS and LID approaches introduce the notion of *browsing*. If browsing is combined with graphics facilities and pointing devices, a powerful end-user interface is provided. Browsing is related to some of the ideas behind *windowing*, which has become popular on micros. One important aspect is the ability to obtain an overall view of the subject area, point to the object or objects of interest, obtain a more detailed or selected view, and return back to the overall view when required. This can be carried down to many levels.

In SDMS (Spatial Data Management System) (Herot 1980), pictorial data (stored on an optical video disc) is supported, in addition to conventional record-based data. A main screen is used for the browsing facility, with icons representing pictorial data objects; when requested, actual pictorial data is displayed on a special screen. A joystick is used for pointing to parts of the screen in order to zoom in on a particular object. In a system such as SDMS, part of the data in the database can be presented to the user at a particular time. He may then 'browse' through the data at the current level by pointing to the edges of the screen to extend the view, or alternatively point to part of the screen to obtain a more detailed view of that part. For example, if the screen contained a set of book titles, the user could obtain full details of a particular book by pointing to a particular title.

In LID (Living in a Database) (Fogg 1984), browsing is carried out via an entity-relationship data model diagram (or part of it) displayed on the screen. If a user points to an entity box (e.g. Person), an occurrence of that entity (e.g. a record relating to a specific person) is displayed in place of the relevant entity box on the screen. Other occurrences of the same entity can then be sequentially or selectively viewed. The user can also use the browsing mechanism to obtain related records of a different type by pointing at the relevant relationship and entity box displayed on the screen; that entity box is then also replaced by an actual record from the database.

The three examples of end-user interfaces presented above are all important in the ways in which they utilise graphics facilities and pointing devices to provide users with access to data in databases, without requiring them to have any more than a basic knowledge of the type of data with which they are working.

7.3.3 Personalising End-User Interfaces — the User Profile

An 'intelligent' user interface (IUI) should be capable of tailoring itself to the needs and idiosyncrasies of individual users, adapting itself to new requirements and new information from the user. In order to do this, the interface must maintain a *user profile*. Most operating systems now provide user profile facilities, in which such things as aliases/synonyms, abbreviations, user-controllable parameters, etc. may be set or altered for individual users. The knowledge base user profile may form part of the operating system profile or may be independent. It will contain individual user aliases, abbreviations, etc., which relate specifically to knowledge base objects and the knowledge base user interfaces.

Users must have control over their own knowledge base profile, in the same way as they have control over their operating system profile. Users profiles should, however, also be updatable by the user interfaces; in this way, an interface can appear to 'learn' about the user from its interaction with him. The importance of this was stressed in section 4.3 in relation to natural language interfaces. It was indicated that a natural language interface should be able to store user definitions which result from some dialogue with the user for future reference, since a user would not tolerate repeating the same dialogue a number of times. The ability to store user definitions is important for all user interfaces, and the profile is an appropriate place for such definitions. A macro facility could be used for this purpose, and users could be allowed to create their own macro definitions.

The separation of the user profiles from the knowledge base itself is important if the user is to have full control over his own profile. He can then create and alter information in it, and even alter information created by the system, without requiring 'permission' from the system. The profile belongs to him, and he has control over it.

7.4 Database Machines

7.4.1 Why Database Machines?

Performance of database systems has been recognised for some time as a problem, in particular in the case of the relational and binary relationship approaches. But it is exactly these approaches which offer the greatest opportunities in the direction of knowledge based systems. As compared with a conventional database, both more data and different types of data will need to be stored in a knowledge base. Hence, the storage and access problems of current DBMSs will be an order of magnitude greater in a KBMS.

Many of the early ideas for improving the performance of database systems were based on a DBMS backend computer using conventional hardware. However, the great interest in the relational approach over the last decade or so, and the more recent interest in the binary relationship approach, has resulted in some major research efforts aimed at producing hardware specifically designed for database management, or to assist in the tasks of database management. With some database operations performed by hardware, rather than software, and some carried out in parallel, rather than sequentially, improvements in performance can be expected. The technology is still fairly new, however, although some prototype systems, as well as commercial systems, do exist.

The different database machine approaches are discussed in the next subsection.

7.4.2 The Different Categories of Database Machine

A *database machine* is a 'backend' computer which takes over from the mainframe (or host) computer the disc input/output routines and in some cases the database management functions as well. There are a number of different approaches to database machines; the following classification has been suggested by Hsiao (1983):
. software single backend approach
. multiple backend approach
. intelligent controller approach
. hardware backend approach
. hybrid approaches (combinations of the above approaches).

The four main approaches are briefly described below, and their likely impact on performance is discussed. Some prototype database machines are described in Hsiao (1983).

Software single backend approach

The software single backend approach utilises conventional hardware (usually a minicomputer). The main DBMS functions reside on the backend computer, with database interface and data communications software residing on both host and backend. The database interface on the host appears to the applications and users just like a DBMS, but it only carries out the user/application interface tasks of a DBMS and sends all database requests to the backend.

A software backend can improve performance and reduce response time, if the host computer is heavily loaded and the volume of database accesses causes bottlenecks to occur when the DBMS is resident on the host. There is an alternative to a backend computer in this situation though; a complete upgrade to a larger and faster computer could be carried out.

The software backend approach is discussed in detail in Maryanski (1980), together with extensions which include the next approach to be discussed.

Multiple backend approach

In the multiple backend approach, the functions of the host computer are the same as in the single backend approach. The backend consists of a 'controller', attached to the host, and a set of computers (possibly micros), attached to the controller.

This approach offers opportunities for parallelism. Various alternatives exist. One possibility is for each backend computer to hold a complete copy of the DBMS functions, but only a portion of the database. Operations can then be carried out in parallel on each portion of the database, thus improving performance. With four processors supporting a relational DBMS, for example, each processor might be responsible for a quarter of the records in each relation, and a complete relation can therefore be processed in approximately a quarter of the time, as compared with a single processor. However, as might be expected, multi-relation operations (such as 'joins') are not so easy (cf. distributed query processing in Chapter 6).

Another alternative for parallelism is for each processor to be responsible for a particular DBMS function or set of functions, with the possibility of pipelining between functions. The processors would all have access to the complete database.

A third alternative is for each processor to be able to carry out all functions, as in the first case, but with access to the complete database. Parallelism in query processing, as discussed in subsection 5.4.1, can take place in this case. The single relation subqueries of the query tree in Figure 5.9 can be carried out in parallel by different processors; the two-relation subqueries must, of course, be processed serially.

Intelligent controller approach

The intelligent controller approach is based on specially designed hardware. The backend machine is designed specifically to support basic database operations, and the software in the backend controls these operations. The top-level DBMS functions (e.g. the user interface, query decomposition, etc.) reside in the host computer, and the lower level database access requests are passed to the intelligent controller for action. The main advantage of this approach is the speed at which operations on complete sets of data may be carried out, as compared with conventional hardware.

Britton-Lee's IDM (Intelligent Database Machine) is an example of this approach. It is based on the relational data model and provides hardware support for relational operations such as selection and join. Another example is ICL's CAFS (Content Addressable File Store).

Hardware backend approach

The hardware backend approach provides the opportunity for the design of special purpose hardware to support the complete database management system. Whereas the software backend approach uses conventional hardware and is constrained by the general purpose nature of the hardware, including the disc input/output facilities, the hardware backend approach can utilise the latest hardware technology. New computer architectures are being designed (e.g. using parallel processors and parallel transfer discs) which specifically support database and related operations.

The constraints imposed on database management by existing conventional general purpose computers have long been recognised. It is these last two database machine approaches — intelligent controller and hardware backend — which therefore offer the greatest possibilities for high performance KBMS support in the future. Examples of various prototype database machines based on these approaches may be found in Hsiao (1983). A further example, which has been designed specifically with knowledge base systems in mind and is based on the binary relationship data model, is the Fact System (McGregor 1984); this system was mentioned in section 5.3.2 in relation to binary relationship storage structures.

7.5 The Intelligent Knowledge Based System of the Future

Putting together what has been discussed in the previous sections of this chapter, a possible architecture for an *intelligent knowledge based system* (IKBS) is beginning to emerge. Figure 7.1 represents this architecture and it is discussed below.

The most important components in Figure 7.1 are, of course, the Knowledge Base Management System (KBMS) and the Knowledge Base which it supports. In section 7.2, it was suggested that the internal language supported by the system should be based on predicate logic, and that the knowledge base should contain both data and metadata.

The KBMS should be designed with the possibility of hardware support in mind. As indicated in section 7.4, special purpose hardware is the way to achieve responsive systems, but research in the field of database machines is relatively new and it is anticipated, therefore, that software KBMSs running on existing hardware will be the first to emerge.

The Intelligent User Interface is part of the IKBS and should provide advanced graphics-based interface facilities such as those discussed in section 7.3, as well as conventional database user interface facilities. It may consist of several modules, one for each type of interface. It should be personalised for individual users by maintaining user profiles as discussed in subsection 7.3.3.

Outside the IKBS are the External Systems Interfaces. It is envisaged that these will be constructed using 'building blocks' provided by the KBMS, and will communicate with the system using the KBMS internal

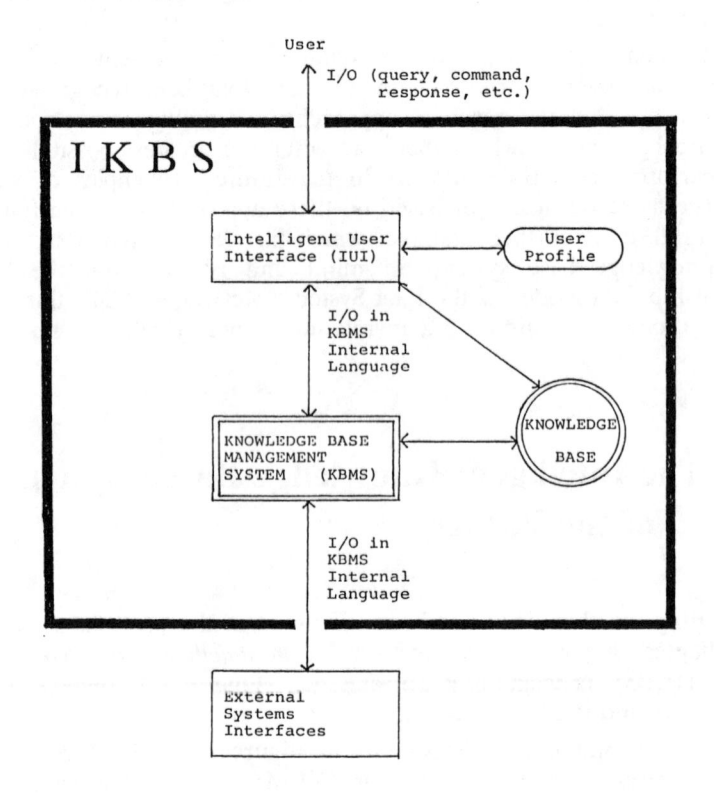

```
              User
               ↑ I/O (query, command,
                      response, etc.)
┌─────────────────────────────────────────┐
│  I K B S                                │
│                                         │
│         ┌──────────────────┐    ┌─────────┐
│         │ Intelligent User │←──→│  User   │
│         │ Interface (IUI)  │    │ Profile │
│         └──────────────────┘    └─────────┘
│              ↕                      ↑
│           I/O in                    │
│           KBMS                      │
│           Internal                  │
│           Language                  │
│                                     │
│         ┌──────────────────┐    ┌─────────┐
│         │ KNOWLEDGE BASE   │←──→│KNOWLEDGE│
│         │ MANAGEMENT       │    │  BASE   │
│         │ SYSTEM  (KBMS)   │    │         │
│         └──────────────────┘    └─────────┘
│              ↕
│           I/O in
│           KBMS
│           Internal
│           Language
└─────────────────────────────────────────┘
               ↕
         ┌──────────────┐
         │ External     │
         │ Systems      │
         │ Interfaces   │
         └──────────────┘
```

Figure 7.1 Architecture for an Intelligent Knowledge Based System

language enhanced as necessary for external systems support. The external systems interfaces will pass appropriate requests to the KBMS for information; for example, the interface to a distributed database system will require database partitioning and distribution information, amongst other things. External systems interfaces may be provided to support any or all of the following:
- application systems, containing embedded knowledge base access commands
- distributed database systems
- interaction with single-user micro-based DBMSs
- intelligent interfaces to existing DBMSs
- office information systems

7.6 Conclusion

Much has been covered in this book, but inevitably, much more could have been covered. The whole field of databases has increased and broadened rapidly in recent years, and looks like continuing to do so in the future, both as a result of the move in the direction of knowledge based systems, and as a result of the impact of micros, distributed systems, and hardware advances on this field.

It has been the objective of this book to give readers a broad view of the field of databases and database systems, rather than the more narrow, traditional view provided by many existing textbooks. Those who wish to specialise in a particular database area should now be able to put their work in the context of the database field as a whole, and also in the context of the environment in which a database is used.

It is hoped that this book, and in particular this last chapter, will stimulate further research in the database field, especially in the direction of more intelligent, user-friendly, and responsive systems.

"The future lies ahead"
John (1986)

Index

access path 37
ACM/PCM 16
Adabas 146
Adaplex 82
advanced user interfaces 232-236
after-images 180
aggregate function 52
aggregation 50-51
alternate key (relational model) 41
architecture
    DBMS architecture 11-13
    DDBS network architecture 194-196
    DDBS software architecture 196-207
Asdas 82, 157
association 22
Astrid 126
attribute 25-26
audit trail 180
authorization 182

B-tree / B^+-tree 154-155
Bachman diagram 69, 73-74
backup copies (of database) 180
BCNF (Boyce-Codd Normal Form) 37, 41
before-images 180
binary relationship model 81-90
    database organisation 155-159
    query processing 172-176
Boyce-Codd Normal Form 37, 41
browsing 233, 234-235

CAFS (Content Addressable File Store) 238
calculus 102
candidate key (relational model) 41
cartesian product (relational algebra) 130

categorization (in data modelling) 49-50
checkpoint 180
Codasyl 68
    schema 74-77
    subschema 96
    database organisation 159-161
    query processing 176-179
communications (in DDBS) 194-196, 213-215
conceptual model 9, Ch.2, 90-93
conceptual schema 13
concurrency control 183-187,
              222-225 (DDBS)
concurrent access 183-187
Condor 126, 146
connection trap 54-56
coset 68
constraint 17, 48, 91-93
cover aggregation 50-51
Cupid 112-114
currency (in Codasyl systems) 135

Daplex 82
data analysis 16 (see also: data modelling)
data base (see: database)
data communications (in DDBS) 194-196,
              213-215
data description language 58
    relational 66-67
    network (Codasyl) 68, 74-77
data dictionary 18-19, 229-230
data distribution 207-210
data independence 7, 38, 230
data investigation 17-19
data manipulation language
    (see: database manipulation language)

data model 9-11
    conceptual 9, Ch.2, 90-93
    external 11, 93-97, 139-140
    internal 11, 148
        (see also: database organisation)
    relational 59-67, 148-155, 164-172
    network 68-77, 159-161, 176-179
    hierarchical 77-81, 161-163
    binary relationship 81-90, 155-159, 172-176
data modelling 19, Ch.2
data sharing 8 (see also: concurrent access)
database 3, 4-9
database administrator 8
database design 19, Ch.3
database development 16-20
    data investigation 17-19
    data modelling 19, Ch.2
    database design 19, Ch.3
    database implementation 19
    database monitoring and tuning 20
database implementation 19
database integrity 179, 183-187
database machines 236-239
database management systems 3, 143-147
database manipulation language 99, 131-138
database monitoring and tuning 20
database organisation 148-163
    relational 148-155
    binary relationship 155-159
    network 159-161
    hierarchical 161-163
database protection 8, 179-187
database reliability 179, 180-182
database security 179, 182-183
Database 2 (IBM) 66, 118, 185
dBase II / dBase III 126, 144, 146, 154
DBMS (database management system) 3, 143-147
DBMS architecture 11-13
DBTG (Codasyl) 68
DDBS (distributed database system) Ch.6
DDBS Data Interface 199, 200, 202
DDBS Message 213-215
DDBS network architecture 194-196
DDBS Nucleus 199-202
DDBS Query Interface 199-201
DDBS software architecture 196-207
DDL (data description language) 58
    relational 66-67
    network (Codasyl) 68, 74-77
DDSS 16
deadlock 185-186

decomposition (of relational queries) 164-167, 216-220 (DDBS)
degree (of relation) 61
degree characteristic (of relationship) 23
Delta 80, 146
dependency 39, 47
determinant 41
Diam 81, 233
dictionary 18-19, 229-230
difference (relational algebra) 130
directory
    data dictionary/directory 18-19, 229-230
    distributed data directory 201
distributed data directory 201
distributed database systems Ch.6
distribution (of data in DDBS) 207-210
division (relational algebra) 130
DML (database manipulation language) 99, 131-138
DMS1100 146
domain 26, 35
domain-oriented calculus 103, 111
D2S2 16

entity 25-26
entity integrity 61
entity set 27
existence characteristic (of relationship) 23
existential quantifier 103, 116
extensional database 59
external model 11, 93-97, 139-140
external schema 13, 93-97, 139-140
external view (see external model)

fact 17, 85, 122, 231
Fact Machine & System 159, 239
failure (disc, system, transaction) 181-182
FDM (Functional Data Model) 82
fifth normal form (5NF) 37, 41
file 4-9
file management system 143-144
first normal form (1NF) 37-38
FMS (file management system) 143-144
foreign key 40, 62
fourth normal form (4NF) 37, 41
fragmentation 209
full functional dependence 39
function (aggregate) 52
function (binary relationship approach) 82
functional analysis 16
Functional Data Model (FDM) 82
functional dependence 39
functional notation 85

functional system   85
    (see also: binary relationship model)

generalization   49-50
generic object   49
global data model (DDBS)   211-213
global conceptual schema (DDBS)   199
global query language (DDBS)   211-213
goal (Prolog)   123, 172-173
graphics-oriented interfaces   109-115, 232-235

hash table   149-152
hashing   149-152
HDAM (IMS)   161-163
heap   149
heterogeneous DDBS   197-203
HIDAM (IMS)   161-163
hierarchical model   77-81
    database organisation   161-163
hierarchical sequence (IMS)   162
hierarchy   77-81
HISAM (IMS)   161-162
homogeneous DDBS   197-198
horizontal fragmentation   209
host language   132, 135-138
HSAM (IMS)   161-162

IDM (Intelligent Database Machine)   238
IDMS   68, 146
identifier   26, 34 (see also: primary key)
IDSII   146
IKBS (intelligent knowledge based system)
    239-240
Image   146
IMS   80-81, 146, 161-163
index   152-155
indexed sequential access mechanism   152
Ingres   116, 146, 149, 150, 154, 169
integrity   179, 183-187
integrity constraint   17, 48, 91-93
intelligent knowledge based systems   239-240
intensional database   59
Interface (DDBS)   199-202
interface (query/user)   Ch.4, 232-236, 239-240
internal model   11, 148
    (see also: database organisation)
internal schema   13, 94
intersection (relational algebra)   130
ISO (International Standards Organisation)
    Open Systems Interconnection   213

join (relational algebra)   126, 127-128, 130
join strategy   169-172

KBMS (knowledge base management system)
    228, 230-232, 239-240
key (see: identifier, primary key)
knowledge base   230-232, 239
knowledge base management system   228,
    230-232, 239-240
Knowledgeman   118, 133-134, 145-147, 154

LBMS-SDM   16, 94
linkage condition   101
lock   184-186, 224 (DDBS)
locking   184-186, 224 (DDBS)
locking granularity   185
log (transaction)   180
logic system   85
    (see also: binary relationship model)

mapping (in database design)   Ch.3
MDBS   120, 135-138, 146, 147, 177
metadata   18, 228-230
metadatabase   228
member (Codasyl)   68
missing value   53-54
model (see: data model)
MRDS   146
multi-attribute identifier   26-27
Multibase   205, 207, 211, 212
multi-database system   198
mutual dependence   39

n-ary relation   60
n-tuple   60
natural join (relational algebra)   130
natural language   104-108
navigational route   37
network architecture   194-196
network model   68-77
    database organisation   159-161
    query processing   176-179
network protocols   213-214
Niam   16, 82
normal forms   37-41, 131
normalisation   37-48
normalised relation   38
Nucleus (DDBS)   199-202
null value   53-54

OBE (Office-By-Example)   112
object graph   166-167
Open Systems Interconnection   213
operator graph   167
optimisation (of relational queries)   167-168,
    220-222 (DDBS)
optimistic concurrency control   186

Oracle 66, 118, 146, 147, 154
organisation (see: database organisation)
OSI (Open Systems Interconnection) 213
owner (Codasyl) 68

partitioning 208
password 182
path (access) 37
pathlist (QRS) 121
physical database (see: database organisation)
pile 149
Planes 104
pointer (Codasyl) 159-161
pointer (IMS) 162
pointer array (Codasyl) 161
Porel 205, 207
predicate 102-103, 231
predicate calculus 102-103
primary key 38, 41, 61, 62-65
privacy key 179
privacy lock 179, 182
project (relational algebra) 126-127
Prolog 82, 85-90, 122-125, 140, 146-147, 172-174
Proteus 206, 207, 211
protocol (DDBS network) 213-214
PRTV 126

QBE (Query-By-Example) 109-112
Qproc 104
QRS 120-122, 177
quadruple 158
quantifier 103, 116
Quel 116-118
Query-By-Example (QBE) 109-112
query decomposition (relational queries) 164-167,
    216-220 (DDBS)
query detachment 166
query interfaces Ch.4
query languages Ch.4
query optimisation (relational queries) 167-168,
    220-222 (DDBS)
query processing 163-179
query tree 165-166
quintuple 158

R* 204, 206
Rapport 118, 146-147, 150
referential integrity 61
relation 38, 60
relational algebra 41, 120, 126-131, 174-175
relational calculus 103, 116-117, 119
relational model 59-67
  database organisation 148-155
  query processing 164-172

relationship 22-25
relationship relation 62
relationship set 27
reliability 179, 180-182
Rendezvous 104
repeated group (unnormalised relation) 38
replication 208
restrict (relational algebra) 126
ring (Codasyl) 159-161
Robot 104
role 26
rule 17, 85, 122, 231

schema 11-13
  relational 66-67
  network (Codasyl) 74-77
  binary relationship 86
SDD-1 204, 206
second normal form (2NF) 37, 39
security 179, 182-183
segment (IMS) 162-163
select (relational algebra) 126-127
selection condition 101
self-contained language 132-134
semantic constraint 17, 48, 91-93
Semantic Hierarchy Model 16
semantics 18, 48-56
semijoin 220-221
Sequel 66 (see also: SQL)
serializable execution 184
set (Codasyl) 68
set (relational model) 60
set attribute 51
shared access 3, 8
    (see also: concurrent access)
singular coset (Codasyl) 71
Sirius-Delta 205, 207, 212
snapshot 52 (history), 140 (user view)
software architecture (DDBS) 196-207
SQL 66-67, 101, 118-120, 139-140
Squiral 129
storage (see: database organisation)
subschema (Codasyl) 96
subset 49
subtype (see: subset)
surrogate 27
system-owned set (Codasyl) 71
System R 118, 182, 185
System 2000 80, 146
systems development methodology 16
synchronisation 222-223

target list   101
third normal form (3NF)   37, 39-41
time   52-53
timestamping   186-187, 224-225 (DDBS)
top-down data modelling methodology   27-37
Total   68, 146
transaction   180
transaction log   180
transitive dependence   39
triple   157-158
tuple   60
tuple-oriented calculus   103, 116
tuple variable   116
two-phase commit   223
two-phase locking protocol   185, 224 (DDBS)

union (relational algebra)   130
universal quantifier   103
universal relation   42
unnormalised relation   38
update dependency (relational model)   47
update synchronisation   222-223
user profile   235-236
user interface   Ch.4, 232-236, 239-240
user view   93-94

validation   183
vertical fragmentation   209
view   9-11, 93-97, 139-140

References

Abrial (1974)   J. R. Abrial, Data Semantics, in *Data Base Management - Proc. IFIP Working Conf. on Data Base Management*, J. W. Klimbie and K. L. Koffeman (ed.), North-Holland, 1974.

Addis (1985)   T. R. Addis, *Designing Knowledge-Based Systems*, Kogan Page, 1985.

Allen (1982)   F. W. Allen, M. E. S. Loomis and M. V. Mannino, The Integrated Dictionary/Directory System, *Computing Surveys vol.14, no.2*, (June 1982), p.245-286.

Anderson (1983)   T. L. Anderson, Modeling Events and Processes at the Conceptual Level, in *Proc. Second Internat. Conf on Databases: ICOD2*, S. M. Deen and P. Hammersley (ed.), Wiley, 1983.

Ashton-Tate (1981)   Ashton-Tate, dBase II User Manual, 1981.

Atkinson (1984)   M. P. Atkinson et al, The Proteus Distributed Database System, in *Proc. Third British National Conf. on Databases: BNCOD3*, J. Longstaff (ed.), Cambridge University Press, 1984, p.225-245.

Babad (1984)   Y. M. Babad and J. A. Hoffer, Even No Data has a Value, *Comm. ACM vol.27, no.8*, (Aug 1984), p.748-756.

Bernstein (1976)   P. A. Bernstein, Third Normal Form Relations from Functional Dependencies, *ACM Trans. Database Systems vol.1, no.4*, (Dec 1976), p.277-298.

Bernstein (1980)   P. A. Bernstein, D. W. Shipman and J. B. Rothnie, Concurrency Control in a System for Distributed Databases (SDD-1), *ACM Trans. Database Systems vol.5, no.1*, (March 1980), p.18-51.

Bernstein (1981a)   P. A. Bernstein and N. Goodman, Concurrency Control in Distributed Database Systems, *Computing Surveys vol.13, no.2*, (June 1981), p.185-221.

Bernstein (1981b)   P. A. Bernstein et al, Query Processing in a System for Distributed Databases (SDD-1), *ACM Trans. Database Systems vol.6, no.4*, (Dec 1981), p.602-625.

Blasgen (1977) M. W. Blasgen and K. P. Eswaren, Storage and Access in Relational Databases, *IBM Systems Journal vol.16, no.4*, (1977), p.363-377.

Bracchi (1976) G. Bracchi, P. Paolini and G. Pelagatti, Binary Logical Associations in Data Modelling, in *Modelling in Data Base Management Systems*, G. M. Nijssen (ed.), North-Holland, 1976.

Bussolati (1983) U. Bussolati et al, Views Conceptual Design, in *Methodology and Tools for Data Base Design*, S. Ceri (ed.), North-Holland, 1983, p.25-55.

Ceri (1984) S. Ceri and G. Pelagatti, *Distributed Databases*, McGraw-Hill, 1984.

Chamberlin (1976) D. D. Chamberlin et al, SEQUEL2: A Unified Approach to Data Definition, Manipulation & Control, *IBM Journal of Res. and Dev. vol.20, no.6*, (Nov 1976), p.560-575.

Chamberlin (1981) D. D. Chamberlin et al, A History & Evaluation of System R, *Comm. ACM vol.24, no.10*, (Oct 1981), p.632-646.

H. Chen (1984) H. Chen and S. M. Kuck, Combining Relational & Network Retrieval Methods, *SIGMOD 84*, 1984, p.131-142.

Chen (1976) P. P. Chen, The Entity-Relationship Model - Toward a United View of Data, *ACM Trans. Database Systems vol.1, no.1*, (Mar 1976), p.9-36.

Chen (1980) P. P. Chen (ed.), Entity-Relationship Approach to Systems Analysis & Design, 1980.

Cheng (1984) J. M. Cheng et al, IBM Database 2 performance: Design, implementation, and tuning, *IBM Systems Journal vol.23, no.2*, (1984), p.189-210.

Clifford (1983) J. Clifford and D. S. Warren, Formal Semantics for Time in Databases, *ACM Trans. Database Systems vol.8, no.2*, (June 1983), p.214-254.

Clocksin (1981) W. F. Clocksin and C. S. Mellish, *Programming in PROLOG*, Springer-Verlag, 1981.

Codasyl (1981a) Codasyl, *Codasyl Data Description Language Committee Journal of Development 1981*, Canadian Gov. Publishing Centre, 1981.

Codasyl (1981b) Codasyl, *Codasyl Cobol Committee Journal of Development 1981*, Canadian Gov. Publishing Centre, 1981.

Codd (1970) E. F. Codd, A Relational Model of Data for Large Shared Data Banks, *Comm. ACM vol.13, no.6*, (June 1970), p.377-387.

Codd (1972a) E. F. Codd, Further Normalization of the Data Base Relational Model, in *Data Base Systems - Courant Computer Science Symposium 6*, R. Rustin (ed.), Prentice-Hall, 1972.

Codd (1972b) E. F. Codd, Relational Completeness of Data Base Sublanguages, in *Data Base Systems - Courant Computer Science Symposium 6*, R. Rustin (ed.), Prentice-Hall, 1972.

Codd (1974) E. F. Codd, Seven Steps to Rendezvous with the Casual User, in *Data Base Management - Proc. IFIP Working Conf. on Data Base Management*, J. W. Klimbie and K. L. Koffeman (ed.), North-Holland, 1974, p.179-199.

Codd (1977) E. F. Codd, A Data Base Sublanguage Founded on the Relational Calculus, *Proc 1971 ACM SIGFIDET Workshop on Data Description, Access and Control*, , Oct 1977.

Codd (1978) E. F. Codd, How about recently?, in *Improving Database Usability & Responsiveness*, B. Shneiderman (ed.), Academic Press, 1978, p.3-28.

Codd (1979) E. F. Codd, Extending the Database Relational Model to Capture More Meaning, *ACM Trans. Database Systems vol.4, no.4*, (Dec 1979), p.397-434.

Comer (1979) D. Comer, The Ubiquitous B-tree, *Computing Surveys vol.11, no.2*, (June 1979).

Crus (1984) R. A. Crus, Data Recovery in IBM Database 2, *IBM Systems Journal vol.23, no.2*, (1984), p.178-188.

Cunningham (1985) M. Cunningham, *File Structure and Design*, Chartwell-Bratt, 1985.

D'Appollonio (1985) V. D'Appollonio et al, The Integration of the Network and Relational Approaches in a DBMS, in *Proc. Fourth British National Conf. on Databases: BNCOD4*, A. F. Grundy (ed.), Cambridge University Press, 1985, p.177-197.

Date (1981) C. J. Date, *An Introduction to Database ystems*, Addison-Wesley, 1981.

Date (1983a) C. J. Date, *An Introduction to Database Systems - Volume II*, Addison-Wesley, 1983.

Date (1983b) C. J. Date, The Outer Join, in *Proc. Second Internat. Conf on Databases: ICOD2*, S. M. Deen and P. Hammersley (ed.), Wiley, 1983.

Fagin (1979) R. Fagin et al, Extendible Hashing - A Fast Access Method for Dynamic Files, *ACM Trans. Database Systems vol.4, no.3*, (Sept 1979), p.315-344.

Falkenberg (1976) E. Falkenberg, Concepts for Modelling Information, in *Modelling in Data Base Management Systems*, G. M. Nijssen (ed.), North-Holland, 1976.

Fitzgerald (1985) G. Fitzgerald, N. Stokes and J. R. G. Wood, Feature Analysis of Contemporary Information Systems Methodologies, *Computer Journal vol.28,no.3*, (July 1985), p.223-230.

Flynn (1985) D. J. Flynn and A. H. F. Laender, Mapping from a Conceptual Schema to a Target Internal Schema, *Computer Journal vol.28, no.5*, (1985), p.508-517.

Fogg (1984) D. Fogg, Lessons from Living in a Database Graphical Query Interface, *SIGMOD 84*, 1984, p.100-106.

Frost (1980) R. A. Frost, *ASDAS: A Simple Database Management System*, Univ. of Strathclyde, Res. Report no.3/80, 1980.

Frost (1981) R. A. Frost, A Simple Database System Aimed at the Naive User, *Proc. 6th ACM European Regional Conf. on Systems Architecture*, 1981, p.234-240.

Frost (1982) R. A. Frost, Binary-Relational Storage Structures, *Computer Journal vol.25, no.3*, (1982), p.358-367.

Gray (1984) P. M. D. Gray, *Logic, Algebra and Databases*, Ellis-Horwood, 1984.

Greenblatt (1978) D. Greenblatt and J. Waxman, A Study of Three Database Query Languages, in *Improving Database Usability & Responsiveness*, B. Shneiderman (ed.), Academic Press, 1978.

Hall (1976) P. A. V. Hall, Optimization of Single Expressions in a Relational Data Base System, *IBM Journal of Res. and Dev.* vol.20, no.3, (1976), p.244-257.

Hall (1981) J. Hall, *System Development Methodology*, Learmouth & Burchett Management Systems, 1981.

Hammer (1981) M. Hammer and D. McLeod, Database Description with SDM: A Semantic Database Model, *ACM Trans. Database Systems* vol.6, no.3, (Sept 1981), p.351-386.

Harris (1977) L. R. Harris, User Oriented Data Base Query with the ROBOT Natural Language Query System, *International Journal of Man-Machine Studies* vol.9, no.6, (1977), p.697-713.

Herot (1980) C. F. Herot, Spatial Management of Data, *ACM Trans. Database Systems* vol.5, no.4, (Dec 1980), p.493-514.

Howe (1983) D. R. Howe, *Data Analysis for Database Design*, Arnold, 1983.

Hsaio (1983) D. K. Hsaio (ed.), *Advanced Database Machine Architecture*, Prentice-Hall, 1983.

Jacobs (1982) B. E. Jacobs, On Database Logic, *J. ACM* vol.29, (1982), p.320-332.

Jacobs (1983) B. E. Jacobs and C. A. Walczak, A Generalized Query-by-Example Data Manipulation Language Based on Database Logic, *Trans. on Software Eng.* vol.SE-9, no.1, (Jan 1983), p.41-57.

Jardine (1977) D. A. Jardine (ed.), *The ANSI/SPARC DBMS Model*, North-Holland, 1977.

Jarke (1984a) M. Jarke, J. Clifford and Y. Vassiliou, An Optimizing Prolog Front-end to a Relational Query system, *SIGMOD 84*, 1984, p.296-306.

Jarke (1984b) M. Jarke and J. Koch, Query Optimization in Database Systems, *Computing Surveys* vol.16, no.2, (June 1984), p.111-152.

Jiang (1985) Y. J. Jiang and S. H. Lavington, The Qualified Binary Relationship Model of Information, in *Proc. Fourth British National Conf. on Databases: BNCOD4*, A. F. Grundy (ed.), Cambridge University Press, 1985, p.61-79.

Johnson (1984) . R. G. Johnson, Integrating Data and Metadata to Enhance the User Interface, in *Proc. Third British National Conf. on Databases: BNCOD3*, J. Longstaff (ed.), Cambridge University Press, 1984.

Katz (1982a) R. H. Katz, Compilation of Relational Queries into CODASYL DML, in *Improving Database Usability and Responsiveness*, P. Scheuermann (ed.), Academic Press, 1982, p.427-450.

Katz (1982b) R. H. Katz and E. Wong, Decompiling CODASYL DML into Relational Queries, *ACM Trans. Database Systems* vol.7, no.1, (1982), p.1-23.

Kent (1979) W. Kent, Limitations of Record-Based Information Models, *ACM Trans. Database Systems vol.4, no.1*, (Mar 1979), p.107-131.

Kent (1983) W. Kent, A Simple Guide to Five Normal Forms in Relational Database Theory, *Comm. ACM vol.26, no.2*, (1983).

Knuth (1973) D. E. Knuth, *The Art of Computer Programming: Volume 3, Sorting and Searching*, Addison-Wesley, 1973.

Kohler (1981) W. H. Kohler, A Survey of Techniques for Synchronization and Recovery in Decentralized Computer Systems, *Computing Surveys vol.13, no.2*, (June 1981), p.149-183.

Kolodner (1983) J. L. Kolodner, Indexing and Retrieval Strategies for Natural Language Fact Retrieval, *ACM Trans. Database Systems vol.8, no.3*, (Sept 1983), p.434-464.

Kowalski (1984) R. Kowalski, Logic as a Database Language, in *Proc. Third British National Conf. on Databases: BNCOD3*, J. Longstaff (ed.), Cambridge University Press, 1984, p.103-132.

Kung (1981) H. T. Kung and J. T. Robinson, On Optimistic Methods for Concurrency Control, *ACM Trans. Database Systems vol.6, no.2*, (June 1981), p.213-226.

Landers (1982) T. Landers and R. L. Rosenberg, An Overview of Multibase, in *Distributed Data Bases*, H. J. Schneider (ed.), North-Holland, 1982, p.153-184.

Larson (1978) P. A. Larson, Dynamic Hashing, *BIT vol.18*, (1978), p.184-201.

Lee (1985) R. M. Lee, Database Inferencing for Decision Support, *Decision Support Systems vol.1, no.1*, (Jan 1985), p.57-68.

Litwin (1978) W. Litwin, Virtual Hashing: A Dynamically Changing Hashing, in *Proc. 4th Conf. on Very Large Data Bases*, 1978, p.517-523.

Litwin (1982) W. Litwin et al, SIRIUS Systems for Distributed Data management, in *Distributed Data Bases*, H. J. Schneider (ed.), North-Holland, 1982, p.311-366.

Litwin (1983) W. Litwin and K. Kabbaj, Multidatabase Management Systems, in *Proc. Internat. Comp. Symposium 1983 on Application Systems Development*, H. J. Schneider (ed.), B. G. Teubner, Stuttgart, 1983, p.482-505.

Lum (1984) V. Lum et al, Designing DBMS Support for the Temporal Dimension, *SIGMOD 84*, 1984, p.115-130.

Lundberg (1983) B. Lundberg, An Analysis of the Concept of Event, in *Proc. Internat. Comp. Symposium 1983 on Application Systems Development*, H. J. Schneider (ed.), B. G. Teubner, Stuttgart, 1983.

Maddison (1983) R. N. Maddison et al, *Information System Design Methodologies*, Wiley Heyden, 1983.

Mahmoud (1979) S. A. Mahmoud, J. S. Riordon and K. C. Toth, Distributed Database Partitioning and Query Processing, in *Data Base Architecture*, G. Bracchi and G. M. Nijssen (ed.), North-Holland, 1979, p.35-54.

Maryanski (1980) F. J. Maryanski, Backend Database Systems, *Computing Surveys vol.12, no.1*, (March 1980), p.3-25.

McDonald (1975) N. McDonald and M. Stonebraker, Cupid - the Friendly Query Language, in *DATA: Its Use, Organisation and Management - ACM Pacific Conference*, ACM, 1975, p.127-131.

McGee (1977) W. C. McGee, The Information Management System IMS/VS, Part II Data Base Facilities, *IBM Systems Journal vol.16, no.2*, (1977), p.96-122.

McGregor (1984) D. R. McGregor and J. R. Malone, An integrated high-performance, hardware assisted, intelligent database system for large-scale knowledge bases, in *Proc. First Workshop on Architectures for Large Knowledge Bases*, Alvey Directorate, May 1984.

MDBS (1981) MDBS Inc., MDBS III Reference Manuals, 1981.

MDBS (1984) MDBS Inc., Knowledgeman Reference Manual (v1.07), 1984.

Neuhold (1982) E. J. Neuhold and B. Walter, An Overview of the Architecture of the Distributed Data Base System "POREL", in *Distributed Data Bases*, H. J. Schneider (ed.), North-Holland, 1982, p.247-290.

Neves (1983) J. C. Neves, S. D. Anderson and M. H. Williams, A Prolog Implementation of Query-By-Example, in *Proc. Internat. Comp. Symposium 1983 on Application Systems Development*, H. J. Schneider (ed.), B. G. Teubner, Stuttgart, 1983, p.318-332.

Olle (1978) T. W. Olle, *The CODASYL Approach to Data Base Management*, Wiley, 1978.

Olle (1982) T. W. Olle, H. G. Sol and A. A. Verrijn Stuart (eds), *Information Systems Design Methodologies - A Comparative Review*, North-Holland, 1982.

Olle (1983) T. W. Olle, H. G. Sol and C. J. Tully (eds), *Information Systems Design Methodologies - A Feature Analysis*, North-Holland, 1983.

Pirotte (1978) A. Pirotte, High Level Data Base Query Languages, in *Logic and Data Bases*, H. Gallaire and J. Minker (ed.), 1978, p.409-436.

Reisner (1981) P. Reisner, Human Factors Studies of Database Query Languages: A Survey and Assessment, *Computing Surveys vol.13, no.1*, (March 1981), p.13-31.

Robinson (1981) H. Robinson, *Database Analysis and Design*, Chartwell-Bratt, 1981.

Rock-Evans (1981) R. Rock-Evans, *Data Analysis*, IPC Business press, 1981.

Rothnie (1980) J. B. Rothnie et al, Introduction to a System for Distributed Databases (SDD-1), *ACM Trans. Database Systems vol.5, no.1*, (March 1980), p.1-17.

Scheuermann (1980) P. Scheuermann, G. Schiffner and H. Weber, Abstraction Capabilities and Invariant Properties Modelling within the Entity-Relationship Approach, in *Entity-Relationship Approach to Systems Analysis & Design*, P. P. Chen (ed.), 1980, p.121-140.

Scholl (1981) M. Scholl, New File Organizations Based on Dynamic Hashing, *ACM Trans. Database Systems vol.6, no.1*, (March 1981), p.194-211.

Senko (1975) M. E. Senko, DIAM II with FORAL, in *Data Base Description*, B. C. M. Douque and G. M. Nijssen (ed.), North-Holland, 1975.

Senko (1976a) M. E. Senko, DIAM as a Detailed Example of the ANSI SPARC Architecture, in *Modelling in Data Base Management Systems*, G. M. Nijssen (ed.), North-Holland, 1976, p.73-94.

Senko (1976b) M. E. Senko and E. B. Altman, DIAM II and Levels of Abstraction, The Physical Device Level, in *Systems for Large Data Bases*, P. C. Lockemann and E. J. Neuhold (ed.), North-Holland, 1976, p.79-93.

Senko (1977) M. E. Senko, Foral LP - Making Pointed Queries with a Light Pen, *Information Processing 77*, 1977, p.635-642.

Shave (1981) M. J. R. Shave, Entities, Functions and Binary Relations: Steps to a Conceptual Schema, *Computer Journal vol.24, no.1*, (1981), p.42-47.

Shipman (1981) D. W. Shipman, The Functional Data Model and the Data Language DAPLEX, *ACM Trans. Database Systems vol.6, no.1*, (March 1981), p.140-173.

Smith (1975) J. M. Smith and P. Y. Chang, Optimizing the Performance of a Relational Algebra Database Interface, *Comm. ACM vol.18, no.10*, (October 1975), p.568-579.

Smith (1977) J. M. Smith and D. C. P. Smith, Database Abstractions: Aggregation and Generalization, *ACM Trans. Database Systems vol.2, no.2*, (June 1977), p.105-133.

Smith (1981) J. M. Smith et al, Multibase: Integrating Heterogeneous Distributed Database Systems, in *AFIPS National Computer Conference*, 1981, p.487-499.

Sordi (1984) J. J. Sordi, Database 2 - The Query Management Facility, *IBM Systems Journal vol.23, no.2*, (1984), p.126-149.

Spaccapietra (1980) S. Spaccapietra, Heterogeneous Distributed Data Base Distribution, in *Distributed Databases*, I. W. Draffan and F. Poole (ed.), Cambridge University Press, 1980, p.155-193.

Stocker (1983) P. M. Stocker and R. Cantie, A Target Logical Schema: The ACS, in *Ninth Int. Conf. on Very Large Data Bases*, 1983.

Stonebraker (1976) M. Stonebraker, E. Wong, P. Kreps and G. Held, The Design and Implementation of Ingres, *ACM Trans. Database Systems vol.1, no.3*, (Sept 1976), p.189-222.

Tanenbaum (1981) A. S. Tanenbaum, Network Protocols, *Computing Surveys vol.13, no.1*, (March 1981), p.453-489.

Thomas (1975) J. C. Thomas and J. D. Gould, A Psychological Study of Query-By-Example, *AFIPS Nat. Comp. Conf.*, 1975, p.439-445.

Todd (1976) S. J. P. Todd, The Peterlee Relational Test Vehicle - A System Overview, *IBM Systems Journal vol.15, no.4*, (1976), p.285-308.

Ullman (1980) J. D. Ullman, *Principles of Database Systems*, Pitman, 1980.

Ullman (1985) J. D. Ullman, Implementation of Logical Query Languages for Databases, *ACM Trans. Database Systems vol.10, no.3*, (Sept 1985), p.289-321.

Unland (1983) R. Unland, U. Praedel and G. Schlageter, Design Alternatives for Optimistic Concurrency Control Schemes, in *Proc. 2nd Internat. Conf. on Databases (ICOD2)*, S. M. Deen and P. Hammersley (ed.), Wiley, 1983, p.288-297.

Verheijen (1982) G. M. A. Verheijen and J. van Bekkum, NIAM: An Information Analysis Method, in *Information Systems Design Methodologies - A Comparative Review*, T. W. Olle et al (ed.), North-Holland, 1982.

Vetter (1981) M. Vetter and R. N. Maddison, *Database Design Methodology*, Prentice-Hall, 1981.

Wallace (1983) M. G. Wallace and V. West, QPROC: A Natural Language Database Enquiry System Implemented in PROLOG, *ICL Technical Journal vol.3, no.4*, (1983), p.393-406.

Wallace (1984) M. Wallace, *Communicating with Databases in Natural Language*, Ellis-Harwood, 1984.

Waltz (1978) D. L. Waltz, An English Language Question Answering System for a Large Relational Database, *Comm. ACM vol.21, no.7*, (July 1978), p.526-539.

Wiederhold (1983) G. Wiederhold, *Database Design*, McGraw-Hill, 1983.

Williams (1982) R. Williams et al, R*: An Overview of the Architecture, in *Improving Database Usability and Responsiveness*, P. Scheuermann (ed.), 1982, p.1-27.

Wilmot (1984) R. B. Wilmot, Foreign Keys Decrease Adaptability of Database Designs, *Comm. ACM vol.27, no.12*, (Dec 1984), p.1237-1243.

Wong (1976) E. Wong and K. Youssefi, Decomposition - A Strategy for Query Processing, *ACM Trans. Database Systems vol.1, no.3*, (Sept 1976), p.223-241.

Yao (1982) S. B. Yao, V. E. Waddle and B. C. Housel, View Modeling and Integration Using the Functional Data Model, *Trans. on Software Eng. vol.SE-8, no.6*, (Nov 1982), p.544-553.

Yormark (1977) B. Yormark, The ANSI/X3/SPARC/SGDBMS Architecture, in *The ANSI/SPARC DBMS Model*, D. A. Jardine (ed.), North-Holland, 1977.

Zloof (1975) M. M. Zloof, Query by Example, *AFIPS Nat. Comp. Conf.*, 1975, p.431-438.

Zloof (1977) M. M. Zloof, Query-by-Example: A Database Language, *IBM Systems Journal vol.16, no.4*, (1977), p.324-343.

Zloof (1978) M. M. Zloof, Design Aspects of the Query-by-Example Data Base Management Language, in *Improving Database Usability & Responsiveness*, B. Shneiderman (ed.), Academic Press, 1978, p.29-55.

Zloof (1981) M. M. Zloof, QBE/OBE: A Language for Office and Business Automation, *IEEE Computer vol.14, no.5*, (May 1981), p.13-22.

Zloof (1982) M. M. Zloof, Office-by-Example: A Business Language that Unifies Data and Word Processing and Electronic Mail, *IBM Systems Journal vol.21, no.3*, (1982), p.272-304.

DATABASES AND DATABASE SYSTEMS
CONCEPTS AND ISSUES

APPENDIX A
OBJECT-ORIENTED DATABASE SYSTEMS

A.1 Introduction

In 1986 when this book was first published, some new research areas were being introduced in database technology. Although substantial advances had been taking place in the provision of data management facilities, in particular highly sophisticated end-user facilities for both mainframe and micro database management systems (DBMSs), the limitations of traditional systems (relational, network, hierarchical) had become apparent and were providing an impetus for research into more advanced approaches to data management. Why was this? The main reason: the change in the pattern of usage of the systems.

The most significant change from the viewpoint of DBMS limitations has been the much wider range of environments in which database techniques are now being utilised. Some of these are far removed from the traditional business data processing environment for which the systems were originally designed. The new application areas include engineering design, project support, electronic office systems, geographical and spatial information systems, expert systems, and others. The nature and requirements of some of these new areas, in particular those just mentioned, are quite different from business data processing and existing DBMSs cannot always adequately satisfy their data management requirements.

The major DBMSs currently available have been designed to support environments in which
- a large volume of data needs to be managed (eg. data relating to real-world objects such as employees, invoices, library books and loans, parts for manufacture, insurance policies, bank accounts, etc)
- the objects are interrelated in fairly complex but predictable ways (as illustrated in Chapter 2 on Data Modelling)
- the data models are relatively stable over time; i.e. data structure changes arising from changes in the relationships amongst entities and attributes are infrequent
- data may be updated by overwriting the old values; i.e. objects are considered to be mutable
- concurrent access to the same data by different application programs and users is frequently required; the data needs to be reliably available, securely stored, and its integrity assured
- access to data by a user is typically of short duration (i.e. transactions are short); the data is held in the form of records containing simple items of data which are stored, retrieved or updated; although a particular database request may involve accessing many related records, transaction times can still be measured in seconds (or possibly minutes if a large volume of data is involved in the transaction).

The main differences in the new non-traditional database applications include:
- the data models involve more complex relationships between different objects, and support for the full semantics of these relationships is often essential
- data cannot always be updated by overwriting; in some of the new applications, the objects are immutable, and hence different versions of the same object need to be maintained; also, support for configurations of object versions may be required
- the data models may not be stable over time; the ability to change the structure of the data may be as important as the ability to change the values of items of data
- transactions are often long, possibly measured in days or even weeks in an environment such as software engineering in which a new module for a large system is being developed
- large volumes of rules rather than large volumes of records are common in expert system environments

The new systems being designed and developed may be grouped into three main approaches:
> logic-based
> enhanced relational
> object-oriented

The logic-based approach is aimed at solving the problem of large volumes of rules needed in expert system environments, while the other two approaches are mainly concerned with the need to support semantically rich and complex data models.

Logic-based approach

The logic-based approach has evolved from work in expert systems. Early applications of expert systems were relatively simple and did not require sophisticated database support, so they were generally based on main memory databases. But it soon became apparent that expert systems need database facilities for the storage and management of large volumes of facts and rules if they are to be effectively used in a wide range of application areas. Thus, some of the recent research has combined AI/logic programming technology with database technology to produce expert or logic database systems (Kerschberg 1986). Some research effort has been based on Prolog and relational databases, e.g. providing a relational interface to Prolog databases or vice versa (as mentioned in Chapter 3), while Zaniolo (1986) and Gray (1985, 1988) have investigated the combination of Prolog with other data models such as Codasyl network and functional data models.

Enhanced relational approach

The success of relational DBMSs over the past decade has led to research aimed at overcoming the limitations by enhancing relational concepts. Early enhancements concentrated on semantic aspects. Codd (1979) proposed extensions in his RM/T model, which included unique identity for entities (via permanent surrogates which are distinct from the attributes of an entity), generalization hierarchies and property inheritance. More recent research has been directed towards support for rules or procedures as data types, e.g. via extensions to INGRES (Stonebraker 1987). Also, POSTGRES (Stonebraker 1986, Rowe 1987), the successor to INGRES, has been designed with features such as enhanced data modelling capabilities, user-defined data types, and procedures as data types; it possesses some object-oriented characteristics but is still heavily based on relational, and hence record-based, concepts.

Object-oriented approach

The object-oriented approach is the subject of this appendix. It is seen as a solution to the problem of providing support for the diverse requirements of the new wide-ranging database application environments.

A.2 Object-Oriented Concepts

For some years now, an object-oriented style of programming has been applied in a number of areas, including simulation, AI, systems design and programming, and more recently database technology. The object-oriented paradigm has been interpreted in various different ways (Stefik 1986), and some inconsistencies and confusion exist. The problem is exacerbated in the case of object-oriented database systems (OODBSs) for two reasons:

1. two technologies have been brought together - object-oriented programming and database technology - both of which have their own collection of recognised terms, some of which have the same names but different meanings
2. since many OODBSs have been designed to support various different specialized environments, the terminology and concepts supported vary widely from system to system.

Although there is, as yet, no standard definition of concepts and terminology, some important concepts relevant to an object-oriented database (OODB) environment can be identified. These are:

> the *object* concept
> the grouping of objects into *classes* and the definition of their *types*
> concepts associated with *complex objects* and *property inheritance*
> *encapsulation* of data and procedures in objects, and *overloading*
> *persistence* of objects

A.2.1 Objects, Classes and Types

The object-oriented approach is based on the *object* concept. Everything in the database is viewed as an object, and each object is uniquely identifiable and complete in itself. Objects may be concrete or abstract, and simple or complex. They are grouped into *classes* according to the 'roles' which they play in the database and according to the properties which they possess. The properties identify the *type* of a particular class of objects, and may consist of data properties (e.g. attributes), constraints, and procedures (which may also be referred to as methods, operations or rules).

It is important to note that the object concept, together with the grouping of objects into classes, is far more general than the relation concept, and hence it provides the basis for a greater degree of flexibility in the area of semantic data modelling. For example, attributes and entities can be considered as independent objects, and it is also possible for relationships to be represented explicitly by defining them as objects (though not all OODBSs provide this latter facility). In addition, the type of an object may be based on other object types, possibly including additional properties, thus providing support for objects with complex structure (more will be said about this later in the section).

The exact definition of the terms 'class' and 'type' varies from system to system, but in an OODBS context, it is appropriate to consider a class as consisting not only of the definition of the class, but also the instances. The object concept implies that each object logically includes not only the description of its properties, but also its instance values, thus making it complete in itself. This is quite different from traditional database approaches in which the definitions of the relations or record types (the metadata) are stored and managed separately from the instances (data). But data is meaningless without the metadata; thus, since metadata and data are integrated in the object concept, it is both semantically meaningful and important.

The term 'type' is used in this appendix to include the complete set of defined properties for an object. The properties of an object could be considered to include a public interface part and a private implementation part, the former being user-visible and the latter hidden from the user. The interface part represents the traditional programming language view of an abstract data type, which provides users with information about how to use the type (names of operators and procedures which can be applied, the functions performed by them, any parameters required, etc.) but not details of how the operators and procedures are actually implemented. Since not all OODBSs distinguish between the interface and implementation parts of properties, this aspect will not be considered further in this appendix.

The library example from Chapter 2 of the main text will be used to illustrate some of the concepts. Figure A.1 is a simplified and slightly modified version of Figure 2.12. The entities and attributes may be considered as objects in their own right. In an OODB, the entities would be represented by unique internal system identifiers (or surrogates), while the

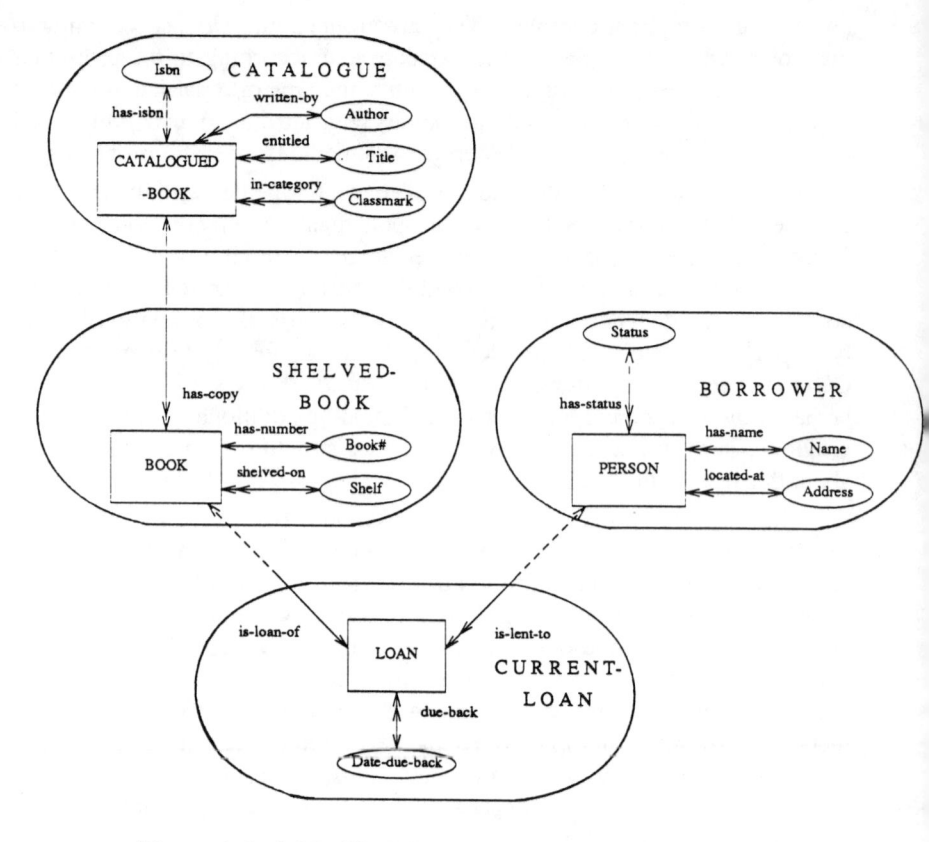

Figure A.1 A Modified Version of the Library Model

attributes would be represented by their actual values. Some OODBSs support relationships as objects or provide facilities for the definition of relationship semantics, so these are shown in the diagram. However, it must be stressed that not all systems provide these facilities, even though the need for them has been recognised for a long time in the field of semantic data modelling (e.g. Abrial 1974, Hammer 1981, Abiteboul 1987, Peckham 1988).

The large ellipses, named CATALOGUE, SHELVED-BOOK, BORROWER and CURRENT-LOAN, represent objects formed from the aggregation of an entity and its associated data properties. Some systems do not distinguish between an entity as an object independent of any properties and the object representing the entity together with some (or possibly all) of its properties. The ability to distinguish between these, though, provides the greatest flexibility for the expression of the data model semantics.

To illustrate the class concept, CATALOGUE in the diagram may be considered to represent the class of catalogue objects whose data properties include the relationships which map a catalogued-book onto the attributes isbn, author, title and classmark (in some systems the data properties are expressed in terms of the attributes only, and not the relationships). The CATALOGUE class may also have constraints defined on the data properties, and procedures (e.g. to create a new catalogue object), but these are not illustrated in the diagram. Each object in the class logically consists of the definition of its properties and any values associated with its properties (e.g. specific values for isbn, author, title and classmark). Figure A.2 represents a definition of the data properties of objects belonging to the CATALOGUE class expressed in the form of relationships, i.e. a catalogue object is a 'catalogued-book' entity which 'has-isbn isbn', is 'written-by author', is 'entitled title', and is 'in-category classmark'.

CATALOGUE

catalogued-book	
has-isbn	isbn
written-by	author
entitled	title
in-category	classmark

Figure A.2 CATALOGUE Class Definition

Note: The notation used for class definitions in this appendix is for illustrative purposes only; it does not relate to any particular system although it is similar to the notation used in KBZ (Oxborrow 1988).

The classes corresponding to the large ellipses in Figure A.1 are similar to relations or record types in traditional database systems, but since the object concept is general, classes may be used to build more complex objects than these, and this subject is discussed next.

A.2.2 Concepts Associated With Complex Objects and Property Inheritance

In the literature on object-oriented systems, a variety of terms are used to encompass concepts associated with complex objects and property inheritance. These include: supertype, subtype, superclass, subclass, IS-A relationship, part-component hierarchy, PART-OF relationship, and others. Since there are no standard definitions, different interpretations are often given to the same term in different systems, or different terms are used for the same concept. The different possible interpretations of the IS-A relationship are clearly illustrated in Brachman (1983), for example. As there is some confusion surrounding the exact meaning of these terms, this appendix will concentrate on the concepts underlying them, rather than the terms themselves. It should be noted though that some effort is currently being put into clarifying the situation and providing formal definitions.

The flexibility of the object and class concepts enables highly structured data models to be built, which incorporate more real-world semantics than is possible with traditional systems. *Complex objects* are objects which are built from other objects. A form of complex object representing a record-like structure has already been referred to, but there are many other ways in which complex objects can be built, although many systems do not provide full flexibility in this respect (often for practical reasons).

Three main forms of complex object will be discussed here. One corresponds to hierarchies or lattices (network structures) based on a single entity, in which the lower the level in the hierarchy/lattice, the greater the specialization with respect to the entity, and the higher the level, the greater the generalization. This form will be discussed under the heading: generalization and specialization. The second form corresponds to part-component hierarchies, in which the object at the root is built from or contains other objects at the next level, and so on down the hierarchy. This form will be discussed under the heading: composite objects. The third form relates to attributes which are non-simple. This will be discussed under the heading: compound attributes.

Generalization and specialization:

In subsection 2.7.1 in Chapter 2, the semantic concepts of generalization and categorization (subsetting) were introduced. Generalization and specialization as introduced here cover a broader set of semantic concepts. Figure A.3 represents a hierarchy reflecting the following information: a university member is a person who possesses properties relevant to all members of a university regardless of their role in the university, while a student possesses not only properties relevant to university members, but also the specialized properties (if any) relevant only to students; and similarly for staff. Also, an undergrad is a student who possesses all the properties relevant to students together with any specialized properties relevant only to undergrads, and similarly for postgrad. Figure A.4 provides some possible class definitions for the university member hierarchy. If a specialized object does not contain any properties of its own (except possibly a constraint), the class containing all objects of this type represents a simple subset. As can be seen in Figure A.4, an undergrad is simply defined as a student, subject to the constraint that its status value must be

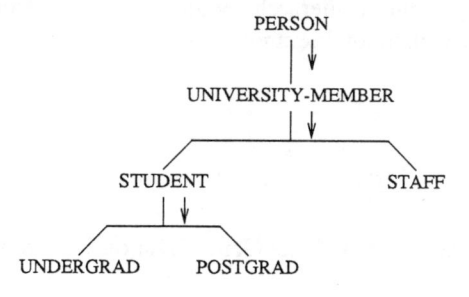

```
                    PERSON
                      │↓
              UNIVERSITY-MEMBER
                      │↓
            ┌─────────┴─────────┐
          STUDENT              STAFF
            │↓
      ┌─────┴─────┐
  UNDERGRAD    POSTGRAD
```

Figure A.3 A University Member Specialization Hierarchy

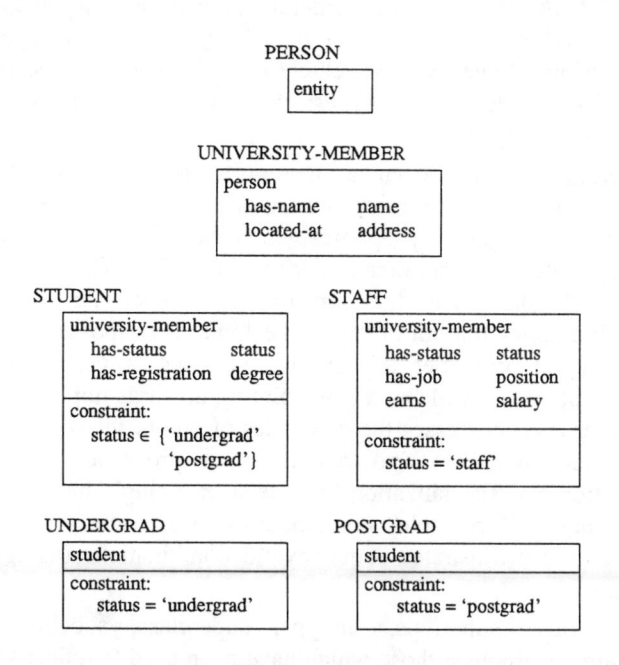

PERSON
| entity |

UNIVERSITY-MEMBER
| person |
| has-name   name |
| located-at   address |

STUDENT
| university-member |
| has-status   status |
| has-registration degree |
| constraint: |
| status ∈ {'undergrad' 'postgrad'} |

STAFF
| university-member |
| has-status   status |
| has-job   position |
| earns   salary |
| constraint: |
| status = 'staff' |

UNDERGRAD
| student |
| constraint: |
| status = 'undergrad' |

POSTGRAD
| student |
| constraint: |
| status = 'postgrad' |

Figure A.4 Example Class Definitions for the
University Member Hierarchy

'undergrad', hence the set of undergrads is a simple subset of the set of students; and similarly for postgrads. Students, on the other hand, do not represent a simple subset of university members, since they have data properties in addition to the university member properties (i.e. a status and degree registration, as well as a name and address); staff also have additional data properties.

Figure A.5 represents a hierarchy with slightly different semantics as compared to the specialization hierarchy.

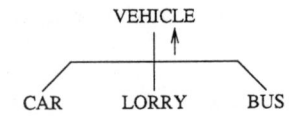

```
           VEHICLE
          ╱   ↑   ╲
        CAR  LORRY  BUS
```

Figure A.5 A Vehicle Generalization Hierarchy

It reflects the following information: cars, lorries, and buses are different types of object but they have a common feature: they are all kinds of vehicle; hence vehicle objects represent a generalization of car, lorry and bus objects; a particular vehicle is either a car or a lorry or a bus and possesses the properties of whichever type of vehicle it happens to be. The vehicle class may have its own defined properties; these will be common to all vehicles, regardless of their type.

Generalization and specialization are often associated with the notion of *property inheritance*. Property inheritance in this context means the possession by an object of properties which 'belong' to some other object to which it is related by generalization or specialization. The arrows in Figures A.3 and A.5 show the direction of inheritance. An arrow pointing downwards implies that an object at the lower level possesses not only its own specialized properties (if any) but also the properties of the object represented above it, while an arrow pointing upwards implies that an object at the higher level possesses the properties of one of the objects represented below it and may also possess its own properties. A mixture of generalization and specialization may exist in a single hierarchy or lattice, although not all possible combinations are necessarily meaningful. Abiteboul (1987) illustrates some invalid combinations (using a different notation).

The terms: supertype, subtype, superclass, subclass, and IS-A relationship are amongst those which have been used to reflect some form of generalization or specialization. The term 'subtype' is generally used in the context of a particular form which is consistent with the object-oriented programming language definition of a subtype.

Before leaving this topic, an important feature of this form of complex object should be mentioned. A generalization/specialization hierarchy or lattice can be used to represent different roles which a particular entity may play in a database. A one-to-one relationship is implied throughout the hierarchy/lattice and the same entity is involved at each level. For example, a particular person who is an undergraduate is at the same time a student and a university member according to Figure A.3 (hence the use of the term IS-A relationship in some systems). In comparison, it should be noted that in a relational database, undergraduates, students and university members would need to be defined as separate relations with a single attribute in common, and with nothing to indicate explicitly what the relationship is between the relations. Also, in a Codasyl network database, these objects would need to be defined as separate record types with Codasyl sets linking them but with nothing to say that the member record type represents the same entity as the owner record type, nor that only a single member can exist in each set occurrence.

Composite objects:

The term 'composite object' refers to an object which is composed of other objects, forming a part-component hierarchy. The components would normally be based on different entities. It should be noted that the two terms 'composite object' and 'complex object' have both been used in the literature to refer to non-atomic objects in general; however, since the part-component hierarchy is very important in certain applications, the term 'complex object' is used in this appendix to refer to non-atomic objects in general, while the term 'composite object' is used to refer to the specific form of complex object which relates to part-component hierarchies. Traditional database systems (relational, network, etc.) cannot directly support the composite object structure, but it is a common occurrence in the real world. Various examples will be used for illustration.

The first example is drawn from a geographical information environment. A region may be divided into districts (cities, towns, villages), and districts may contain buildings, parks, woodland, roads, etc. These are all objects with their own properties, based on different entities, but they are related to each other by spatial containment (e.g. a district is part of a region, and buildings, parks, etc are contained in the districts). To take another example drawn from an electronic publishing environment, a book contains chapters, chapters may contain sections, and sections may contain paragraphs, figures, etc. Again, these are all objects with their own properties, related to each other by spatial containment. This is, in fact, true of all 'parts' and 'components' in a part-component hierarchy.

In a relational or network database, there is no difference in representation between a relationship involving spatial containment and one involving non-spatially related objects. But from a semantic viewpoint, these are quite different relationships. Consider, for example, the relationship between a book reservation and a book; this is not the same as the relationship between a district and a region, since a reservation is not 'contained in' a book but a district is contained in a region. Both of these relationships would be represented in a relational or network database in the same way; in a relational database, the primary keys of region and book would be placed in the district and reservation relations respectively, as foreign keys, giving the impression that the semantics underlying the two relationships are the same.

Figure A.6 illustrates the spatial containment inherent in composite objects.

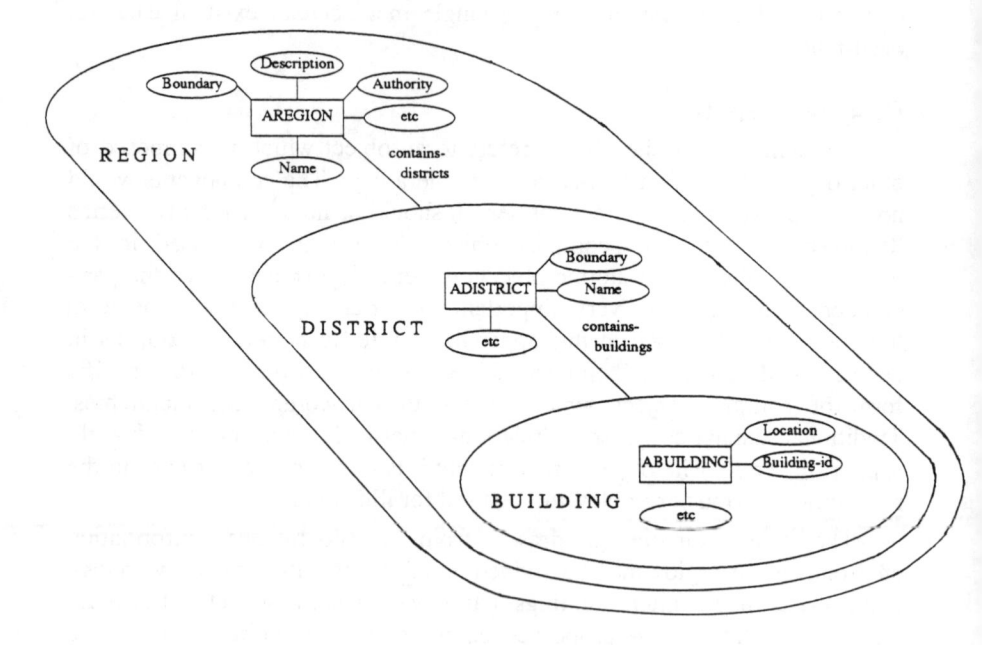

Figure A.6 A Region Composite Object Hierarchy

It shows a region composite object hierarchy, with districts in the regions and buildings in the districts. Although not illustrated in the diagram, the districts could also have had woodland, roads, etc. contained within them, as well as buildings. Note that the 'contains-districts' relationship maps the 'aregion' entity onto district objects, each of which represents a district together with all of its properties, i.e. a complete district is contained in a region; and similarly for the 'contains-buildings' relationship.

It may be thought that the components of a composite object cannot exist independently. This may be true in certain circumstances, but in others, it may be important for the components to be able to exist on their own without being 'attached' to any composite object. For example, in the manufacture of a particular car or a computer, the components which make up the car or computer may be held in stock initially and only later incorporated into the manufactured object. Also, a defective component may be removed for repair and temporarily replaced by another copy of the component. Such situations can be modelled with full relationship semantics. For example, the function mapping a computer entity onto a complete disc drive might be mandatory, while the inverse function, mapping a complete disc drive onto a computer entity would be optional (if disc drives can exist without being connected to a computer at a particular point in time), as shown below:

$$ACOMPUTER \longleftarrow \text{-----}\twoheadrightarrow DISC\text{-}DRIVE$$

Compound attributes:

Traditional DBMSs generally only support simple attributes (i.e. attributes which are single-valued and based on a standard type such as string or integer. Most do now provide a date data type, which consists of day, month, year (and also hours, minutes and seconds if time is not a separate type). However, it is often the case that a single logical attribute is made up of a number of separate components which need to be user-defined. These are referred to here as 'compound attributes' and some examples are

- a person's name in reality consists of a surname and initials, or surname and forenames.
- an address is composed of a building name or number, street, town, county and postcode.
- a grid reference for a point on a map is composed of an 'easting' and a 'northing', both of which may be represented either as integers or as strings.

One environment in which compound attributes are important is a geographical/spatial environment. A geographical information system (GIS) must provide facilities for representing such spatial objects as a point, a line, an arc (non-straight line), a boundary, etc. To the user of a GIS, these are types of attribute, but they are compound attributes. In the diagram in Figure A.6, for example, the location attribute associated with a building might be represented as a spatial point (grid reference) and the boundaries associated with regions and districts might be represented as a set of ordered points (implicitly connected to form a closed boundary).

A.2.3 Encapsulation of Data and Procedures in Objects

The previous subsection has illustrated the potential of the object-oriented approach in the field of semantic data modelling. The flexibility of the object concept and class structure provides complex data structuring capabilities; although not all systems support all forms of complex object, the potential still exists. However, the concept which really makes object-oriented systems powerful is the *encapsulation* concept. This, when fully applied, means that the only procedures which can be performed on an object are those which have been declared in the definition of that object (or in an 'inherited' definition). However, encapsulation is often applied more loosely in OODBSs to mean that users may define procedures as properties of objects.

Support for the encapsulation of data and procedures in objects enables objects to be defined completely, both in terms of their structural/static properties (attributes and relationships) and in terms of their behavioural/dynamic properties (rules, operators, procedures). The implications of this are important for application programming. All the standard procedures in an application system which are associated with specific objects in the data model can be built into the database and simply 'called' by application programs when required.

An example will be used to illustrate encapsulation. Figure A.7 shows class definitions for catalogue and borrower objects, which include procedures (in skeleton form).

CATALOGUE			BORROWER		
catalogued-book			person		
has-isbn	isbn		has-name	name	
written-by	author		located-at	address	
entitled	title		has-status	status	
in-category	classmark				
constraint:			constraint:		
create:			create:		
list:			delete:		
			display:		

Figure A.7 Encapsulation of Procedures in Object Definitions

In this diagram, the data properties (in the form of relationships) are in the top part of each definition, and the constraints and procedures are in the bottom part. The constraints and procedures have not been fully specified in this illustrative example, only their names have been provided. The procedure appropriate to 'create' in CATALOGUE might be as follows (expressed in pseudocode):

> input attribute values for the catalogue instance to be created
>   (i.e. isbn, author, title, classmark)
> check if an instance for the specified isbn already exists
> if so
>   output a warning message (since isbn should be unique)
> otherwise
>   create a new catalogued book entity object
>   create new instances of the catalogue data properties
>   output a completion message

Note that a 'create' procedure has been specified in both CATALOGUE and BORROWER, but there is no problem regarding unique reference to the procedures since they may be referred to uniquely by specifying the name of the object in which they are encapsulated, for example, 'catalogue.create' and 'borrower.create'. The ability to define procedures with the same name for different objects is known as *operator overloading*.

A.2.4 Persistence of Objects

The last concept to be discussed is *persistence*. Persistence is inherent in all OODBSs as in all DBMSs, though it is not inherent in object-oriented systems in general. Persistence simply means the permanent storage and maintenance of the objects which are created. In general, data created by a program only exists during the execution of that program, while data created by a DBMS is normally permanently stored in a database. The database community takes persistence for granted, but it is only quite recently that the programming language community has recognised the importance of persistent data.

A.3 The Future for Object-Oriented Database Systems

Possibilities

From the discussion in the previous section, it should be clear that one of the important features of the object-oriented approach is the ability to directly support a variety of forms of complex object. The semantic richness of the object-oriented approach enables data models to be built which more closely reflect the real-world environment which they model. In contrast, such facilities do not exist in traditional record-oriented database systems. The relational approach, for example, offers only the simple relation construct and the ability to represent just one type of implicit relationship between relations. It is the user of a relational database who holds the semantic information, not the relational database! And similar comments can be made regarding network and hierarchical DBMSs.

Some OODBSs which have been designed only contain structural object-oriented features, but although these are important, the full power of the object-oriented approach cannot be realised without support for behavioural features. If both the structural/static and the behavioural/dynamic characteristics of particular types of object can be built into a database, it will be more complete and contain more real-world knowledge than is possible with traditional DBMSs. Thus, a system is not considered to be properly object-oriented unless it supports both structural and behavioural object-oriented facilities. It is worth noting that some of the ideas behind the object-oriented concepts described in the previous section have individually been the subject of much research in the past (e.g. semantic data modelling, procedures as data types, behaviour modelling, etc.). The object-oriented approach brings these ideas together in a consistent manner.

With the provision of more powerful and flexible facilities, the object-oriented approach simplifies the task of providing specialized environments. Attempts have been made in the past to build environments such as project support, engineering design, and geographical information systems (GIS) on top of existing DBMSs, often with limited success due to the restrictions imposed. An example from a GIS environment will illustrate the importance of the object-oriented features for this purpose. A GIS built on top of an OODBS could provide object definitions to represent the types of object of interest to its users, for example, the spatial objects: point, line, arc, etc. These might be represented as compound attributes, but in addition, the object definitions could include procedures which define appropriate operators for such objects, e.g. 'intersect' for lines, 'overlap' for boundaries, and so on. Users could then build their data models using the GIS-defined objects such as point, line, etc. as though they were standard data types.

Current problems

This appendix would be incomplete without some mention of the current problems of the object-oriented approach. Firstly, the lack of standard definitions for the concepts and terminology has led to some confusion and inconsistency (as mentioned earlier), and some of the early OODBSs are not truly object-oriented, but are more like enhanced relational systems. Thus, there are large differences between the systems which have so far been implemented or designed. Secondly, OODBSs are more sophisticated than traditional DBMSs and hence more complex. This may lead to performance problems if large volumes of data are involved, although in some of the new application environments (e.g. project support), large volumes of data may not be involved and OODBSs can be used quite successfully in these cases.

However, widespread research is currently taking place which should have a significant impact on both of these problems. Effort is being put into the clarification of concepts and definition of terminology. The many systems currently being implemented will lead to new software techniques specially suited to the management of objects. And research in the field of hardware support is already taking place. It should be mentioned that about a decade before relational systems became widely used, some people thought that the relational approach would never be commercially viable for performance reasons. But advances in hardware and software technology have resulted in the development of a number of successful relational systems. There seems little doubt that, with the high level of research currently taking place, significant improvements in the performance of OODBSs will be achieved during the next decade, as well as improvements in the end-user facilities.

Conclusion

This appendix has provided a brief introduction to the subject of object-oriented database systems. For those who wish to investigate the subject further, there have been many papers published covering recent research. Some useful material may be found in (TOIS 1987, Dittrich 1986, Shriver 1987, Kim 1989).

September 1989

Appendix References

Abiteboul (1987)   S. Abiteboul and R. Hull, IFO: A Formal Semantic Database Model, *ACM Trans. Database Systems vol.12, no.4*, (Dec 1987), p.525-565.

Abrial (1974)   J. R. Abrial, Data Semantics, in *Data Base Management - Proc. IFIP Working Conf. on Data Base Management*, J. W. Klimbie and K. L. Koffeman (eds.), North-Holland, 1974.

Brachman (1983)   R. J. Brachman, What IS-A Is and Isn't: An Analysis of Taxonomic Links in Semantic Networks, in *IEEE Computer*, (Oct 1983)), p.30-36.

Codd (1979)   E. F. Codd, Extending the Database Relational Model to Capture More Meaning, *ACM Trans. Database Systems vol.4, no.4*, (Dec 1979), p.397-434.

Dittrich (1986)   K. Dittrich and U. Dayal (eds.), *Proc. Internat. Workshop on Object-Oriented Database Systems*, Sept 1986.

Gray (1985)   P. M. D. Gray, Efficient Prolog Access to Codasyl and FDM Databases, in *Proc. ACM SIGMOD 85*, 1985, p.437-443.

Gray (1988)   P. M. D. Gray et al, A Prolog Interface to a Functional Data Model Database, in *Proc. Internat. Conf. on Exending Database Technology*, Mar 1988.

Hammer (1981) M. Hammer and D. McLeod, Database Description with SDM: A Semantic Database Model, *ACM Trans. Database Systems vol.6, no.3*, (Sept 1981), p.351-386.

Kerschberg (1986) L. Kerschberg (ed.), *Proc. First Internat. Workshop on Expert Database Systems*, 1986.

Kim (1989) W. Kim and F. Lochovsky (eds.), *Object-Oriented Languages, Applications, and Databases*, Addison-Wesley, 1989.

Oxborrow (1988) E. A. Oxborrow and H. M. Ismail, KBZ - An Object-Oriented Approach to the Specification and Management of Knowledge Bases, in *Proc. Sixth British Nat. Conf. on Databases (BNCOD 6)*, W. A. Gray (ed.), Cambridge University Press, 1988, p.21-46.

Peckham (1988) J. Peckham and F. Maryanski, Semantic Data Models, *ACM Computing Surveys vol.20, no.3*, (Sept 1988), p.153-189.

Rowe (1987) L. Rowe and M. Stonebraker, The POSTGRES Data Model, in *Proc. Thirteenth Internat. Conf. on Very Large Databases*, 1987, p.83-96.

Shriver (1987) B. Shriver and P. Wegner (eds.), *Research Directions in Object-Oriented Programming*, MIT Press, 1987.

Stefik (1986) M. Stefik and D. G. Bobrow, Object-Oriented Programming: Themes and Variations, *The AI Magazine*, (Jan 1986), p.40-62.

Stonebraker (1986) M. Stonebraker, Object Management in POSTGRES Using Procedures, in *Dittrich (1986)*, p.66-72.

Stonebraker (1987) M. Stonebraker et al, Extending a Database System with Procedures, *ACM Trans. Database Systems vol.12, no.3* (Sept 1987), p.350-376.

TOIS (1987) *ACM Trans. Office Information Systems vol.5, no.1*, (Jan 1987).

Zaniolo (1986) C. Zaniolo, Prolog: A Database Query Language for All Seasons, in *Kerschberg (1986)*, p.219-232.

JOHN ASHFORD & PETER WILLETT
Text Retrieval and Document Databases

An accessible account of *text databases* (available for searching, selection, transmission, and eventually archiving) and their development into *document databases,* i.e. documents incorporating words, numbers, drawings and pictures. These offer *total information management* with conventional data processing included through the use of gateways to other software.

The volume of published text is now huge. More than 420,000 new books are published each year in English and other European languages by about 10,000 commercial publishers. There are at least 100,000 journals in the same languages. Add to these the non-commercial publications,the internal technical, administrative and operational papers of government and industrial organisations, and the great importance of textual material becomes apparent. Moreover, text management applications are growing at around 60% a year.

Early chapters of this highly practical and detailed book fully introduce the established nucleus of the subject. A flavour of systems in use is given (indeed, several applications are explored, as well as a variety of text retrieval packages available). The technical aspects of design are carefully and clearly covered in detail. Applications of Optical Disk Storage and special purpose hardware are discussed, and the most promising current research and development is examined. Finally, a basis for system evaluation and selection is offered. Main sources of further information are given, and a separate software index is included.

The book will appeal to computer scientists, information scientists and librarians, but will also be of value to computer managers and systems analysts dealing with office automation and document management projects, and to users planning to get the best from their Computer Departments.

Attractively priced, 1989, 132 pages, ISBN 0-86238-204-1

Available from your local bookshop, or direct from **Chartwell-Bratt** (Publishing & Training) Ltd, Old Orchard, Bickley Road, Bromley, Kent, BR1 2NE, England, Tel: (0)1-467 1956, Telecom Gold 84:KJM001, Telex: 9312100451 Fax: (0)1-467 1754

COMPUTER SYSTEMS MODELLING & DEVELOPMENT:
A disciplined approach
Volume 1: Language, mathematical modelling and logic
by David Cornwell

This highly readable approach to disciplined computer systems modelling and development particularly highlights how *mathematics* can help in these related activities. Volume one covers language, mathematical modelling and logic. The author demonstrates a range of powerful and highly relevant mathematical and logical techniques in a very readable, informative and entertaining style. Primarily intended for students of computing and related disciplines, the book will also be of considerable use to practising analysts, designers and programmers. All the techniques presented are *relevant practical tools* - there is no maths for maths' sake. In addition to experience as a Senior Lecturer, the author has very wide industrial experience. Chapter summaries and end of chapter exercises, with answers, consolidate learning and are a valuable teaching aid.

Contents: Mathematics and language; Introduction to modelling and development; Introduction to sets, functions, relations and logic; Propositional logic; Normal forms, theorem proving, propositional Prolog and natural deduction; Predicate logic; Proof procedures and natural deduction for predicate logic; Answers to questions; Bibliography; Index.

1989, approx 200 pages, ISBN 0-86238-220-3

Database Analysis and Design: 2nd Edition
by Hugh Robinson

An undergraduate text describing the techniques and methods needed in analysis and design of database systems. The working environment for a database system is established. A wide range of approaches to databases techniques are outlined. The use of a generalised architecture for database systems is emphasised to provide a framework within which the various approaches may be examined. Topics covered in the substantive areas of analysis and design include data analysis and functional analysis, conceptual data models, the use of normalisation, logical database design, and physical database design. Concludes with an examination of the wider issues in the development of database systems, such as the role and responsibilities of DB administration and importance of data dictionary systems.

Contents: Preface; FUNDAMENTALS: The need for the database approach; The architecture of a database system; Relational database systems; Codasyl database systems; Other database systems; ANALYSIS; Conventional systems analysis; Conceptual models; Data analysis; DESIGN: Logical database design; Physical database design; Database administration; Data dictionaries.

Lecturers' comments: *"A very good introduction to databases. Easy reading" ..." strongly recommended" ... "Well written, well laid out and reasonably priced" ... "Useful and suitable for introductory course" ... "I will recommend the book very strongly to students " ... "Good theoretical background, nice methodology" ... "Excellent value for money. Well balanced and appropriate text."*

2nd Edition, 1990, ISBN 0-86238-232-7

RING OR WRITE FOR OUR FREE CATALOGUE !!

Computing Books from Chartwell-Bratt

GENERAL COMPUTING BOOKS

Compiler Physiology for Beginners, M Farmer, 279pp, ISBN 0-86238-064-2
Dictionary of Computer and Information Technology, D Lynch, 225 pages, ISBN 0-86238-128-2
File Structure and Design, M Cunningham, 211pp, ISBN 0-86238-065-0
Information Technology Dictionary of Acronyms and Abbreviations, D Lynch, 270pp, ISBN 0-86238-153-3
The IBM Personal Computer with BASIC and PC-DOS, B Kynning, 320pp, ISBN 0-86238-080-4

PROGRAMMING LANGUAGES

An Intro to LISP, P Smith, 130pp, ISBN 0-86238-187-8
An Intro to OCCAM 2 Programming, Bowler, et al, 109pp, ISBN 0-86238-137-1
Cobol for Mainframe and Micro: 2nd Ed, D Watson, 177pp, ISBN 0-86238-211-4
Comparative Languages: 2nd Ed, J R Malone, 125pp, ISBN 0-86238-123-1
Fortran 77 for Non-Scientists, P Adman, 109pp, ISBN 0-86238-074-X
Fortran 77 Solutions to Non-Scientific Problems, P Adman, 150pp, ISBN 0-86238-087-1
Fortran Lectures at Oxford, F Pettit, 135pp, ISBN 0-86238-122-3
LISP: From Foundations to Applications, G Doukidis et al, 228pp, ISBN 0-86238-191-6
Prolog versus You, A-L Johansson, 296pp, ISBN 0-86238-174-6
Simula Begin, G M Birtwistle et al, 391pp, ISBN 0-86238-009-X
The Intensive C Course, M Farmer, 167pp, ISBN 0-86238-114-2
The Intensive Pascal Course, M Farmer, 111pp, ISBN 0-86238-063-4

ASSEMBLY LANGUAGE PROGRAMMING

Coding the 68000, N Hellawell, 214pp, ISBN 0-86238-180-0
Computer Organisation and Assembly Language Programming, L Ohlsson & P Stenstrom, 128pp, ISBN 0-86238-129-0
What is machine code and what can you do with it? N Hellawell, 104pp, ISBN 0-86238-132-0

PROGRAMMING TECHNIQUES

Discrete-events simulations models in PASCAL/MT+ on a microcomputer, L P Jennergren, 135pp, ISBN 0-86238-053-7
Information and Coding, J A Llewellyn, 152pp, ISBN 0-86238-099-5
JSP - A Practical Method of Program Design: 2nd Ed, L Ingevaldsson, 204pp, ISBN 0-86238-107-X
JSD - Method for System Development, L Ingevaldsson, 248pp, ISBN 0-86238-103-7

Programming for Beginners: the structured way, D Bell & P Scott, 178pp, ISBN 0-86238-130-4
Software Engineering for Students, M Coleman & S Pratt, 195pp, ISBN 0-86238-115-0
Software Taming with Dimensional Design, M Coleman & S Pratt, 164pp, ISBN 0-86238-142-8
Systems Programming with JSP, B Sanden, 186pp, ISBN 0-86238-054-5

MATHEMATICS AND COMPUTING

Fourier Transforms in Action, F Pettit, 133pp, ISBN 0-86238-088-X
Generalised Coordinates, L G Chambers, 90pp, ISBN 0-86238-079-0
Linear Programming: A Computational Approach: 2nd Ed, K K Lau, 150pp, ISBN 0-86238-182-7
Statistics and Operations Research, I Schagen, 300pp, ISBN 0-86238-077-4
Teaching of Modern Engineering Mathematics, L Rade (ed), 225pp, ISBN 0-86238-173-8
Teaching of Statistics in the Computer Age, L Rade (ed), 248pp, ISBN 0-86238-090-1
The Essentials of Numerical Computation, M Bartholomew-Biggs, 241pp, ISBN 0-86238-029-4

DATABASES AND MODELLING

Computer Systems Modelling & Development, D Cornwell, 200pp, ISBN 0-86238-220-3
Database Analysis and Design, H Robinson, 378pp, ISBN 0-86238-018-9
Databases and Database Systems, E Oxborrow, 256pp, ISBN 0-86238-091-X
Data Bases and Data Models, B Sundgren, 134pp, ISBN 0-86238-031-6
Text Retrieval and Document Databases, J Ashford/P Willett, 125pp, ISBN 0-86238-204-1
Information Modelling, J Bubenko (ed), 687pp, ISBN 0-86238-006-5

UNIX

An Intro to the Unix Operating System, C Duffy, 152p, ISBN 0-86238-143-6
Operating Systems through Unix, G Emery, 96pp, ISBN 0-86238-086-3

SYSTEMS ANALYSIS AND DEVELOPMENT

Systems Analysis and Development: 3rd Ed, P Layzell & P Loucopoulos, 272pp, ISBN 0-86238-215-7

SYSTEMS DESIGN

Computer Systems: Where Hardware meets Software, C Machin, 200pp, ISBN 0-86238-075-8
Distributed Applications and Online Dialogues: a design method for application systems, A Rasmussen, 271pp, ISBN 0-86238-105-3
Microcomputer Systems: hardware and software, J Tierney, 168pp, ISBN 0-86238-218-1

SSADM Techniques, M Leijk, *et al*, 350pp, ISBN 0-86238-224-6

HARDWARE

Computers from First Principles, M Brown, 128pp, ISBN 0-86238-027-8
Fundamentals of Microprocessor Systems, P Witting, 525pp, ISBN 0-86238-030-8

ELECTRICAL & ELECTRONIC ENGINEERING

Analogue and Digital Signal Processing and Coding, P M Grant, *et al*, 450pp, ISBN 0-86238-206-8
Handbook of Electronics, J de Sousa Pires, 800pp, ISBN 0-86238-061-8

NETWORKS

Communication Network Protocols: 2nd Ed, B Marsden, 345pp, ISBN 0-86238-106-1
Computer Networks: Fundamentals and Practice, M D Bacon *et al*, 109pp, ISBN 0-86238-028-6
Datacommunication: Data Networks, Protocols and Design, L Ewald & E Westman, 343pp, ISBN 0-86238-092-8
Data Networks 1, Ericsson & Televerket, ISBN 0-86238-193-2
Telecommunications: Telephone Networks 1, Ericsson & Televerket, 147pp, ISBN 0-86238-093-6
Telecommunications: Telephone Networks 2, Ericsson & Televerket, 176pp, ISBN 0-86238-113-4

GRAPHICS

An Introductory Course in Computer Graphics, R Kingslake, 146pp, ISBN 0-86238-073-1
Techniques of Interactive Computer Graphics, A Boyd, 242pp, ISBN 0-86238-024-3
Two-dimensional Computer Graphics, S Laflin, 85pp, ISBN 0-86238-127-4

APPLICATIONS

Computers in Health and Fitness, J Abas, 106pp, ISBN 0-86238-155-X
Developing Expert Systems, G Doukidis, E Whitley, ISBN 0-86238-196-7
Expert Systems Introduced, D Daly, 180pp, ISBN 0-86238-185-1
Handbook of Finite Element Software, J Mackerle & B Fredriksson, approx 1000pp, ISBN 0-86238-135-5
Inside Data Processing: computers and their effective use in business, A deWatteville, 150pp, ISBN 0-86238-181-9
Proceedings of the Third Scandinavian Conference on Image Analysis, P Johansen & P Becker (eds) 426pp, ISBN 0-86238-039-1
Programmable Control Systems, G Johannesson, 136pp, ISBN 0-86238-046-4
Project Skills Handbook, S Rogerson, approx 100pp, ISBN 0-86238-146-0
Risk and Reliability Appraisal on Microcomputers, G Singh, + G Kiangi,

142pp, ISBN 0-86238-159-2
Statistics with Lotus 1-2-3, M Lee & J Soper, 207pp, ISBN 0-86238-131-2

HCI

Human/Computer Interaction: from voltage to knowledge, J Kirakowski, 250pp, ISBN 0-86238-179-7
Information Ergonomics, T Ivegard, 228pp, ISBN 0-86238-032-4
Computer Display Designer's Handbook, E Wagner, approx 300pp, ISBN 0-86238-171-1

INFORMATION AND SOCIETY

Access to Government Records: International Perspectives and Trends, T Riley, 112pp, ISBN 0-86238-119-3
CAL/CBT - the great debate, D Marshall, 300pp, ISBN 0-86238-144-4
Economic and Trade-Related Aspects of Transborder Dataflow, R Wellington-Brown, 93pp, ISBN 0-86238-110-X
Information Technology and a New International Order, J Becker, 141pp, ISBN 0-86238-043-X
People or Computers: 3 ways of looking at information systems, M Nurminen, 1218pp, ISBN 0-86238-184-3
Transnational Data Flows in the Information Age, C Hamelink, 115pp, ISBN 0-86238-042-1

MATHS & SCIENCE HANDBOOKS

Alpha Maths Handbook, L Rade, 199pp, ISBN 0-86238-036-7
Beta Maths Handbook, L Rade, 425pp, ISBN 0-86238-140-1
Nuclear Analytical Chemistry, D Brune *et al,* 557pp, ISBN 0-86238-047-2
Physics Handbook, C Nordling & J Osterman, 430pp, ISBN 0-86238-037-5
The V-Belt Handbook, H Palmgren, 287pp, ISBN 0-86238-111-8

Chartwell-Bratt specialise in excellent books at affordable prices.

For further details contact your local bookshop, or ring Chartwell-Bratt direct on **01-467 1956**(Access/Visa welcome.)

Ring or write for our *free* catalogue.

Chartwell-Bratt (Publishing & Training) Ltd, Old Orchard, Bickley Road, Bromley, Kent, BR1 2NE, United Kingdom.
Tel 01-467 1956, Fax 01-467 1754, Telecom Gold 84:KJM001,
Telex 9312100451(CB)